Dissident Voices

Edited by Mike Wayne

Dissident Voices
The Politics of Television and Cultural Change

Pluto Press
LONDON • STERLING, VIRGINIA

First published 1998 by Pluto Press
345 Archway Road, London N6 5AA
and 22883 Quicksilver Drive,
Sterling, VA 20166–2012, USA

British Library Cataloguing in Publication Data
A catalogue record for this book is available from
the British Library.

ISBN 0 7453 1329 9 hbk

Library of Congress Cataloging in Publication Data
Dissident voices: the politics of television and cultural change/
    edited by Mike Wayne.
        p.   cm.
    Includes bibliographical references.
    ISBN 0-7453–1329–9 (hardcover)
    1. Television broadcasting—Social aspects—Great Britain.
I. Wayne, Mike.
PN1992.6.D57   1998
302.23'45—dc21   98–24898
                                                                          CIP

Designed and produced for Pluto Press by
Chase Production Services, Chadlington, OX7 3LN
Typeset by Stanford DTP Services, Northampton
Printed in the EC by T.J. International Ltd, Padstow

Contents

Notes on Contributors   vii
Introduction   1
Mike Wayne

1   'Reality or Nothing'?: Dennis Potter's *Cold Lazarus*   12
    Glen Creeber
2   Counter-Hegemonic Strategies in *Between the Lines*   23
    Mike Wayne
3   Crisis and Opportunity: Class, Gender and Allegory
    in *The Grand*   40
    Mike Wayne
4   Bare Necessities and Naked Luxuries: The 1990s Male
    as Erotic Object   58
    Kenneth MacKinnon
5   'The Fierce Light': The Royal Romance with Television   72
    Deborah Philips and Garry Whannel
6   'Progressive' Television Documentary and Northern
    Ireland – The Films of Michael Grigsby in a 'Postcolonial'
    Context   91
    David Butler
7   The Exquisite Corpse of Rab(Elais) C(opernicus) Nesbitt   107
    Colin McArthur
8   The Politics of Ridicule: Satire and Television   127
    Peter Keighron
9   Not a Lot of Laughs: Documentary and Public Service   145
    Brian Winston
10   Dissidence and Authenticity in Dyke Porn and Actuality TV   159
    Tanya Krzywinska
11   Downloading the Documentary   176
    David Chapman

Index   184

Notes on Contributors

David Butler teaches media studies at the University of Ulster. He is the author of *The Trouble With Reporting Northern Ireland* (1995).

David Chapman is a lecturer in video production at the University of East London and a documentary producer in the independent sector.

Glen Creeber is a lecturer in media and television studies at the University of East Anglia. His publications include *Dennis Potter: Between Two Worlds, A Critical Reassessment* (1998). He is currently compiling a reader on television drama and researching on the films and television of Mike Leigh.

Peter Keighron is a television documentary researcher and scriptwriter and freelance journalist. He has written for the *Guardian*, the *Independent*, *Broadcast* and *Media Week*.

Tanya Krzywinska is currently subject leader for the Film/TV Studies degree programme at Brunel University. She has published articles on vampires, pornography and fantasy, and is now working on Voodoo and Witchcraft in film.

Kenneth MacKinnon is Professor in Film Studies at the University of North London. He has had five books on aspects of film and other media published, including *Misogyny in the Movies* and *Uneasy Pleasures: The Male as Erotic Object*, as well as two books of translations of modern Greek drama, and many articles on both Classics and Film Studies.

Colin McArthur was formerly head of the distribution division of the British Film Institute. He is now a freelance writer and lecturer. His publications include *Underworld USA* (1972), *Television and History* (1978), *The Big Heat* (1992) and as contributing editor to *Scotch Reels* (1982).

Deborah Philips teaches in the Department of Arts at Brunel University. She has written on popular fiction and is co-author, with Ian Haywood, of *Brave New Causes, Postwar Popular Fictions* (1998) and, with Liz Linnington and Debra Penman, of *Writing Well* (1998). She is currently researching the function of narrative in carnival sites.

Mike Wayne lectures in Film and Television Studies at Brunel University. He has special responsibility for developing the interface between theory and practical work. His publications include *Theorising Video Practice* (1997). His current research is on British film and modernity.

Garry Whannel is a Reader in Sport and Culture and Co-Director of the Centre for Sport Development Research in the School of Sport Studies, Roehampton Institute. He has published widely on the media and sport and is the author of *Fields In Vision: Television, Sport and Cultural Transformation* (1992).

Brian Winston is Head of the School of Communication, Design and Media at the University of Westminster. *Claiming the Real: The Documentary Film Revisited* was published by the BFI in 1996. Winston began his career at Granada Television in 1963 on *World In Action*. In 1985 he won a US prime time Emmy for documentary script writing (for WNET New York). His latest book is *Media Technology and Society: A History from the telegraph to the Internet* (1998).

Mike Wayne

Introduction

Dissidence and popular culture: the two terms appear to be mutually exclusive, especially if we are talking about popular *television* culture. While film has acquired the status of an art which has made the study of it intellectually respectable, television still, even amongst students and academics, struggles to be taken seriously and struggles to be understood as having anything serious to say. So what can dissidence and television have to do with one another? Dissidence is after all associated with calling into question prevailing norms; it is by definition sceptical of what officially constitutes popular opinion and it is often associated with the individual voice. The associations which cluster around popular culture and television however tend to suggest the exact opposite: consensus, conformity and against the individual voice, the machine of mass production and the blandishments of mass appeal. I do not propose that we replace this vision of cultural pessimism with an upbeat, celebratory vision of television as radical and heterogeneous, a vision which must ultimately shrink any critical perspective to an absolute minimum. Instead I would suggest that the relationship between dissidence and popular television is a shifting and complex terrain of possibilities and blockages, subversion and incorporation, successful articulations of dissidence and equally successful eviscerations of such voices. Why dissidence sometimes wins and often loses on television is complicated and although generalisations are helpful, indeed imperative, it is a process that can only be fully answered on a case by case basis. Part of the difficulty of any such assessment is that it is by no means clear what counts as a dissident voice these days. For it is true, although the extent is often exaggerated, that some of the established political demarcations have shifted, blurred and are in the process of being redrawn. At the political level, the key event which accounts for these shifts in Britain was the rise of the New Right during the 1980s.

The rise of Thatcherism shattered the political consensus that had been in place since 1945. Yet while Conservative governments were successful electorally throughout the 1980s and early 1990s, there were

1

always more people voting against them than for them. While they battled successfully against organised labour – particularly in the public sector which Conservative governments were committed to reducing – popular opinion was never uniformly won over by the case that the private sector was inherently more efficient and delivered better quality services, or that fairness and equality of access to public provision would have to go. In short, the Conservatives did not fashion popular opinion into a new consensus uncritically reflecting their own agenda. High levels of anxiety and resistance to Conservative shibboleths, such as the necessity for social and economic inequality, remained to be tapped into and rearticulated by television.

Anxiety is perhaps a key word. We live in a time of political closure, where individual leaders come and go, where even governing parties may change, but where core economic imperatives and policies remain much the same, hemmed in as they are by what some people euphemistically call 'the real world' (by which they mean the world of a triumphant global capitalism). There is now a new political consensus but, as in America,[1] it is largely shared by political and economic elites, increasingly split off from ordinary people, who nevertheless tirelessly invoke the mantra that there is no alternative. And even amongst the elites one finds some peculiar dissidents, like Prince Charles or George Soros, the financial dealer warning us of the dangers of unbridled capitalism even as he makes billions speculating against another country's national currency. Unhinged from this political consensus, popular opinion and culture become increasingly contradictory and fissiparous as social, cultural and technological changes gather pace.

The extent to which individual voices involved in television production and/or iconic figures on television screens can be at all dissident depends on their voices striking a chord with the collective discontents and shifts which such a situation produces. To what extent has television represented these changes as they manifest themselves in specific institutions, such as the police and the monarchy; in social identities such as gender; and in definitions of national identity? To gauge these questions, we do need to locate television inside and not outside these material and cultural changes.

If television's texts were once transitory and ephemeral, its institutions were once stable and permanent with long-term investment in large pools of labour and fixed capital the norm. Today it is the programmes, the cultural commodities themselves that are more permanent. Television culture has been 'materialised', partly as a means of increasing its exchange value (racking them up on the video shelves of music stores throughout the country, raiding and reframing archival material as cult classics) and partly, as a result of this, building into the use value of television a self-referential quality (from *Teletubbies* to *Rab C. Nesbitt*) as an awareness of its centrality and pervasiveness takes hold. What this means is that assessing the politics of cultural change on television often requires assessing television's own awareness of its role in culture and its intervention in cultural change. The institutions themselves meanwhile have been liquefied, constantly restructuring themselves in a bid to adapt to rapidly changing technological, legislative and economic agendas. This in turn has an effect on how, when and where television registers or handles significant cultural shifts, articulates or recuperates dissident voices. While some essays suggest that there are spaces for leftist or liberal dissent on television from political orthodoxies (see, for example, Creeber, Keighron, McArthur and Wayne), others suggest that what may look like a dissident voice upon closer examination is recuperated (see MacKinnon) or flawed (see Butler). In such cases it is the writers themselves who become the dissident voice.

It is tempting to say that television is currently poised between two modes of production, possibly a transitional moment where a strong residual public service ethos still animates cultural workers and commissioning editors in various departments within the broadcasting institutions, while at the same time it is increasingly interlocked with an emerging and rapidly dominating market-led television. These two modes of production were for several decades meshed together with some success. But from the introduction of ITV to Channel 4, extending market principles as a way of challenging the paternalism of public service television was always a substitute for more accountable and democratic public service possibilities. Today public service and market-led television are increasingly two halves which, in a profound sense, do not add up. The tensions and relations between the cultural and economic dynamics of television surface as a theme in a number of essays collected here.

Glen Creeber's essay on Dennis Potter's final work, *Cold Lazarus*, sums up many of the prevalent themes of Potter's *oeuvre*. Creeber argues that Potter's work straddles a powerfully nostalgic 'Hoggartesque' liberal view of national identity while trying to come to terms with and offer a critique of a Thatcherite, media saturated, privatised Britain of the future in social and cultural disintegration. *Cold Lazarus* places television at the centre of this conflict between a liberal organic cultural agenda and a Thatcherite economic one, both within the text – with its thinly disguised attack on Rupert Murdoch and the culture of commerce – and in the very production and scheduling of *Cold Lazarus* and *Karaoke*. Potter asked that Channel 4 and the BBC make the unprecedented move of collaborating on the two dramas, each episode being shown twice a week by each broadcaster. As Creeber notes, this last request – immediately agreed by Alan Yentob (BBC1) and Michael Grade (Channel 4) – was an attempt by Potter to reconstruct the so-called 'Golden Age' of public service television when the weekly drama was often the highlight of the week, drawing large audiences and often provoking controversial reactions: certainly a pre-digital, pre-multichannel age.

Potter of course represents one of the founding if not necessarily one of the most explicitly political figures of that exploratory and critical current that broke through into television drama in the late 1960s and early 1970s. As the preeminent television *auteur* his work was always guaranteed to be taken seriously by the institutions that produced his television dramas. Just as crucially, his work was taken seriously by popular critical discourses and, while reviews of his work became increasingly mixed in his later years, it was always assumed that his work needed to be taken seriously.

This is not the case for television generally. The discourses which frame television fall into two types and both function to the detriment of the medium. While some popular commentary on television may be genuinely funny, there has to be something amiss when such a major cultural institution (claiming around 23 hours of people's weekly leisure time) seems to only ever function as a convenient object on which the critic's wit may be honed. The exception to that of course is when television is catapulted out of the realm of 'mere' entertainment and caught up in wider political debates and rows. The problem here is the tendency to see television as a simple reflection of the world and then usually to decry its lack of accuracy, its misrepresentation in a particular programme of a group, institution, event or place. The response of some Muslims to Salman Rushdie's *The Satanic Verses* is a relatively rare example of this happening in literature, but it happens all the time to television (although with less devastating consequences for writers). This reductionism bypasses the medium's own specificity – the complexity of its language, history and the possible meanings it may have at the point of consumption – precisely its 'materiality'. If the dissident voices which do exist on television are to have any recognition and amplification beyond simplistic denunciation, then mainstream critical discourses on the medium are going to have to undergo change.

It is the specificity of the medium and how this intertwines with its contexts of production and consumption that I try to address in my discussion of *Between the Lines* as a counter-hegemonic text. This police drama is a flawed and problematic multiple text, but in my essay I attempt to amplify those strategies which successfully produce a different kind of relationship between programme and viewer in the hope that these strategies may be developed in the future. In particular I focus on the concept of the 'flawed hero' and argue that the most interesting aspect of this which the series developed is not its notion of personal flaws (*Cracker*'s hero has many of those) but the blockage of the hero's function as 'problem solver' due to institutional, sociostructural constraints. The ethnic and gender identity of the hero/heroine gives significant inflections to their representation in the genre. Thus I compare the hero of *Between the Lines*, Tony Clark, to examples of the black male detective and the white female detective in *Black and Blue* and *Prime Suspect* respectively.

My second contribution to this anthology is on *The Grand*, a period drama set in a large Victorian Manchester hotel shortly after the First World War. My essay explores the dual referents invoked by the series: on the one hand the disruptions in class and gender wrought by the traumas and transformations of the War; on the other, first broadcast over the period of the 1997 General Election, *The Grand* is also a coded rumination on the traumas and transformations of our own contemporary moment. Through this notion of dual focalisation my essay explores *The Grand*'s mobilisation of popular memory, television's relation to history as myth and the possibilities for counter-hegemonic representations of the past on television. Critical discourses on television have been dominated by the thematics of postmodernism (nostalgia, metatextuality, surface, paranoia) but *The Grand* seems to require the deployment of concepts associated with the critical realism advocated by Georg Lukács, in particular the concepts of totality and typicality. These concepts and their wider sociocultural referents are integrated into an analysis of the specificity of television, both as a text and with regard to the production conditions under which the text was made.

One thing that is very clear in *The Grand* is that gender roles are to some extent in crisis and changing. Precisely to what extent is a question Kenneth MacKinnon explores in his essay. MacKinnon identifies a phenomenon which has a growing circulation both in television and other media. Indeed one of the television programmes MacKinnon discusses, *The Bare Necessities*, obviously inspired the box office hit *The Full Monty*. This phenomenon is male exhibitionism which, MacKinnon argues, is both increasingly displayed but also cunningly disavowed. The invitation to look at the male body as an erotic object is given special frames of explanation which help diffuse some of the anxieties which such an invitation generates. MacKinnon finds three such explanatory alibis. First, there is the appeal that this is some kind of popular culture response to the feminist critique of female objectification; secondly there is the 'it's only a laugh' alibi which reaffirms traditional components of masculinity by temporarily transgressing them; lastly, male exhibitionism has been explained as a response to economic necessities and aspirations. MacKinnon suggests that these frames negotiate all sorts of anxieties around power and desire which the male as erotic object generates.

Deborah Philips and Garry Whannel's essay offers a historical contextualisation to the changing relations between broadcasting and the monarchy. The forging of such a relationship was ineluctable and it seemed beneficial to both institutions. When television supplanted radio as the chief medium for royal coverage during the 1953 Coronation, it bathed in the glow of royal mystique. The royals in turn achieved a massive amplification of their image, cementing their popularity and underlining their ideological role as a point of consensus and unity for what was to become an increasingly divided nation. What could go wrong? After all, television was nothing if not rigorous in policing itself, in excluding or marginalising any dissident perspective on the monarchy. Yet, as Philips and Whannel show, television ended up undermining the monarchy despite itself.

The amplification of pageantry is only one dynamic in the mass mediation of the royals. As Walter Benjamin argued in relation to art, that which withers in the age of the mass media is the 'aura' of remoteness, distance and uniqueness attached to the art object or, we may say, to a whole institution such as the monarchy. Its reproduction and dissemination prises it away from the 'domain of tradition', the domain of the sacred, and brings it in touch with the secular and everyday world of the masses.[2] This second dynamic means that all media stars, even royal ones, cannot only be extraordinary and unique; they must also be ordinary, just like us.[3] Thus Philips and Whannel juxtapose the 1969 Investiture of the Prince of Wales, with all its grandeur, with the 1987 *It's a Royal Knockout*, a bizarre televisual concept, and one hardly designed to lift the monarchy into the realm of the immutable.

Interacting with the tension between the extraordinary and the ordinary was a second dynamic: the tension between tradition and modernity. During the 1980s it became increasingly hard to marry the two just as the marriage between Charles and Diana was also unravelling. For Thatcherism had an impact on the monarchy every bit as significant as on other British institutions. The traditional ideological function of the monarchy as an image in which an apparently unified nation can celebrate itself began to resemble the One Nation Toryism which Thatcherism excoriated. By the early 1990s the Thatcherite ethos of 'value for money' for taxpayers was also opening the royals up for criticism.

The response of the two most significant royals apart from the Queen was contradictory. While Charles attempted to invoke the past in his views on the present (extolling, for example, the virtues of traditional architecture in a special edition of *Omnibus*), Diana was constructed, in countless news bulletins, as a modernising force: informal, caring, in touch with the people. Yet it was Charles who was first on television to confess adultery; and in her own celebrated *Panorama* interview Diana was throwing stones at the House of Windsor although she had no intention of bringing the edifice down. The traditions and rituals of royalty were pulling one way, what it meant to be modern, another: the royals as desperately ordinary versus the royals as worthy of extraordinary status. What no one had expected when television and the monarchy first embraced was that discord and dissent *within* the Royal family would become the subject of television, flowing from the screens and into the watching public and then ramifying into widespread criticism of the royals after the death of Diana. The meanings around her death and her subsequent funeral were fundamentally generated through television and the watching public, as Philips and Whannel argue. Post-Diana, the monarchy is adapting in an alliance with New Labour and, for the time being, survives. But the tensions between television and the monarchy will remain despite the best efforts of both institutions.

The monarchy is one of the most important elements in a traditional and dominant version of national identity. David Butler and Colin McArthur address the question of national identity from the imperial 'margins', as it were, trying to step out of the shadows of a dominant Englishness without tipping over into an equally problematic nationalism.

David Butler's essay engages questions of 'progressiveness' in connection with debates about the British media and Northern Ireland. He recontextualises those debates by acknowledging the impact which postcolonial studies have made to questions of identity. Whatever constitutional future Northern Ireland has and however one might define what exactly would count as a 'postcolonial' context, it is clear that postcolonialisation cannot be conflated with the delegitimisation of Britishness as an *identity* within Northern Ireland. As Butler argues, if the region is to enjoy a peaceful future then the postcolonial context is one which shall have to embrace hybridity and reject exclusivist conceptions of national identity.

The question of how such identities can be articulated in a television text and discussed in a critical language brings Butler to reflect on methodology. Here he suggests that both television texts and critical methods have focused on Ireland through the lens of British definitions, reflecting histories and politics ill suited to a simple transference onto Northern Ireland. Butler takes the work of British documentary filmmaker Michael Grigsby as a case study for this argument. He sensitively explores the complex relations between cultural forms and politics (socialist-humanist in the case of Grigsby) by locating Grigsby's work in its contradictory relations to the British documentary film movement. Grigsby's eloquent, moving and nostalgic portrayals of British working-class life deracinated by Thatcherism are not unproblematic however, as Butler notes. The moral centre in Grigsby's work is that of an authentic homogeneous community, a vision that begs questions about ethnic diversity and becomes doubly difficult when he turns his lens to understanding the politics of identity and difference in Northern Ireland.

Colin McArthur argues that Scotland has an ambiguous relation to the United Kingdom's imperial past. A material beneficiary in many ways, Scotland, as a junior partner, was also subject to a cultural colonisation that produces a psychological estrangement with some analogies to the type analysed by Franz Fanon and Edward Said. Language and the power of self-imaginings is a key site in the struggles for decolonisation and thus McArthur begins his discussion of *Rab C. Nesbitt* with the word. Although sound has often been unjustly marginalised in film studies, it is even more crucial to the study of television. Here, the range and limitations of accents and dialects tells us something about television's relations to the regional and class-based coordinates of cultural power as it manifests itself in the dominance of Standard English. The relationship between cultural specificity and class is a close one because the higher one climbs in the class hierarchy, the more the voice tends to gravitate towards the accepted norm irrespective of regional location. McArthur notes how *Rab C. Nesbitt* juxtaposes the vernacular English laced with Scots words which Rab, his family and immediate friends speak, and the Received Pronunciation of various authority figures. This awareness of class difference within Scotland helps the series circumvent the dangers of nostalgia and sentimentalism which McArthur sees in the work of other cultural producers who have turned to the vernacular. McArthur goes on to discuss the cultural specificity of the programme's vernacular, crucially its blending of the scurrilous with 'high culture' references and a general philosophising register. McArthur also speculates whether one might be able to think of gesture and body language as having culturally specific elements as much as the vocal performance. The issues of cultural specificity are also imbricated with the formal strategies of the medium; the way, for example, that Rab's philosophising is underwritten by his direct-to-camera address. McArthur discerns an occasional complexity and sophistication in the series' *mise-en-scène* which is still unusual in a situation comedy but which is perhaps becoming more common across television generally as cultural producers begin to exploit the medium's imaginative possibilities.

In part, *Rab C. Nesbitt* is a satire, as Peter Keighron notes, about surviving Thatcherism. As Keighron explains in his essay, political satire is the mode of showing the absurdity of prevalent ideas, figures of authority and dominant values by ridiculing them. However, 'stand-up' satire has an uneasy relationship to television generally and particularly to its public service traditions of entertainment and education. Its literary, 'high culture' roots, but more crucially the fact that satire is not necessarily *funny*, makes it sit oddly in the entertainment mode. On the other hand, its use of derision makes it sit askance orthodox notions of education. In short, it can be too serious for comedy while its mode of delivery seems too frivolous, informal or just inappropriate for it to be 'seriously' educational. Despite the difficulty of accommodating satire within television's divisions of labour and competitive pressures, it does manage to survive in a variety of manifestations. While acknowledging that there is a looser definition of the term 'satire' which would legitimately incorporate such programmes as *One Foot In The Grave* and *Blackadder*, Keighron focuses on the cultural and political implications of 'hardcore' leftist satire and how it negotiates or is blocked by conservative forces and practices inside television (such as 'balance') and outside television (libel laws, newspapers, politicians). Keighron's methodology includes making refreshing use of empirical material in the form of interviews with comedians, writers and commissioning editors.

Another genre which has had a marginal but well-established place on British television is the documentary. Brian Winston believes that reports of the imminent or actual 'death' of documentary, or its transformation into trivia, are exaggerated. It has proved remarkably resistant to attack and erosion despite the wider Thatcherite attack on the values of public services generally and broadcasting specifically. Given that the documentary has comparatively limited audience appeal (ratings for documentary programmes above 5 million remain the exception rather than the norm), survival is perhaps the best one could have hoped for. Unlike America, where documentary on network television has diminished precipitously, British television retains a regulatory framework for which documentaries signify 'quality' television and public service. Winston wonders if the inertia of broadcasting institutions might not be the main explanation for the documentary's puzzling persistence. This is a salutary reminder that the 1980s did not wind the clock back to a Thatcherite Year Zero. Without underestimating the profound effects on British institutions which marketisation has had, or the fact that Thatcherism triggered changes which are still working themselves through under New Labour, not every aspect of life was uniformly levelled by Thatcherism.

If inertia explains the commitment of institutions to documentary, how might we account for audience investment in the genre? Perhaps the desire for knowledge becomes increasingly important to audiences precisely at the moment when the authenticity of the image has been undermined by digital technology, by cultural shifts towards pastiche and self-referentiality, and by the sheer manipulation of information as politics and marketing converge. However, these explanations do not quite address the *jouissance* of documentary which, Winston suggests, both the practice and the theory of the genre have largely ignored.

With this in mind we can turn to Tanya Krzywinska's essay. She explores lesbian pornographic video, situating its formal strategies and content in relation to broadcast television, particularly 'actuality' TV and access programming, both of which draw on the signifiers of realism associated with video footage. Broadcast television has tapped into the codes of authenticity which have accrued to amateur, low budget, 'underground' video practice, recuperating them for various represen-tations which reinforce dominant social norms like the family or institutions such as the police. If the transgressive, dissident content of dyke pornography is clear enough, the formal strategies it shares with the normative content of *You've Been Framed!* suggests a wider cultural investment in the desire to catch reality in the raw, with a minimum of mediation.

Krzywinska explores the psychical roots of this fascination with this video aesthetic and its promise to reveal what is normally hidden. Her closely observed analysis of a dyke pornographic video identifies how the sounds and images connote an authentic capturing of the real, an overhearing and overseeing which can be traced back to the unconscious fantasy of the primary scene (parental coitus). The power of this fantasy which the video aesthetic is mobilising is that it imagines our own origins. The political implications of this fantasy can be directed in ways that both shore up and, alternatively, call the existing social order into question. On the one hand, it produces a desire to know our origins, who our 'authors' are, and therefore it confirms the legitimacy of who or what has *authority* over us. Yet there is an element of transgresssion in this drive to knowledge, in this very image of coming upon the primal scene, that can work in more critical and liberatory directions. Thus the normative content of broadcast television's use of the video aesthetic is mobilising deeply secreted psychical energies to authenticate the social order, to know it in its real unmediated truth. On the other hand, the same texts draw on an aesthetic which depends on the *frisson* of transgression, thus inviting the viewer to glimpse the social order at the moment where it breaks down (the accident in *You've Been Framed!*, the car chase in numerous police videos such as *Police, Camera, Action!*).

Yet if the progressive potential of these texts seems severely attenuated, the dialectic between transgression and knowledge, between overhearing and overseeing the forbidden and social/cultural authority, is worked out in more progressive directions in underground and alternative video practices. In the case of Krzywinska's porn text, the forbidden/hidden calls the sexual norms of the social order into question while its transgressive aura does not produce the 'truth' about lesbian sex, but through certain devices, such as the enigmatic whispering between the two women, withholds a position of mastery and closure from the spectator.

A similar psychical dynamic is operating, I would suggest, in the work of *Undercurrents* – a video news magazine specialising in documenting the environmental activism which broadcast news marginalises. When activists record their invasion of a company's offices because of its involvement in unethical trade, then the revelation calls into question the social order, while their ejection from the premises produces that enigma which reminds us how bourgeois property relations keep protected and unaccountable their secret workings. The position of mastery being withheld, the desire to know these secrets has been reinforced. In tracing links between such disparate texts as *You've Been Framed!*, lesbian pornography and *Undercurrents*, psychoanalysis reminds us that politically and creatively the unconscious, or rather the way it is mobilised, is a site of struggle.

David Chapman's concluding piece peers into the future, when technological developments transform television into a multifunctional information receiver and producer. What are the prospects for a critical cultural practice in such a world? Chapman focuses on the documentary in an increasingly fragmented and deterritorialised television environment.

Postmodernists used to claim such a future as their own. Their celebratory confidence in the actuality and potentiality of the new order combined with a political quietism. This perversely inverted Gramsci's famous aphorism into something like 'optimism of the intellect, pessimism of the will'. Even in a television future where origins become blurred and destinations more unknown, Gramsci's own formulation ('pessimism of the intellect, optimism of the will') serves still as a better guide to the future. Thus Chapman's essay reminds us that technological change extends and alters the terrain of cultural struggle, determining nothing in itself, but creating new sites of contestation between those forces which seek to make communications defer to the domination of the market, ideological dominants and/or the state and those currents that seek to construct a television culture that is questioning, critical, pulling into representation the marginalised and cutting through the layers of passivity, cynicism and consensual norms that predominate elsewhere.

Notes

1   Christopher Lasch, *The Revolt of the Elites and the Betrayal of Democracy* (W. W. Norton and Company, 1995).
2   Walter Benjamin, 'The Work of Art in the Age of Mechanical Reproduction', in J. Curran, M. Gurevitch and Janet Woollacott (eds) *Mass Communication and Society* (Edward Arnold/Open University Press, 1977), pp. 384–408.
3   R. Dyer, *Stars* (BFI, 1979).

1

Glen Creeber

'Reality or Nothing'? Dennis Potter's *Cold Lazarus* (1996)

> More than the coming of the bus and the train, or even the daily newspaper, it was the voices out of the air which, as though by magic, pushed out those constricting boundaries. You could hear a play that made the back of your neck tingle as well as a dance band that made your foot tap, a brow-furrowing talk about something I'd never heard of, as well as an I-say-I say-I say music-hall routine, or even (and how bizarre) a ventriloquist's dummy as well as a not wholly dissimilar news reader. And none of it trying to sell you anything.
>
> Dennis Potter, 'The James MacTaggart Memorial Lecture', 1993[1]

The history behind Dennis Potter's last two television serials are well known. Diagnosed with incurable cancer, he appeared on Channel 4's *Without Walls* in April 1994, interviewed by Melvyn Bragg.[2] Memorably he concluded the BAFTA award-winning programme by promising two new screenplays before his imminent death. Some two months later, not only were they both completed but the playwright had already influenced important areas of their subsequent production. Not just involving himself in crucial areas of the casting, he also insisted that both serials be directed by Renny Rye, responsible for *Lipstick on Your Collar* (1993) and *Midnight Movie* (1994).[3] When, after Potter's death in June 1994, the serials' producer Kenith Trodd tried to have Rye replaced by a more experienced director (some rumours had Martin Scorsese up for the job), the wishes of the dead dramatist still managed to triumph.[4] It is perhaps no exaggeration to say that the scripts themselves were adhered to with almost religious reverence, and the £10 million budget helped to faithfully reproduce the finest details of location and design.[5] But perhaps Potter's greatest coup was to have the BBC and Channel 4 co-produce the two serials, each broadcaster showing a repeat of the episode first screened by the rival company.[6] Such a feat may have been partly influenced by the fact that Alan Yentob (Head of BBC1) and Michael Grade (then Chief Executive of Channel 4) were well-known Potter fans, but it also paid testament to Potter's immense standing in television and his endless powers of persuasion. However, with the ultimate deadline to meet, it is perhaps not surprising that Potter was unable to achieve the sort of quality which had typified his finest work. Yet, *Cold Lazarus* (1996), the second of the two serials, did draw together themes and techniques which not only characterised his unique dramatic landscape but reflected his passionate belief in the power and significance of the medium to which he had doggedly devoted his life.

While *Karaoke*'s (1996) story of a drunken and dying television writer brought together the well-known Potter themes of sex, death and biography, *Cold Lazarus* appeared to offer a completely new departure for the writer. Set in the year 2368, this science fiction pastiche is centred around a group of British scientists intent on tapping into the memories of a cryogenically frozen head.[7] Yet despite its futuristic setting, comically kitsch costumes and seductive sci-fi music composed by Christopher Gunning (which, according to Trodd, attempted to remind us of *Star Wars* and *Blade Runner*),[8] its conception of the future is seen unmistakably and inevitably from the point of view of the present. Greatly undervalued by its critics, *Cold Lazarus* offers a complex satire on the state of contemporary Britain. In particular, it portrays a society where Milton Friedman's monetarist economics (the type favoured by Thatcherite and even more recent 'Blairite' policies) has reduced everything to a commercial transaction.[9] Above all, the serial is Potter's final comment on the sort of 'management culture' and its desire for 'market efficiency' which he felt was eroding the basic ideals of British life and slowly corrupting the fundamental principles of British broadcasting.

In 1989 Rupert Murdoch delivered the James MacTaggart Memorial Lecture at the annual Edinburgh International Television Festival. 'Most of what passes for quality on British Television', he argued, 'is no more than a reflection of the values of the narrow elite which controls it and has always thought that its tastes are synonymous with quality.'[10] British TV, he said, was 'obsessed with class', tended to 'hark back to the past' and was dominated by 'anti-commercial attitudes'. According to Murdoch,

the television set of the future will be a global cornucopia of programming and nearly infinite libraries of data, education and entertainment. The arguments that have recently dominated British broadcasting ... will soon sound as if they belong in the Stone Age.[11]

It came as no surprise, then, that when Potter (a great adversary of Murdoch) took the stand for his own James MacTaggart Memorial Lecture in 1993, the earlier speech became the target for much of his personal contempt and passionate rhetoric. For Potter, Murdoch's commercially financed media empire symbolised the total destruction of state-funded public service broadcasting as he knew and understood it. Funded by a licence fee rather than advertising revenue, the BBC of Potter's childhood remained the very model upon which he believed British broadcasting should still be founded. Above all, Potter seemed concerned that the increased commercialisation of both television and radio would finally eradicate the unique power of British broadcasting to both 'educate' and 'inform', as well as 'entertain':

> On the old Light Programme you could suddenly, maybe reluctantly, collide with a play or a discussion or an embryonic drama-documentary. The now totally pervasive assumptions of the market-place, which have stiffened into something close to natural law, had not by then removed the chance of being surprised by something you didn't know, or – better still – by something you didn't know that you knew.[12]

It is with this background in mind that *Cold Lazarus* is best understood. Set 400 years hence, it takes Murdoch's broadcasting practice and philosophy to its most logical and extreme conclusions. Potter's media mogul is David Siltz (Henry Goodman), a vacuous American and the president of UTE (Universal Total Entertainment). Siltz is the most powerful man in a wholly privatised world, intent on transforming the entire planet into a global entertainment industry. 'He's like the ... Tsar of All the Russias,' a character observes; 'Genghis Khan's a better analogy,' replies another.[13] As Potter told Bragg, this is his dramatisation of a Murdoch-type figure, whose own global entertainment empire already stretches across the UK, USA, Germany, Asia, Latin America, Australia and the Pacific Basin.[14] Siltz's media empire is even more global, but the type of programming it offers is essentially limited. Above all, his entertainment business is driven by the all-consuming need to keep audiences *watching*, regardless of the quality of the programmes they receive. 'If I lose nought point two of an audience in any of my shows,' he declares, 'we calculate we lose nought point *three* of advertising revenue ....'[15] Seat sensors tell his programme-makers exactly how the viewer or 'interactivator' is reacting. 'We know,' he explains, 'when a killing or a fuck or a droplet from the tear duct is needed.'[16] Such a vision of the world reflects Neil Postman's *Amusing Ourselves to Death: Public Discourse in the Age of Show Business* (1985), his own nightmarish vision of a media-saturated planet. According to Postman, the future will not resemble Orwell's *Nineteen Eighty-four* where terror is the ruling edifice but Huxley's *Brave New World* where people 'are controlled by inflicting pleasure'.[17]

Slitz's fellow marketer is Martina Matilda Masdon (Diane Ladd) who, like Siltz, is a symbol of a world which has allowed the pressures of economic forces not only to control people's entertainment but also to infiltrate their bodies and minds. She is the head of a powerful pharmaceutical company which has recently produced a Prozac-like drug to obliterate 'anxiety'. As a result, she asks Siltz if she could sponsor a television programme specifically designed to produce the highest level of fear, thereby ensuring the greatest demand for her new product. '[Y]ou gotta make a whole damn zillion of folks mighty *anxious*,' she tells him, '[a]nd that's where your TV and VR ... comes in.'[18] A combination of Margaret Thatcher and the Wicked Witch of the West, she seems to spend most of her time being massaged by semi-naked muscular young men and admonishing her employees for going over budget. 'You've tilted tit-up into overspend,' she cries in frustration at her demoralised British scientists.[19]

However, as we gradually discover, these scientists are in the process of unearthing a form of 'media' no longer conceived by such a commercially obsessed industry. They have in their possession the head of Daniel Feeld (Albert Finney) which had been cryogenically frozen at his death in 1994. In contrast to the sort of inane and revenue-led programming currently on offer from Siltz and sponsored by the likes of Masdon, Daniel's fragmented memories from the late twentieth century (which they are able to project onto the 'living wall' of their laboratory) conjure up images of an immensely human and organic world. Possessing both a physical and psychical resemblance to the psoriatic Philip Marlow in *The Singing Detective* (1986) (whose head, at times, also seemed divorced from his body),[20] Daniel's recollections of a postwar working-class childhood offer a distinct contrast to the media-manipulated world of the future. His memories provoke some of them to be more critical of the present, forcing them to ask why, as one of the scientists puts it, 'we can't mingle and touch and hope in the way our forefathers and mothers used to do?'[21]

Daniel's memories are familiar even to the most casual of Potter's viewers. The Forest of Nead ('Dean' reversed), with its chapel, dance halls and dense woodland, portrays, as the script puts it, 'another land', one infinitely more 'natural' than Britain's dehumanised and commercialised future. As elsewhere in Potter's work, this postwar working-class community somehow embodies Britain's own 'land of lost content'.[22] With its coal mines and working-men's clubs there is the sense of a world which, despite its narrowness of horizon and expectations, was fundamentally more 'organic' and 'authentic' than the present. The British scientists of the future can only look on bewildered by this reminder of a time when comradeship, courtship, citizenship and community were the staple ingredients of British life. As Daniel and his future wife sit talking on the grass near Wordsworth's Tintern Abbey, so the beauty and innocence of a rural British summer comes drifting across the centuries, highlighting the urban isolation at the heart of their future dystopia.[23] Not surprisingly, one scientist spies an opportunity to use Daniel's memories for their own salvation. '[I]f we wear our VR helmets,' she excitedly explains, 'we will live for hours at a time in the *real* past, the *authentic* past ... and perhaps escape.'[24]

Potter's serial then, dramatises the potential dangers of a world obsessed and controlled by the entertainment business, a business in every sense of the word which cares more for present and future profit than preserving the cultural and social traditions of the past. Put crudely, it dramatises the contemporary conflict between a form of public service broadcasting which possessed and dictated a national, historical and cultural identity (represented here by Daniel's 'authentic' memories), and Murdoch's market-led form of broadcasting (here represented by Siltz's global entertainment empire) which has dispensed with any such cultural mission in the pursuit only of increased advertising revenue. As Anthony Weymouth explains in *Markets & Myths: Forces for Change in the European Media*, such a division can be understood in terms of a 'modernist' and 'postmodernist' divide. As Weymouth puts it:

> According to some contemporary thinkers, public service broadcasting was conceived within the final phases of what has come to be known as the 'modernist era'. By this they mean that PSB developed in a time of clearly defined national identities as well as of strongly held views of historical destiny (i.e. Marxist and capitalist theory). It is currently a *fin-de-siècle*, postmodernist argument to assert that such cultural and ideological certainties, which gave the states of Western Europe their sense of mission, were illusory. If this is the case, then a large part of that illusion ... was reinforced by the media and by public service broadcasting in particular.[25]

In this sense, *Cold Lazarus* can be seen as offering a deliberate and conscious critique of contemporary broadcasting in particular and 'postmodernism' in general.[26] The serial constructs a nightmarish and satirised vision of a world in which so-called 'postmodernism' has overwhelmingly triumphed, displacing any notion of historical identity or even '*reality*' as simply illusory or ideological. 'Postmodernism', Fredric Jameson writes, 'is what you have when the modernisation process is complete and nature is gone for good ....'[27] However, in Potter's future dystopia 'nature' and 'reality' come back (via Daniel's memories) with a vengeance, and threaten to disrupt the entire premise of people's distorted and media-saturated perceptions. This can help explain why many viewers were apparently not convinced by Potter's knowledge and understanding of the science-fiction genre. *Cold Lazarus* was an attempt to parody perhaps the most 'postmodern' of all genres in order to re-assert the very notion and possibility of 'truth' and 'reality' which so many contemporary science-fiction dramas attempt to destabilise.[28] From this point of view, one can see Potter's final screenplay as offering a conscious subversion of a science-fiction dystopia like *Blade Runner* (1982), by providing, at its very centre, an *actual* and *authentic* sense of 'history' which Ridley Scott's 'replicants' (with their implanted memories) so conspicuously lack.[29]

As one might expect, then, Potter's narrative does uncover a group of activists intent on returning a sense of 'truth' to this morally decentred world. Deriving their title from an acronym of 'Reality or Nothing', the RONs (with their 'power base' in England) are a terrorist organisation intent on overthrowing this deluded society, preferring 'reality' to the mindless mass entertainment on offer via Siltz's global media empire. Potter argued in his James MacTaggart Memorial Lecture that 'drama or fiction' could offer 'one of the last few remaining acres of possible truth-telling left to us in our over-manipulated and news-stuffed world ...'.[30] So it is that Daniel's memories (particularly in their seemingly chaotic disregard for chronology, almost mimicking Potter's own particular style of television drama[31]) offer the British scientists a sort of 'fiction', an antidote to the media-manipulated world of Britain's future. Although limited in their resources, the RONs do finally free Daniel's head from its virtual imprisonment and even manage to kill Siltz, finally dramatising Potter's own deeply held wish to inflict a similar demise on Murdoch. As Potter told Bragg,

> I'd call my cancer, the main one, the pancreas one, I call it Rupert, so I can get close to it, because the man Murdoch is the one who, if I had the time – in fact I've got too much writing to do and I haven't got the energy – but I would shoot the bugger if I could. [32]

However, there are hints in Daniel's childhood that even here all is not well at the heart of British life. As the young Marlow graphically witnessed his mother's sexual infidelity in the Forest of Dean, so the boy Daniel is seemingly the victim of a traumatic sexual attack. As elsewhere in Potter's work, this child abuse signifies a resounding loss of innocence, a sudden, irretrievable and traumatic fall from grace. But it is not just a sexual innocence which has been lost; the event also signals Daniel's wider isolation from the warm and communal Forest of Nead. Like his predecessors, Nigel Barton and Philip Marlow, Daniel grows up to be a 'scholarship boy' who will soon lose forever the communal embrace of his working-class roots when he gains a scholarship to study at Oxford University. Only his wife-to-be, a 'blue-eyed dazzler' from the Forest of Nead, will forever remind him of what he has irretrievably lost. As a whole, Potter's drama tended to suggest that Britain too experienced a 'Fall' at roughly the same time. Reflecting the work of Richard Hoggart's *The Uses of Literacy* (1957), Potter tended to conceive the 1950s, with its sexualised rock 'n' roll and rampant consumerism, as heralding Britain's *cultural* Fall.[33] As charming and innocent as the decade may seem now, Potter clearly saw the 1950s as a dangerous turning point in British culture. Symbolised by the national humiliation of the Suez Crisis, Potter's drama conceives it as the time when Britain (and England in particular) began to first lose touch with its historical traditions, forsaking much of its organic 'folk culture' and replacing it with an empty and Americanised 'mass culture', what Hoggart famously referred to as the new 'Candy-Floss World'.[34] As Potter suggested to Graham Fuller when describing his use of rock 'n' roll in *Lipstick on Your Collar*, set in 1956:

> To show that music and to be *in* that music while Suez is going on is a good example of how, dramatically, the music can show what is happening in terms of the breaking of the shell, or the fracturing of the egg, and some new, ugly little chick coming out. What it is we don't know, but it isn't the old England. It's England with blue suede shoes.[35]

Seen in this light, Daniel's' gradual alienation from his past is also suggestive of a wider loss of innocence. As he was tempted away from the communal harmony of his roots so England has forsaken the deep-rooted values and traditions of its past. Four hundred years into the future and the country, as one character points out, no longer 'exists as a political entity'.[36] The first thing one notices is that the British scientists are a mixture of ethnic groups, suggesting a multiculturalism perhaps at odds with Daniel's 'authentically' British memories. The serial, then, seems to suggest that Britain is in danger of losing touch with its past. Not the history of Empire or monarchy, but the organic history of its people and traditions. There has, it suggests, been a national or cultural 'repression' which has allowed Britain to forsake some of its most treasured beliefs and culture. As a result, Daniel's memories act as a reminder of what Britain has lost, a glimpse of 'Eden' before the Fall. 'Oh, we have so much to learn or relearn from the past,' a scientist explains, 'Daniel Feeld ... could have been our ... teacher!'[37] And as elsewhere in Potter's work, Daniel's distorted and fragmented memories (projected onto the 'living wall') illustrate how the past, present and future can never be successfully separated from each other, that each depends on the other for its own particular meaning and significance.

Here, then, is a treatment of personal consciousness which offers a parallel with human history – denial or repression being as unhealthy for a particular society or community as it is for the individual. Whether national or personal, in Potterland repression will amount to distortion, psychosis and finally mental and physical breakdown. This could also be interpreted as setting itself directly against the popular conception of postmodernism which has tended to proclaim 'the end of history'.[38] Some critics have even attempted to explain the individual experience of 'postmodernism' in terms of a 'schizophrenic' disorder. According to poststructuralist theorists like Jacques Lacan, the persistence of personal identity is an effect of discourse.[39] However, because of the postmodern uncertainty centred around language, the normal temporal sequence of the sentence (which gives us our sense of past, present and future) has been disrupted, producing a sense of temporal fragmentation. As Madan Sarup puts it, the individual is therefore 'condemned to live in a perpetual present with which the various moments of his or her past have little connection and for which there is no future on the horizon'.[40] According to the historian Eric Hobsbawm,

> [t]he destruction of the past ... is one of the most characteristic and eerie phenomena of the late twentieth century. Most young men and women at the century's end grow up in a sort of permanent present lacking any organic relation to the public past of the times they live in.[41]

Perhaps Daniel's ultimate dilemma is that he is *literally* forced to live in such a predicament; cast adrift in time, his own and unique 'schizophrenic' condition reflects a society which has lost all sense of its national identity and historical destiny; a reading further emphasised by the presence of Daniel's mysterious twin brother Christopher, who, eventually committed to a mental asylum, seems to represent a hidden and repressed side of Daniel's complex psychological make-up.[42]

It is this continual conflict between past, present and future which provides the real impulse behind Potter's futuristic melodrama. Four hundred years into the future and England has clearly lost touch with its most precious ideals and political principles. In particular, there is the sense that postwar British idealism has been forsaken and corrupted by the ever-increasing encroachment of American commercialism and economic Darwinism. The great reforms of welfare and nationalisation set in motion in Britain after the Second World War are now nothing but a distant memory. Talking to Bragg, Potter spoke glowingly of the 1945 Labour government which helped piece together the principles of the welfare state.[43] Daniel's Forest of Nead is the physical embodiment of those ideals, a tight-knit, working-class community whose strong sense of identity and its vibrant 'folk culture' suggests a country still in touch with itself and proud of its historical traditions. But this postwar idealism is perhaps best encapsulated by Potter's notion of public service broadcasting which he believed could unite the nation, projecting a paternal but essentially *democratic* vision.[44] Potter was particularly inspired by Raymond Williams's notion of a 'common culture', the idea that Britain could be connected through broadcasting by a common bond and identity.[45] However, cast adrift in this totally privatised world, Daniel's projected memories provide the final reminder of what has been lost, a form of British 'television' which is still able to fulfil its basic requirement to act as a public service, a 'keeper of folk memory' and the 'guardian of the national conscience'.[46]

It is this essentially 'modernist' vision of broadcasting which clearly lay behind Potter's unusual request that *Karaoke* and *Cold Lazarus* be shown both by the BBC and Channel 4. Such a demand was surely an attempt to take British broadcasting back 30 years, to recreate the so-called 'Golden Age' of British television drama. In particular, the move can be seen as an attempt to reconstruct the circumstances of the BBC's *Wednesday Play* when the whole country seemed to be watching this new 'national theatre'.[47] Indeed, both serials yearn for a mythical past, nostalgic for an 'innocent' and 'simpler' world whose notions of identity and community were seemingly more stable and secure. Daniel's 'folk memories' appear to offer a last glimpse of this forgotten world, a reminder of a time when Britain (at least, in comparison with the present or the foreseeable future) was apparently united in a shared vision and a common goal. In contrast, the commercialised and 'postmodern' world offered by digital broadcasting (producing the possibility of 500 television channels) suggests a national fragmentation which threatens to destroy the sort of cultural cohesion which the BBC may have once symbolised. Although *Cold Lazarus* failed to receive the sort of critical acclaim lavished upon some of Potter's earlier work, perhaps it does finally act as a 'fitting memorial' for a writer and a public figure who continued to champion and defend the founding ideals upon which British broadcasting and perhaps even postwar British society were established. As bizarre and outlandish as it might at first seem, Potter's last screenplay offers us a chilling critique of British television and politics as they both stand facing an uncertain and turbulent future.

Notes

1   See Dennis Potter, *Seeing The Blossom: Two Interviews, a Lecture and a Story* (Faber & Faber, 1994) p. 45. The Lecture was first given at the Edinburgh International Television Festival 1993.

2   'Dennis Potter – An Interview with Melvyn Bragg', *A Without Walls Special*, was first broadcast by Channel 4 on 5 April 1994. Such was the demand for a transcript of the interview that Faber & Faber published it a few months later (see Potter, *Seeing the Blossom* (1994)). A Channel 4 video of the interview was also subsequently released.

3   Potter had insisted that the comedian Roy Hudd and Louise Germaine (who had appeared in *Lipstick on Your Collar* and *Midnight Movie*) be given parts. In fact, the part of Sandra Sollars was actually written for Germaine who had to turn it down because of pregnancy. The part then went to Saffron Burrows. Hudd, however, remained to take the place of Ben Baglin.

4   For background to the debate over the Renny Rye and Kenith Trodd feud, see Mike Ellison, 'Potter dramas under threat', *Guardian*, Saturday, 9 June 1994.

5   For example, many scenes in *Karaoke* were set in central London which is a notoriously expensive location. However, the dramatist's wishes were preserved.

6   *Karaoke* was principally the responsibility of the BBC, while Channel 4 took responsibility for *Cold Lazarus*. *Karaoke* was therefore shown first on BBC and repeated on Channel 4, while for *Cold Lazarus* this running order was reversed.

7   This was Potter's way of bringing the two serials together, thereby uniting the two channels and the apparently different story-lines.

8   See Kenith Trodd's sleeve notes to the sound-track of *Karaoke* and *Cold Lazarus* (Channel 4 and BBC Records).

9 Milton Friedman (b. 1912) is an American economist, particularly associated with the concept of monetarism and a forceful advocate of free market capitalism.

10 All quotations from the lecture are cited by 'John Heliemann: Can the BBC be Saved?' (www.wired.com/wired/2.03/features/bbc.html). For a review of the lecture, see 'Home Truths', *Broadcast*, August 1989. For futher information on Murdoch, see 'The Rupert Murdoch Information Page' on www.cusn.edu/~kab42291/

11 Ibid.

12 Potter, *Seeing the Blossom* (1994), p. 47.

13 Dennis Potter, Karaoke *and* Cold Lazarus (Faber & Faber, 1996) p. 271.

14 Murdoch has more recently moved his attention to China. In terms of the UK alone, Murdoch owns *The Times, The Sunday Times,* the *Sun, News of the World, The Times Educational Supplement, The Times Higher Educational Supplement, The Times Literary Supplement, The Times Scottish Education Supplement, Trader, Sky Television, Sky News, Sky Movies, Sky One, Eurosport, Sky Radio,* as well as several publishing houses and a number of other operations.

15 Potter, Karaoke (1996), p. 232.

16 Ibid., p. 231.

17 Neil Postman, *Amusing Ourselves to Death: Public Discourse in the Age of Show Business* (Methuen, 1985), p. viii.

18 Potter, Karaoke (1996), p. 234.

19 Ibid., p. 205.

20 In *The Singing Detective* Philip Marlow suffers (like the playwright himself) from psoriatic arthropathy, a crippling form of psoriasis and arthritis which makes it practically impossible for him to move his head.

21 Potter, Karaoke (1996), p. 307.

22 This is a quotation from A. E. Houseman's *A Shropshire Lad*, a section of which Potter recites with great pathos at the end of *Blue Remembered Hills* (1979).

23 Potter's work abounds with Romantic allusions in general. The name of Emma Porlock (one of the leading British scientists) may also refer to Coleridge's writing of *Kubla Khan* in which the poet is awoken from an opium dream 'by a person on business from Porlock'.

24 Dennis Potter, Karaoke (1996), p. 204.

25 Anthony Weymouth and Bernard Lamizet, *Market & Myth: Forces of Change in the European Media* (Longman, 1996), pp. 11–12.

26 Potter made no bones about his dislike of the phrase or term 'postmodernism'. 'In the long, grey, ebb tide of so-named Post-modernism', he wrote in 1984, 'pseudo-totalitarian, illiberal, and dehumanising theories and practices lie on top of the cold waters like a huge and especially filthy oil slick' (Dennis Potter, *Waiting for the Boat: On Television* (Faber & Faber, 1984), p. 26).

27 Fredric Jameson, *Postmodernism or, The Cultural Logic of Late Capitalism* (Verso, 1991), p. x.

28 According to Chris Baldick, postmodern fiction such as Thomas Pynchon's *Gravity's Rainbow* (1973) and Vladimir Nabokov's *Ada* (1969) 'employ devices reminiscent of science fiction, playing with contradictory orders of reality or the irruption of the fabulous into the secular world'(Baldick, *The Concise Oxford Dictionary of Literary Terms* (Oxford University Press, 1990), p. 175.

29 In *Blade Runner* (a film generally regarded by critics as typically postmodern) the 'replicants' (androids who are apparently 'more human than human') are provided with memory implants which artificially give them a sense of their own history and individual identity. However, as a number of them gradually find out, their identity is fundamentally illusory and artificially induced.

30 Potter, *Seeing the Blossom* (1994), p. 41.

31 Because Daniel's memory does not remember events in a logical and chronological manner, we are given the past through a series of typically Potteresque 'flashbacks' and 'flash forwards'. The distortion of memory is also emphasised by Daniel appearing

as a child yet played by a fully grown man, a technique Potter originally employed in *Stand Up, Nigel Barton* (1965) and *Blue Remembered Hills* (1979).

32   Potter *Seeing the Blossom* (1994), p. 14.

33   Like Potter, Hoggart was also a scholarship boy who regretted the changes in working-class culture which he saw taking place during the 1950s. As John Storey has put it, 'Hoggart shares with the Leavisites a belief in a cultural *Fall* – from healthy culture to corrupt and corrupting mass culture' (John Storey (ed.), *Cultural Theory and Popular Culture: A Reader* (Harvester and Wheatsheaf, 1994), p. 47). For a further discussion of Potter's ambiguous relationship with mass culture generally, see Glen Creeber, "Banality With a Beat": Dennis Potter and the Paradox of Popular Music', *Media, Culture and Society*, vol. 18, no. 3, July 1996.

34   Richard Hoggart, *The Uses of Literacy* (Penguin Books, 1990), p. 206.

35   Potter cited by Graham Fuller (ed.), *Potter on Potter* (Faber & Faber, 1993), p. 103.

36   Potter, Karaoke (1996), p. 237.

37   Ibid., p. 243.

38   This phrase has been used by several contemporary commentators to suggest that the project of a 'single' history has come to an end. See, for example, Francis Fukuyama, *The End of History and the Last Man* (Penguin, 1992).

39   See Jacques Lacan, *Écrits: A Selection* (Tavistock, 1977), pp. 1–7.

40   Madan Sarup, *An Introductory Guide to Post-Structuralism and Post-Modernism* (Harvester Wheatsheaf, 1988), p. 134.

41   Eric Hobsbawm, *Age of Extremes: the Short Twentieth Century 1914–1991* (Michael Joseph, 1994), p. 3.

42   'He is me. And I am him,' Daniel cries at one point, '... I should be put away!' Potter, Karaoke (1996), p. 386.

43   'But we were, at that time both a brave and steadfast people, and we shared an aim, a condition, a political aspiration if you like, which was shown immediately in the 1945 General Election, and then one of the great governments of British history – those five, six years of creating what is now being so brutally and wantonly and callously dismantled was actually a period to be proud of, and I'm proud of it.' (Potter, *Seeing the Blossom* (1994) p. 9)

44   Potter liked to refer to television, because of its power to address different classes, as the most 'democratic medium'.

45   See the conclusion of Raymond Williams, *Culture and Society: 1780–1950* (Penguin, 1958).

46   According to Anthony Weymouth, public service broadcasters have been '[a]cting simultaneously as entertainers, interpreters of events, and ...' offering '... to the peoples of Europe a mediated reflection of themselves as national communities' (Weymouth and Lamizet, *Market & Myth* (1996), p. 11).

47   It was for the *Wednesday Play* that Potter began writing television drama. In Britain in the early 1960s there were only two television channels (BBC2 was introduced in 1964), making it much easier for a television programme to become a 'national event'. For example, Ken Loach's *Cathy Come Home* (1966) made such an impact that it is often associated with helping establish Shelter, the registered charity for the homeless.

2

Mike Wayne

Counter-Hegemonic Strategies in *Between the Lines*

The police genre, like most genres, depends on a high level of recurrent visual imagery (or iconography), thematic obsessions and recycled narrative strategies.[1] Despite this standardisation, the police genre, like all genres, is not fixed and static but dynamic and changeable. The possibilities for 'bending' the genre have attracted left cultural workers who have wanted to both dramatise contemporary social and political issues and reach large audiences. Writers, directors and producers like John McGrath, Troy Kennedy Martin, G. F. Newman, Tony Garnett and John Wilsher have all worked within the genre for this purpose. One of my intentions in this chapter is to give, as far as space allows, some voice to the intentions and perspectives of such cultural workers in the television industry. Yet such 'authors' do not work in a vacuum. The accumulated history of the police genre pushes the cultural worker in certain directions, determining how and what can be said. But at the same time, a genre is more or less malleable and open to reinscription. How far the genre can be inflected in new directions depends on the wider contexts of production and consumption as much as on the individual cultural workers concerned. The context of consumption, for example, asserts itself via the conventions of genres which establish a kind of 'contract' with audiences, mapping out the terms on which cultural workers and audiences meet and communicate in the semiotic space of the text. To paraphrase Martin Barker, a whole range of social relationships are implicitly sedimented into generic conventions.[2] Thus we can expect wider sociocultural contradictions to be inscribed into the terms of the contract which such conventions establish with their audiences. I will explore this in relation to the role of the police hero/heroine in the narrative structure.

As far as the context of production is concerned, writers, producers, directors, etc., also work with and within definite industrial facilities, constraints and pressures. Central to this context is the way the text is enmeshed in processes that produce and define it as a *cultural commodity*. 'Cultural' because television's texts are – in the broadest sense of the term – symbolic goods, resonating with the meanings, values, desires and anxieties in wider social circulation. 'Commodity' because television's texts are also economic goods, attempting to accumulate profits, if advertising funded, and/or (for the BBC) to compete in the ratings wars. The cultural and economic dimensions of the text are often pulling in different directions and, as has been argued in relation to the single play, economic considerations may transform or even erase the text.[3] I will trace some of the tensions between *Between the Lines* as a cultural good and as an economic good, across a few key textual strategies. Essentially, I have been summarising Tom Ryall's recasting of Marxian theory into the model illustrated in Figure 2.1.[4] This offers a methodology for exploring the relationships between cultural workers, audiences, genres, texts and contexts. As can be seen from the diagram, Ryall completes the methodology by circumscribing cultural production and consumption within the wider sociopolitical context. I want to start with a brief sketch of this wider context.

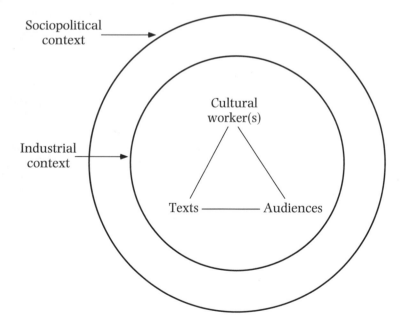

Fig. 2.1   Ryall's Model

Hegemony, *Ubermensch*, and Gramsci

A classic study of the media's portrayal of law and order and its relationship to the wider social context can be found in *Policing the Crisis*.[5] It was Antonio Gramsci who initially developed the concept of hegemony into an analytical tool for Marxism and it is the framing concept for the authors of *Policing the Crisis*. Gramsci argued that capitalist democracies reproduced themselves through a combination of consent and coercion. In 'normal' times, it is the mode of consent which predominates, which is to say that the political and economic elites are successful in providing the cultural, intellectual and moral leadership necessary to secure consent from the subordinate classes for their socioeconomic agenda. However, it is also the norm for capitalism to undergo periodic economic crises (such as the downturn of the business cycle) with all the attendant social problems that that brings. Typically, in such a context, the dominant economic and political elites have to resort more to coercion, as their moral, intellectual, and cultural roots wither in the parched terrain of economic, social and political conflict. The authors of *Policing the Crisis* argue that this indeed was the case in the 1970s. They chart a modification in the operation of hegemony, detecting 'a tilt in the operation of the state away from consent towards the pole of coercion ... and the powerful orchestration, in support of this tilt ... of an *authoritarian* consensus'.[6] Their focus is on the print media's representation of the phenomenon of 'mugging'. They argue that the image of mugging constructed served both to articulate a feeling of law and order breakdown, while also *concealing* the social forces and contradictions accumulating within the crime and responses to it, as well as the wider historical context in which it occurs.

History, it seems, really does repeat itself as farce. In the 1990s we find Jack Straw, then Labour's shadow Home Secretary, making a speech in which he attacked 'winos', drug addicts, 'aggressive' begging and 'squeegee merchants' as 'obstacles faced by pedestrians and motorists in going about their daily business'.[7] The speech produced a number of responses in articles and letters that were deeply critical of Straw's targets and emphasis. Some responses, like Suzanne Moore's, were supportive. I want to address some of her arguments as a way into the question of 'the popular', into hegemony and left interventions.

Suzanne Moore defended Jack Straw by arguing that he was in touch with the common experience of the decaying urban environment. The article is full of appeals to recognise the *emotional* charge of this experience, arguing that attempts to explain and account for the causal factors underpinning it are inevitably insufficient and implicitly the luxury of the middle class.

> the presence of such people [the homeless, unemployed, drug addicts] in our midst may serve as a reminder of the failure of government

policy, of inequalities of the way we live, but I doubt it. Those who can afford to, avoid face-to face confrontation if they can. They don't use public transport. They don't live in areas in which adolescent crusties huddle with decrepit winos .... They don't take their kids to playgrounds covered in dog shit and broken bottles, screwed up tin foil and used condoms. They don't see it the same way. Those of us who do can't help but feel uneasy in our streets. We feel that no one cares, that there is no one or nothing to stop bad things happening, that it's all out of control.[8]

This discourse resonates with the impulses and desires which Adorno recognised to be susceptible to irrational authoritarianism. Along with the intellectual retrogression which underpins the rejection of rational explanation, there is the increasing aggression evident in the reiterated use of 'they', directed towards those who can 'afford' to avoid coming face to face with this appalling vista of social decay. The emphasis on feelings and emotions divorced from rational explanation is linked to the sense that things are out of control, that 'bad' things are happening, and therefore implicitly requiring the need for someone to intervene in this hour of crisis and assert their authority. Jack Straw, it seems, is Moore's *Ubermensch*. Moore's argument is that we must not be afraid to articulate our fears and anxieties in relation to crime, for such a denial 'plays into the hands of the right more than anything else'.[9] Yet while Gramsci would have agreed that the left must engage with the 'elemental passions of the people' in order to strike a popular chord,[10] he also argued that the left's intervention cannot reside at the level of emotion and feeling alone. That way lies the route of the demagogue, something Gramsci, languishing in Mussolini's jails, knew a little about. Although Moore claims not to know how this law and order debate 'divides up on traditional left–right lines',[11] any left position worthy of the name must surely begin by tracing the roots of people's feelings back to their institutional causes and the macrostructures and social relationships which frame them.

This is the basis of any counter-hegemonic intervention such as *Between the Lines* attempts. For the left, the state apparatus constitutes a rather more substantial locus of oppressive power than 'squeegee merchants'. The task is to touch the people where they fear, not to frighten them further but to raise political and social questions rather than promote mythological solutions.[12] Thus *Between the Lines* focuses on the Complaints Investigation Bureau (CIB). According to Tony Garnett, the producer of the series, this focus allowed 'us to pose the fundamental political question, which is, who shall police the police?'[13] Clearly, the space for such a question to be posed has been prised open in the context of growing public unease about the police which mushroomed in the 1980s. It became clear in the wake of the miners' and print workers' strikes that the police were being harnessed to contain the social fall-out generated by the free market policies of the Thatcher governments. The debates about the 'politicisation' of the police (a problematic term insofar as it assumes a once neutral arm of the state apparatus) had barely subsided when, in the 1990s, a whole string of convictions were found to be 'unsafe' – in legal discourse – or to be 'fit-ups', as they are known in television fiction. The routine competence and honesty of the police came into question in the wake of a series of successful appeals by the Birmingham Six, the Guildford Four, the Tottenham Three, the Taylor sisters, Judith Ward, and others.

The Context and Process of Production

Between the Lines ran for three series of 13 parts each. The first episode was broadcast on 4 September 1992 and episode 13 of the first series concluded on 4 December 1992.[14] The second and third series ran over similar periods in 1993 and 1994. It was produced by Tony Garnett's Island World Productions for BBC1. Across the three series there is a definite progression. The first series introduces us to the three main characters; Tony Clark (Neil Pearson), his 'bag man' Harry Naylor (Tom Georgeson) and Maureen Connell (Siobhan Redmond), all newly arrived at CIB. At one level the first series is quite 'local' in its focus on accusations of and actual police malpractice at various police stations. But the series culminates by uncovering a web of corruption, hypocrisy and cover-ups, with CIB Chief Superintendent John Deakin at its head. The second series continues to move the focus away from individual police stations and increasingly situates its narratives within a national and even international context. This is achieved by looking at the relationships between Special Branch (an arm of the Metropolitan Police) and MI5, and the struggles between the two agencies for 'turf', with CIB trying to hold the ring of accountability. The final series sees all three principal characters leave the police force and move into the world of private security, corporate sabotage, and the drugs and arms dealing industries. I want to concentrate on the first two series.

At one level, *Between the Lines* is very much the product of the dominant economic logic coursing its way through the television industry. As Tony Garnett argues:

I think television's changing and there will be more and more long-running series for commercial reasons of cost per thousand viewers. With big sets you can amortise over a number of weeks and audiences can identify with regular characters. There will be fewer one-off films which are very expensive and probably even fewer mini-series except at the more glossy commercial end.[15]

But within this logic *Between the Lines* tries to articulate cultural values which run against the grain of the industry's economics. The proof of this is to ask whether the series would have existed at all on British television in the early 1990s were it not for BBC1. The short answer is surely, no. The viewing figures for *Between the Lines* hovered between 7 and 8 million, which would have been considered reasonably satisfactory by the BBC. But at that time BBC2 was not investing in long-running series (this was several years before the nine-part series *Our Friends in the North*). Similarly, so many episodes of high-budget drama would have been prohibitively expensive for Channel 4.

That leaves ITV. One of the paradoxical outcomes of recent government broadcasting legislation is that it has left ITV at the centre of a television system powered, more than it has ever been before, by the narrowly economic logic of market forces. Yet, at the same time, ITV now 'enjoys' a fractious, conflictual relationship with its governing body, the Independent Television Commission (ITC). ITV and the ITC are the odd couple of television. The ITC is trying (vainly) to maintain a cultural dimension to television. It is, to be sure, a very conservative notion of culture but, nevertheless, it offers some kind of discourse about television as a cultural good, as well as an economic good. In its 1995 review of ITV's cultural performance, the ITC concluded that ITV should take more risks, particularly in the areas of drama, entertainment and comedy. David Glencross, ITC's chief executive said: 'ITV can afford to take occasional risks with one offs, they do not need to win every slot, every night.'[16] Revealingly, Paul Jackson of Carlton replied: 'It's all very well for people to say we do not have to win every slot every day, but the system is that way.'[17] It is inconceivable then that *Between the Lines*, an expensive series (costing around £450,000 per hour) would have found a home with ITV based on projected audience figures of around 8 million.

So BBC1 was the only place where *Between the Lines* could have found a home. And even here there are commodifying pressures to be negotiated. The pressures for a text to function as a commodity are inscribed into the product at inception (in the case of *Between The Lines*, for example, there was a need to have a 'hero') and are modulated to a particular level of intensity (how, if at all and in what ways will the hero be 'flawed'?) which will vary according to a whole range of variables (e.g. commissioning organisation, place in the schedules, etc.). The potential and the tendency is for that pressure to increase over the lifetime of the commodity with ever-diminishing cultural returns. One has immediately to qualify the last statement for two reasons. First, it is not only organisations and texts which define the cultural uses and values of symbolic goods. Audiences also play a part, and may be working to quite different agendas and priorities. Secondly, and within limits, commodifying pressures at the point of production can be resisted. As Tony Garnett says:

We consciously pay the price in the ratings for having a flawed hero and for all the ambiguities. I could do this show and guarantee to put at least 3 million, maybe 5 million on the house if we did certain things, but the stories are complicated and it's not easy viewing.[18]

Interestingly, not all the pressures to make a text easy viewing come from the sponsoring organisation. Commenting on how writers for *Between the Lines* often approached the central character of the series, Garnett complains how many tried to 'turn him into a Boy Scout so that he's more and more, in an uncomplicated way, someone you can root for'.[19] There is perhaps a generation gap here. If it is true that many new writers are already attuned to an increasingly ratings-dominated television system, Garnett's experience in television gives him a reference point back to previous struggles between television as cultural good and television as economic good.

This is particularly true of the first series of *Z-Cars* which went on air in the early 1960s. This series has become a celebrated instance of the possibilities for and difficulties involved in a left intervention into popular culture. The key figures here were John McGrath and Troy Kennedy Martin. As director and writer respectively, they both wanted to use the police in *Z-Cars* as a device for representing the wider social community, for exploring its social problems and, in McGrath's words, for 'finding out about people's lives'.[20] According to Stuart Laing, this interest in the way the wider community is lived, allowed for 'a level of latent critical social analysis' just below the surface of the narrative.[21] However, the very success of the series determined its future development and to a large extent closed the space for such critical possibilities. As the BBC realised they had found a popular product, the more the pressure increased to stabilise that product around a particular set of imagery and concerns. The only imagery and themes which appeared each week were the police themselves. Thus, gradually, the police as known, familiar quantities, became the main subjects of *Z-Cars* rather than the vehicle for exploring the vicissitudes of wider social relationships.

That experience has stayed with Tony Garnett, but in John Wilsher he found a writer who could devise some textual strategies which might keep the series moving in new directions so as to keep it fresh and attuned to exploring contemporary social realities. Wilsher set to work constructing a narrative framework which would have enough shape to appeal to commissioning editors, while still leaving room for the writers of individual episodes to have some creative input. Here he is describing his role:

I provided a fairly extensive overall outline, laying down the basic format which says who these characters are and what the context is that they work in. I then lay out what I describe as a dummy magazine, that is to say 12 or 13 possible individual stories which also indicate overall plot and character developments. I said to the other writers, 'If you like those individual ideas, pursue them. If you can come up with something that will carry on our overall plot in a satisfactory way, by all means do that.' Some people followed my suggestions and some people came up with entirely new notions of their own.[22]

The idea of the first series, and it is one which Garnett and Wilsher concede did not always work, was an ambitious one. It was to operate on three levels. Watching the entire 13 episodes, the text would hang together as a single narrative 'like an episodic nineteenth-century novel', according to Garnett. At another level, there was a strong serial element whereby storylines would play out across a number of different episodes (for example, Jenny Dean's story). 'What we're at least attempting to do,' Garnett suggests, 'is allow the characters to grow through the experiences they are having – the serial element is helpful there.'[23]

At the third level there was a series structure whereby there would be at least one narrative that would get resolved each week. It was through this multilayered, dynamic structure that *Between the Lines* tried to keep open creative possibilities for its producer, writers, directors and actors. The linchpin is the serial element, linking individual episodes and the resolution of individual storylines, to the macrostructure which is much more ambiguous, ambivalent and shifting than some of the parts which make up the whole. It is a lesson in thinking strategically about cultural form that the serial device plays such an important role in setting up resistances to the pressures of commodification, when the serial as soap opera is the television system's main weapon in the ratings war of attrition.[24]

Narrative and the Concept of 'the Hero'

The police have a contradictory position in social life under capitalism. On the one hand they are supposed to function for the protection of the public, implementing the law fairly and impartially; yet they also function as part of the state's coercive apparatus. So many people inevitably experience the police in ways which contradict the protective, public service function. It may be as a worker on a picket line, as a black person getting stopped in the street, as a legitimate demonstrator, or as an anti-road and veal export protester, or other such flashpoints, but wider layers of society are coming into contact with the police in ways which force them to ask 'Whose law and whose order?' Outside a revolutionary context, such a question will, in all likelihood, co-exist with the dominant representation of the police which, after all, is a deeply appealing and reassuring image. This tension is captured by veteran writer G. F. Newman when he says,

Individuals are afraid of all sorts of things and they want to believe that there is this thin blue line that can protect us from the marauding hordes. The problem is, the thin blue line very often is the marauding horde.[25]

As Geoffrey Hurd has argued, it is possible to trace the contradictory position of the police and public perceptions of policing in television's police genre.[26] We can trace such contradictions, embedded in the terms of the contract which genres establish between texts and audiences, around the figure of the police as hero/heroine.

Take, for example, the classic 1970s cop show *The Sweeney*. The central character, Jack Regan, is an iconic but contradictory type. On the one hand he seems to represent one of the currents flowing into that authoritarian consensus which Hall *et al.* mapped out in *Policing the Crisis*. Tempting as it may be, it would be a mistake to situate *The Sweeney* as simply preparing the ground for that 'tilt' towards the rule of coercion. For *The Sweeney* does not 'reflect' that wider social reality but reconstructs it within the genre's *own* rules. One of those 'rules' is that the hero be clearly separable from the institution of law and order which he serves. Regan's appeal lies largely in the fact that, like the earlier lawman in the western genre, he is an *outsider*.[27] In the Western genre, the sheriff struggles to establish the law against the complacency, cowardice, opposition or plain ineffectualness of the town. Whereas in the Western the individual *is* the law, in the modern urban setting of the police drama the individual is only one component of a larger organisation. Here it is the institution of the law itself which is characterised as complacent and ineffectual because of its massive inertia under the weight of bureaucracy, its sensitivity to political pressures and its adherence to 'the rules' which the Regans of the world will break, if necessary, to establish social order. This deep attachment to the integrity of the individual complicates the series' relationship with the shift towards the more authoritarian state. For indeed, anything which suggested a more general, systematic and *institutionalised* coerciveness would make identification with Reganesque characters, for most of the audience, deeply problematic. In the contradictory world of popular culture, the flipside of Regan, the anti-hero, reveals the sinister image of the state apparatus casting its menacing shadow over the people, instead of protecting them.

It is precisely this flipside which the police genre has to register in the 1980s, while not entirely relinquishing the sociopsychic appeal of 'the thin blue line'. This tension is again resolved by the outsider motif, but now reversed. In one-off dramas such as *Black and Blue* and mini-series such as *Prime Suspect* and its sequels, the central characters are outsiders not because they 'bend the rules' and are coercive where the institution is weak, but rather because they are black, or are women, encroaching into the bastions of white male power. In Lynda La Plante's *Prime Suspect*, the male detective initially in charge of the murder case is a Reganesque character, cutting corners and boisterously boosting his masculinity by engaging in 'laddish' record-breaking games (for example, trying to break the record time for receiving a murder case to charging a suspect). When DCI Tennison (Helen Mirren) takes over the case after the male detective has a heart attack, the prime suspect has to be released precisely because, as Tennison finds, procedures have not been adhered to and the evidence has not been accumulated in the proper manner. If the defining characteristic of the outsider in the 1970s was the cop who transgresses the rules, in the 1980s the ethnic and gender identities of the cops are mapped onto an argument that the outsider is someone who believes in the effectiveness of the law as an *institution* and practises its legal procedures. This allows the drama to highlight problems with police malpractice, which is then often linked with the wider discriminations of race and sex which the institution has internalised. Of course this still allows the police drama to hold out the possibility that the institution can be reformed by the good practice of the lead characters. This route, taken by *Prime Suspect*, obviously leads the drama in an affirmative, consolatory direction.

In formal terms, the police hero/heroine is defined as the narrative's problem-solving agency. The more interesting police dramas are those which call into question the hero/heroine's capacity to resolve the multiplying and overlapping problems of corruption, sexism and/or racism which the crime and the pursuit of the criminal throw up. In G. F. Newman's bruising representation of the police in *Black and Blue*, the black police officer at the centre of the narrative, Maurice Knight (Christopher John Hall), is torn between the principle of law enforcement and the black community who suffer the practice of law enforcement in 1990s Britain. Unlike the Western 'knights' (for example, *Shane*), Maurice Knight is an outsider not by choice but because he cannot belong to both his ethnic and professional community. He is stranded between them, caught in the racist wilderness that separates the black community from a white-dominated police force. As far as the prospect of reform is concerned, the ending is decidedly ambiguous. The hero returns to the community centre on the estates where he has been working undercover. A youngster tries to steal his recently awarded Queen's Medal for bravery, but when caught, tosses it back saying, 'It ain't worth shit,' to which the black cop replies, 'That's for sure.' The tensions between registering systemic corruption *and* maintaining the appeal of 'the thin blue line' have in this drama become so acute that it is not clear whether our narrative hero is still in the force, and if he is, whether his presence makes for anything more than a *token* difference. It is this tension between making a real difference and having only a token effect, between reforming pressures within the force and a deeply entrenched institutional paralysis and self-serving stagnation, between having a hero who resolves narrative problems and a hero who is confronted with overwhelming, pervasive corruption, which *Between the Lines* tries to sustain in over two dozen episodes.

Between the Lines

Like DCI Tennison, Tony Clark is a massively ambitious and upwardly mobile career cop, something which the Jack Regans of the world rarely are. But the gendering of police heroes/heroines, which is pervasive in the genre, means that this attachment to procedures threatens to emasculate Clark, installed as he is in the upper echelons of the police bureaucracy and tasked with policing the Jack Regans of the force.[28] One of the least successful aspects of the first series was the wild sexual adventures which Clark enjoyed in his personal life, as if the series was trying to 'prove' his masculinity in the light of his professional location. It could be argued that the sexual betrayals in which Clark engages (he is initially married) raise the possibility of whether he would betray his professional life. This appears to be where the series is heading as it is gradually revealed that his lover, another police officer, Jenny Dean, is also implicated in corruption. However, the question of whether his personal life would overwhelm his professional conduct is closed off by the suicide of Jenny Dean. This leaves Clark successfully to pursue his corrupt boss at CIB, John Deakin. In other words, although Tony Garnett complained that some writers tried to 'whiten Clark', Clark is already fairly 'pure' in that his professional integrity remains untarnished, no matter how dubious his personal conduct might have been.

In the first series, it is not the personal moral shortcomings of Clark which make him an interestingly flawed hero. Rather, it is in the hints and glimpses we are given as to the limits in which he operates, limits which check his ability to function in the conventional heroic mode and resolve problems. For the problems identified are often not amenable to individualistic solutions, or are held by his bosses to be outside his brief. Thus the real flaws, it is implied, are structural and institutional. This is further developed in the second series which consolidates and extends the strengths of the first series while avoiding some of its weaknesses. It becomes increasingly clear that CIB is not a crusading department, but rather a pragmatic one, whose investigations into corruption become weighed down by trade-offs and deals between various parts of the political, judicial and security apparatus.

Title Sequence

It is worth considering the title sequence of *Between the Lines* for it tells us, as title sequences often do, an awful lot about the kind of programme we are about to watch. The sequence consists of a mix of images beginning with a shot of the River Thames at Battersea Power Station and finishing with the Houses of Parliament. Given that this series is about the circumvention of democratic power and accountability, beginning the sequence with an image of the abandoned power station and finishing with the Houses of Parliament is a provocative way of raising questions about the status and role of the House in relation to the state and wider society. In addition to weaving this metaphor about power out of the physical landscape of London, we see clips of the central characters 'in action' and various images of urban conflict (mounted police, riots, etc.). The images of the police we see are not about resolving individual crimes (as, for example, in the way the opening sequence of *The Sweeney* dramatises); rather they are images which foreground social and political relationships which are in crisis. There is also the intriguing image of Tony Clark himself watching these images which suggests that he himself is troubled by them and that his relationship to these social conflicts and the police is problematic and uneasy. These images are placed within a 'widescreen' ratio, with the titles 'Between the Lines' sliding repeatedly above and below the image, right to left. Thus the sequence offers the images (and the programme which follows) as a reading 'between the lines' of the official reports, documents and public announcements which constitute the state's relationship with the public. The reiterated theme in episode after episode is that the full story never gets told.

The prominence and importance of London in the title sequence is typical. The city is a crucial component of the symbolic geography of the police genre. It almost always figures in title sequences, including American police dramas such *NYPD Blue*, *Homicide* and *Hill Street Blues*. This is because, as we have seen, the streets of the city, with its various and diverse 'recesses and labyrinths',[29] provide the crucial testing ground for the hero's masculinity. The authors of *Policing the Crisis* also regarded the image of the city – or rather a specific location within the city, the ghetto/slum – as playing an important role in the print media's representation of 'mugging'. They suggest that the image of the city that was mobilised with its 'apparent richness of description and evocation stood in place of analytic connections'.[30] The authors argue that posing some answers to the relationship between crime and the environment would require 'calling into question some fundamental characteristics of society'.[31] The image of the city offered by the print media blocked off systematic analysis in favour of presenting the city as a vast amorphous place of fear and fate, secreting crime as naturally as it presents the diversity of humanity. The title sequence of *NYPD Blue* is a particularly striking example of this representation of the city. Something very similar is, arguably, operating in most television crime drama. By contrast, *Between the Lines* (as the title sequence implies) does try to make analytic connections and reveal something of the political topography and power relations of London.

'New Order'

The first episode of the second series was 'New Order' written by J. C. Wilsher. The hints at fascism in the title are immediately confirmed in the first image as a skinhead climbs to the top of a mosque and fastens a pig's head onto one of the minarets. In the streets below, a Moslem self-defence group clash with a group of fascists. The police arrive. In the ensuing melee the fascist who planted the pig's head, and who has now joined the fighting, is arrested by a police officer. But then there is mutual recognition between them. 'For Christ's sake, Steve,' implores the fascist. Shocked, the arresting officer releases him, but is seen by one of the Moslems. Immediately then the narrative has set up a question in the mind of the audience concerning the relationship between the police and fascist organisations. This theme will run throughout the episode but only as part of a more complex, more contradictory and bigger picture.

There is however an important sub-plot to this episode which is part of the serial element of the series. This concerns the 'new order' within CIB itself. Having arrested his own boss at the end of the first series, Tony Clark is now Acting Chief Superintendent of CIB and is hoping that the position will be made permanent. His old boss, Deakin, is still on trial and a new officer, Graves, has joined the CIB team. Graves is a 'university man' or 'flyer' as Clark calls him, and as such is also seeking rapid promotion within the force. Traditionally in the genre a figure from such a background is suspect, particularly in terms of their masculinity. But in *Between the Lines* Clark's animus towards Graves is just one of many references to the class tensions that exist within the police. Clark does however appear to be on an upwardly mobile trajectory himself, answering the phone as 'Acting Chief Superintendent' with evident relish and assigning Graves and Harry the job of looking into the 'Mosque trouble'. In the first half of this first episode, then, Clark is increasingly associating himself with 'the office', while his subordinates work on the streets. This desk-bound trajectory would appear to undermine his qualifications to be a 'hero' in the genre.

Gradually Harry, Maureen and Graves find out that the fascist released by the police officer is called Joe Rance, that he is himself in the force and later they discover he is working undercover for Special Branch. Clark comes into conflict with Special Branch, believing that Rance may have 'gone native', something which various shots of Rance (in bed with his Union Jack bedspread, engaging in military-style fitness programmes, etc.) appear to imply. But this is not simply a question of an individual loose cannon since the episode maps out the wider political relationships in which Rance moves. Rance has become a driver for Derek Lee-Metford, the national organiser for a fascist grouping called New Order. The role of driver for Rance allows the text to map a set of political relationships. For example, we see Rance collecting a suitcase of money for his boss and we later learn that this is a donation from an Arab embassy towards anti-

Zionist and anti-Semitic propaganda. When Rance expresses surprise at the source of money, Metford argues that, 'a political movement has to make strategic and tactical alliances, even with its enemies'. Contacts, networks, alliances; this is the substance of what *Between the Lines* likes to explore.

The scene then cuts to the lawns in front of the Houses of Parliament where a Conservative MP, Douglas Carter, is being interviewed by a television crew about the case of a Mr Ingram, an American fascist historian whom the Home Office has granted a visa to enter the country to promote his new book. Carter evidently has a reputation as a right-winger because his interview is cut short by anti-fascist demonstrators. In the next shot we see Carter being interviewed in a television studio about Ingram's book *A 20th-Century Myth* in which (like the real life 'historian' Robert Faurisson) Ingram argues that the Holocaust was an invention of Germany's wartime enemies.[32] The scene then cuts to a bar where Harry and Clark are playing pool; the television interview with Carter is playing in the background. They are discussing Clark's prospects for promotion. This sequence of shots is significant. Most police dramas (such as *The Bill* and *NYPD Blue*) never have a scene without the presence or imminent presence of the police. The narration's perspective is thus anchored in their experiences, which makes for exciting drama certainly but is structurally unable to explore the contexts in which policing takes place. By contrast, *Between the Lines* does not feel compelled to locate the police in every single shot of the programme. This allows the text to sketch the wider sociopolitical forces whose alliances and conflicts the police are caught up in but cannot, in any simple way, control. Thus we have moved from an opening image which is very local, that of the London mosque and the struggle to defend it against the fascists, up to the national (Douglas Carter) and international (Patrick Ingram) context.

Metford, of course, also wants his fascist movement to move from the local to the global and so he visits Carter to give him a signed copy of Ingram's book. He persuades Carter that it would be beneficial to everyone if he and Ingram were to meet. Carter agrees, but only if the meeting is secret. On the doorstep of Carter's plush country home, the combination of this most 'English' of *mise-en scènes* with Metford's discourse creates an unsettling picture of alliances being forged. Metford declares of Ingram:

> He's changing the climate. After all, we represent three different paths to the same broad goal. I can speak for the lads at the sharp end, on the streets. Ingram's engaged in the battle for ideas and you are part of the political establishment, although not compromised by it. ... who knows what might be allowed to speak its name next.

Metford has obviously read Gramsci! Political leaders, the intelligentsia and 'the masses' were, Gramsci argued, three key social forces involved in the struggle for hegemony (whether it be a fascist, parliamentary or socialist hegemony). *Between the Lines* situates the police as occupying a contradictory position in relation to these wider social forces and this is evident in the final scenes of the episode.

The climax builds. In the light of Deakin being found not guilty in court, Maureen warns Clark that perhaps, with his promotion prospects under consideration, Clark should not challenge Special Branch's undercover operation. Clark however argues the case that Rance is still subject to the law and so continues surveillance of Rance's movements. With Special Branch pulling one way, CIB (under Clark) another, the local police are facilitating Ingram's arrival at a New Order meeting by smuggling him through the anti-fascist demonstrators in a police uniform. 'Your British police are wonderful,' Ingram declares to Metford once inside the hall. During the subsequent meeting the anti-fascists break into the hall. Fights between the police, New Order and anti-fascists break out. On Metford's instructions, Rance leads Ingram out of the back of the hall, intending to drive him to his secret meeting with Carter. But once outside, Rance assaults photographers and anti-fascist demonstrators as he bundles Ingram into a van. Clark, Harry and Graves arrive and arrest him. However, the indications that Rance has become too immersed in the fascist culture seem to be contradicted when they discover recording equipment taped to his body.

The conclusion of this narrative problem does not however operate as a vindication of Special Branch, their Reganesque man, Rance, or even CIB. Back at the office (traditionally the police narrative's moment of closure) a number of questions and outcomes remain unanswered and problematic. Maureen, wondering what Special Branch would have done with the recording that Rance was going to obtain, is told by Harry (who is ex-Special Branch) that they would have kept it for their own purposes of leverage over a political figure, rather than 'going public' with it. It then becomes clear that the professional relationship between Clark and Graves has altered. We find Clark protesting that Rance is not going to be charged with assault. Graves appears to be handing information down from superiors. 'Not in the public interest,' he declares; Rance has left the force, he informs Clark/the audience, and Special Branch now believe he was working for MI5 all along. The final image confirms why Graves has suddenly become the authoritative source of such information. As Clark, Maureen and Harry file into the room for him to 'spell out the lessons' of the Rance case, Graves shuts the door of the Chief Superintendent's room. It has his name on it.

Conclusion

The problem for Clark is that he never learns his lesson. He does not see a conflict between his career ambitions and what CIB is supposed to stand for. He is, rather like Maurice Knight in *Black and Blue*, something of a naive character. This naivety is a crucial component of the text's generic contract with its audiences. It represents the audience's sociopsychic investment in the possibility of reform even as episode after episode reveals CIB's complicity in undermining democratic sanctions, its emphasis on institutional survival over and above accountability, and its public relations function. The lesson for the audience, is simply this. The police operate (albeit contradictorily) within the institutional and cultural hegemony of the *status quo*. Irrespective of the good intentions of individuals, they are part of the problem, not part of the solution. By revealing this on prime-time television, *Between the Lines* can be said to be a counter-hegemonic text.

Notes

1   For a discussion of iconography, see Ed Buscombe, 'The Idea of Genre in the American Cinema', in *Film Genre Reader* (University of Texas Press, 1986).
2   Martin Barker, *Comics, Ideology, Power and the Critics* (Manchester University Press, 1989), p. 275.
3   Carl Gardner and John Wyver, 'The Single Play: From Reithian Reverence to Cost-Accounting and Censorship', in *Screen*, vol. 24, nos 4–5, 1983.
4   Tom Ryall, *Teachers' Study Guide 2: The Gangster Film* (BFI, 1979).
5   Stuart Hall, Chas Critcher, Tony Jefferson, John Clarke, Brian Roberts, *Policing the Crisis: Mugging, the State and Law and Order* (Macmillan, 1978).
6   Hall *et al.*, *Policing*, p. 217.
7   *Guardian*, 5 September 1995, p. 1.
8   Suzanne Moore, 'On The Real Mean Streets', *Guardian*, 2, 7 September 1995, p. 5.
9   Moore, ibid.
10 Gramsci, quoted in James Joll, *Gramsci* (Fontana, 1977), p. 101.
11 Moore, 'Mean Streets', p. 5.
12 Richard Sparks discusses how in the police genre 'the invocation of fear is deeply integrated in both the discursive structures and saleability of cultural goods', thus heightening the consolatory powers of the texts when we see effective police action. See *Television and the drama of crime: moral tales and the place of crime in public life* (Open University Press, 1992), p. 159.
13 Tony Garnett, interviewed by Peter Keighron and Mike Wayne, 6 April 1993.
14 The first series is now available on video.
15 Garnett, interview, 6 April 1993.
16 *Guardian*, 12 April 1995, p. 6.
17 Ibid.
18 Garnett, interview, 6 April 1993.
19 Ibid.
20 Quoted in Stuart Laing, 'Banging in some reality: the original Z-Cars', in John Corner (ed.) *Popular Television in Britain* (BFI, 1991), p. 127.
21 Ibid, p. 134.
22 John Wilsher, interviewed by Peter Keighron, 15 April 1993.
23 Garnett, interview, 6 April 1993.
24 Mike Wayne, 'Television, Audiences, Politics' in Stuart Hood (ed.) *Behind the Screens: The Structure of British Television in the Nineties* (Lawrence and Wishart, 1994), pp. 58–62.
25 G. F. Newman, interviewed by Peter Keighron, 16 April 1993.

26 Geoffrey Hurd, 'The Television Presentation of the Police' in Tony Bennett, Susan Boyd-Bowman, Colin Mercer and Janet Woollacott (eds) *Popular Television and Film* (BFI, 1981), pp. 64–5.
27 Alan Clarke, '"This is not the boy scouts": Television police series and definitions of law and order' in Tony Bennett, Colin Mercer and Janet Woolacott (eds) *Popular Culture and Social Relations* (Open University Press, 1986), pp. 219–21.
28 Hurd, 'The Television Presentation of the Police', p. 67.
29 Sparks, *Television and the Drama of Crime*, p. 126.
30 Hall *et al.*, *Policing the Crisis*, p. 118.
31 Ibid.
32 For Faurisson's theories see Christopher Norris, *Uncritical Theory: Postmodernism, Intellectuals and the Gulf War* (Lawrence and Wishart, 1992), pp. 71–4.

3

Mike Wayne

Crisis and Opportunity: Class, Gender and Allegory in *The Grand*

If cultural practitioners working within television want to have a dissident voice, then they will need to think strategically about their institutional location and the generic and formal strategies which they deploy. The limit case for what can and cannot be achieved must surely be the commercial heartlands of terrestial television: ITV. If my argument about *The Grand* has any validity, then it may serve as an antidote to the dangers of cultural pessimism in difficult times. Produced by Granada Television for ITV, *The Grand* is set in the period shortly after the First World War, in a large Victorian Manchester hotel. This essay explores the dual referents invoked by the series: on the one hand the disruptions in class and gender wrought by the traumas and transformations of the war; on the other, broadcast over the period of the 1997 General Election, *The Grand* is also a coded rumination on our own contemporary moment.[1] Thus the series explores the way the post-First World War period was informed by the war years precisely at the moment when questions of change and continuity were being dramatised in contemporary politics. In offering a critical account of the continuities in class and gender domination in 1920 and, by allusion or allegory, their persistence in the contemporary period, *The Grand* deploys certain formal strategies which need analysing. While television critical discourses have been dominated by the thematics of postmodernism (nostalgia, metatextuality, surface, paranoia), *The Grand* seems to require the deployment of concepts associated with the critical realism advocated by Georg Lukács. I will offer a tentative explanation why this may be the case at this particular historical moment. The prime motive though for this essay is to insist that the wide disrepute which the period drama has fallen into, the conflation between the genre and nostalgia *per se*, is debilitating. With audiences of between 8 and 9 million a week,[2] *The Grand* is significant because it combines a popular cultural form with a sociologically complex and politically progressive analysis of the past.

Realism: Some Earlier Debates

The relations between representations of the past and the political implications of the *formal* strategies chosen to figure those representations, were crystallised in the 1970s by the debate between Colin MacCabe and Colin McArthur around Ken Loach's *Days of Hope*. This serial charted the rise of British working-class militancy from the First World War through to the General Strike of 1926. MacCabe polemicised against what he termed the classical narrative, in which category he placed *Days of Hope*. He argued that the various 'voices' or discourses of the classical narrative text are organised into a hierarchy of graduated 'truths' with a master discourse or metalanguage at the top, embracing and evaluating all the others within the text. This has two consequences, according to MacCabe's article. The classical realist text is both unable to deal with the real as contradictory, and it offers the spectator a simple position of 'truth' *vis-à-vis* characters and events thanks to their access to the metalanguage.[3] In effect MacCabe was arguing for modernist formal strategies which would disrupt the spectator's easy access to the 'truth' of things, would require them to work to evaluate the relative weight and validity of different discourses and positions within the text without the text doing so on their behalf, and which would consequently be able to present the real as a set of contradictory social forces which required an 'active' spectator if those forces were to be understood.

In a not unsympathetic response, Colin McArthur warned against the dangers of formalism, whereby a text's progressive or reactionary implications are mechanically read off against its use of certain formal techniques. Widening the analysis to include the context of reception, the debates which *Days of Hope* generated, and the wider political context could suggest a considerably more complex relationship between text and spectator *vis-à-vis* knowledge than MacCabe's account allowed.[4]

What is remarkable is how closely this debate reworked an earlier set of debates in Marxist cultural theory around the relations between form and politics and the traps of formalism. The key protagonists here were Bertold Brecht and Lukács. If modernism set the terms for the debate in the 1970s, it was Lukács, with all his considerable authority, who set the terms for the debate in the 1930s with his advocacy of classical narrative forms. Both Lukács and Brecht shared a common goal: they wanted to see representations that were both realist and popular. Indeed it is often unremarked how closely these two concepts were connected for these theorists. For Brecht 'popular' forms (and by extension, realism) required connecting with the contemporary modern urban world, its rhythms, its multiple stimuli, its shifting perspectives, its pace, its unexpected connections and disjunctions. Modernist forms seemed worth engaging in to capture the contradictory dynamics and potentialities of social life. As Brecht argued, art,

> cannot be forbidden to employ skills newly acquired by contemporary man, such as the capacity for simultaneous registration, bold abstraction, or swift combination.[5]

Above all, the principle of montage appeared to exemplify such newly acquired skills.

For Lukács, by contrast, 'popular' culture required working in those mainstream classical storytelling forms which the bourgeosie had disseminated through the novel. It was these forms which were rooted in the historical experiences of the broad masses. At their most analytical these forms could depict, in the microcosm of the story, the fundamental dynamics of wider society. By contrast, modernism for Lukács merely reproduced the fragmentation, chaos and disparate quality of modern society. For Lukács, different strategies were needed if art was to penetrate beneath the surface of life and draw the various represented phenomena into a network of socioeconomic relationships, tracing their pulsating interactions and conflicts. It was this which would facilitate the reader/spectator's understanding of the world as complex and multifaceted.

Thus Lukács advocated formal strategies that emphasised unity and coherence, believing that *they* (rather than modernist strategies) better correlated with the profoundly systemic and tightly interconnected social relations and forces that characterised the inner core of capitalism, beneath the fragmentation and transience of its surface life.[6] Lukács also made a distinction between realist and naturalist representation. He criticised the latter as severely as he did modernism. He claimed that naturalism's aspirations to a phoney objectivity, its fetishisation of appearance and immediacy, its investment in the mundane and ordinary were all symptomatic of its acceptance of capitalist society as inevitable.

With some qualifications, the arguments of these Marxist theorists, many decades old now and formulated prior to television's advent as a mass medium, are surprisingly relevant if we are still interested in the notion of 'progressive television'.[7] For debates about modernism, we have *This Life*, for debates about naturalism, we have soaps like *EastEnders* and for debates about Lukácsian realism, we have *The Grand*. Having situated this essay in a theoretical tradition, though, I would just like to indicate one departure from that tradition. Brecht's argument, that Lukács' inflexible attachment to what he called, witheringly, 'a few bourgeois novels of the previous century',[8] made Lukács more of a formalist than the modernist experiments in form which he condemned, was devastating and unanswerable. Nevertheless, it no longer seems necessary to adopt an exclusively Brechtian or Lukácsian position on the general issue. First, the circumstances of their writing and the passage of time has concealed the key point of convergence between them: both championed the possibility of art having some cognitive potential in relation to the real world. As we shall see, this argument has come under attack in recent times. Secondly, it is best to see the arguments they made in relation to particular strategies as indicative of strengths and weaknesses on both sides and as requiring qualification according to particular case studies, changing historical and cultural circumstances and the cultural tastes of the audiences who are being addressed.

Allegory

One of the advantages of the concept of allegory is that it expands our notion of text from the solitary individual film or cluster of television programmes to a broader canvas of representations, images, discourses and memories. And it is precisely this connection with history and contexts which capitalism frustrates. In *The Political Unconscious* Fredric Jameson argues that under capitalism storytelling is confronted with a dilemma. How, in a privatised world, are stories to be meaningful and transcend the monadic subject's *anomie*, given the split between the private and the public, the psychological and the social, the personal and the historical?[9] Traditionally, allegory is a type of storytelling which refers its representations back to broader moral and spiritual codes. Allegory then is a *transcoding* of a metatext into the specific dramatic configurations of a particular text. It is this process of transcoding which moves interpretation from the individual text and the individual characters it dramatises to a transindividual, *collective* story. Thus allegory can be seen as having a relationship to the concept of popular memory. Here the individuals' memories are the text, locating their own lives, friends and family in relation to a larger collective story.

However, the collective story of allegory (or popular memory) is not history in any direct sense, since we cannot know the real except 'through its prior textualization, its narrativization'.[10] Thus while transcoding reconnects the privatised subject to a collective narrative, the operation is also essentially an intertextual one. Representations of the historical past are allegorical structures in exactly this sense. For, such representations of the past are not some unmediated window onto distant events; rather, such images and discourses are routed through the images, imaginings and counter-imaginings of the present, while the anxieties and aspirations of the present are not accessed in their pristine immediacy but are in turn routed through a representation of the past. There is then a kind of dual focalisation at work in historical allegory.

Thus far, though, we have yet to articulate the term 'allegory' in a way compatible with a realist epistemology, which, for political reasons, I intend to do. The intertextuality of the term, as I have sketched it should not be taken to form a closed circuit, only referring endlessly to a textual process. Jameson deploys Lacan's notion that the Real is that which resists symbolisation, and therefore can only be traced in its effects within the text as symptoms. This is perilously close to the immanent hermeneutics by which cultural studies has become increasingly nervous of postulating a relationship between discourse, text, language and the real. This trend is already evident in MacCabe's 1974 article. Today the situation has worsened. When relationships are suggested (for example, by linking cultural change to historical change) then it is often logically in contradiction with the implicit or explicit argument that there is no evidence, better than any other evidence, for making such a claim (a tell-tale sign here is when the real is put in inverted commas). Yet as we shall see, there are historical reasons why this relativism has become so *de rigueur*. Indeed, if there were no real world historical causes involved in the rise and rise of relativism, how else would we explain its (re-)emergence?

One of the claims of relativism is that since there are no neutral, natural disinterested perspectives on the world, all perspectives are rendered equally valid/invalid: all are equally ideological (composed of values and assumptions). The argument is that the plausibility of a discourse lies not in any congruence it may have with the real but in its own internal coherence and rhetorical power. Reading of recent work which has tried to rebut this line of thinking suggests that the persuasive power of a text or discourse resides not only in its internal coherence and rhetorical strategies, but also in the plausibility of its congruence with the real.[11] The notion of plausible congruence returns us to history: for under what circumstances does a discourse or set of images or stories become persuasive? What is the relationship between those circumstances and the unequal distribution of power in societies? Ideology, understood *not* as all and any values but as the legitimation of unequal relations of power has two advantages over the more expansive sense of the term. First, as I have indicated, we are more likely to understand ideology as historically contingent. Secondly, we give back to the human subject and culture the *possibility* of self-reflexivity. This is the weak spot of ideology. For its plausible congruence with the real is not seamless, suffering as it does in *varying degrees* from gaps, discrepancies, hesitations and logical flaws. It is only through an implicit comparison with the real that discourse/image(s)/narratives can be subjected to some 'internal' critique and, in the case of ideology, an understanding of the pressures, dislocations and sheer textual *work* that goes into trying to assert a plausible congruence.[12]

Under some historical conditions, the possibilities for a plausible congruence between an ideological discourse and the real are greater than others. The Second World War, for example, provides very favourable terrain for a *retrospective* mythologising of national unity, not least because of the way the conflict could be plausibly framed (democracy *vs.* fascism) as well as the actual and discursive formation of the Home Front, which at the time and subsequently (consolidated in the economic boom of the 1950s, for example) could be plausibly interpreted as the sign of collective cooperative effort transcending differences of class, gender and region.[13] Indeed, so effective has been the mythologising (in the Barthesian sense of a draining away of history, the extirpation of conflict)[14] that it takes an act of critical labour to reactivate the distant social antagonisms preserved for the cultural historian in films made during the war.[15] Once these antagonisms have been recognised, however, these films are usually less secure in their mythologising of national unity than postwar films and television programmes. Retrospective mythologising could fasten onto representations of the period but from a historical position safely insulated from the social tensions and conflicts which made contemporaneous representations of the war years so fraught and problematic for a mythologising project.

Alternatively, a retrospective account can be receptive to its own contemporary social conflicts and allow the representations of the past to be informed by them, thus prising the past away from nostalgia and using it as a way to critically discuss the present. This kind of dual focalisation is exactly the strategy of *The Grand,* but it is rarely deployed in representations of the Second World War. Trevor Griffiths's television drama *Country* (BBC 1981) is one of the few exceptions. Made in the early years of Thatcherism, the entire action is located in the country house retreat of a rich brewing family, the Corlions (itself an intertextual reference to that other famous nexus of family and business relations depicted in *The Godfather* films).[16] The story turns on the problem of succession within the family business and this itself is an allegory for the question of succession for capitalism itself. For the date is 1945 and that other 'country' has just given Labour a landslide General Election victory. The people, observes the prodigal son of the business patriarch, 'have just declared war on us'. The presence of 'the people' in the conventional Second World War storytelling frame and the invisibility of the business-owning class is of course a hegemonic strategy which Griffiths's drama here seeks to reverse and undermine by focusing on the Corlions.

There are some interesting comparisons to be made between *The Grand* and *Country*, not least in the way that they suggest that conflict between nations during the war gives way in the postwar period to a resurfacing of conflicts *within* the nation. However, *The Grand*'s temporal location means that it is working with cultural material that has been subjected to less ideological closure than that associated with the Second World War.

The First World War presents problems of plausible congruence for a mythologising discourse. For it has never been entirely rescued from its widely perceived complicity with imperialist rivalry. Such popular intuitions received their theoretical exposition in Lenin's 1916 book *Imperialism: The Highest Stage of Capitalism.*[17] The subsequent Russian Revolution only further served to impede national mythmaking in the immediate postwar period. Indeed, according to Wrigley, there was widespread fear amongst the propertied classes that the legitimacy of the social order had been badly damaged by the war and by revolutions in the East. There was widespread unrest, not only in various industries (the dockers, railway workers, the miners) but also in the armed forces and the police and a general level of discontent and lack of deference amongst the working class.[18] For this and for other reasons, the immediate post-First World War setting of the television drama *The Grand* is promising terrain for telling a story about the social order and social change, which explores rather than conceals collective fissures and tensions.

Structure and Typology in *The Grand*

The importance of temporal location and how that activates the ideological opportunities and counter-hegemonic possibilities of a text was well understood by key creative personnel involved in the production of the series. Here is Anthony Wood, producer of the series:

> Although we had toyed with the idea of setting it [*The Grand*] during the war, we felt that that only really left people not fighting the war, waiting for news. By setting it in 1920 the drama becomes much more about a society trying to put itself back together again. But the pieces are not going to fit in the same way. The series is really set around the birth of the modern era where the political conflicts then about the kind of society Britain was are recognisable to us now at the end of the millennium.[19]

The birth of the modern era emerges painfully with the emotional and social fall-out of the war informing the present. It's this concern with the dynamics between *The Grand*'s diegetic present and its immediate past which gives the drama a sense of historical depth that is unusual for television. It's more typical to find television drama curiously bracketed from history. *The Grand* however saturates the diegetic present with references to the war; it anchors its vision of the disruptions in the class and gender order to the traumas and transformations wrought by the First World War.

However, *The Grand* of course enunciates on the past from our own contemporary present and that context informs our reception of the drama as much as the knowledges, discourses and images it mobilises from the past. *The Grand* opened on television at 9 p.m. Friday, 4 April 1997. The last episode was televised on Friday, 23 May so that it straddled the General Election – which in turn was a somewhat truncated debate on 18 years of Conservative hegemony. A number of themes that were in circulation at that time seem to find their way into the television text. There is the 'good' (New Labour?) employers *vs.* ruthless employers; the question of whether, to what extent and what kind of aspirations one should have in a class and gendered society; the issue of corruption (the first episode starts with a financial scandal); and the perennial running gag of the Major years – the sexual peccadillo (images of a Madam spanking her gentleman client). These are fairly obvious, and at one level, quite superficial references to our contemporary moment. The interplay between a representation of the past and a more profound rumination on our own contemporary moment is something that I will want to tease out. For, just as *The Grand* is concerned with the way the post-First World War period was informed by the war years, so we today are assessing the impact and continuing influence of the Tory years in the field of class and gender relations.[20]

Structurally *The Grand* combines elements from both the series and the serial – a combination that is increasingly popular with television drama. The serial element, in which storylines are developed across several episodes, helps give a complexity to how we interpret characters and their actions. This is further underlined by *The Grand*'s use of the series structure, where a particular story is begun and completed within each episode. However, in *The Grand* the conclusion of the episode's featured story is often open-ended, leaving the social and economic problems fundamentally unresolved. Indeed, frequently the most that has been achieved is that characters come to an understanding that they cannot intervene to change for the better another character's dire circumstances. They come, in other words, to an appreciation of how their ability to help others is limited by the social structure and moral conventions of society. For example, when a young woman recovering at the hotel from the scandal of an abortion leaves the hotel in the embrace of her father, her friend, the daughter of the hotelier, realises (as we now do) that the true scandal is that the father raped and impregnated the daughter. The final scene has a shot/reverse-shot between the two characters just as the abused young woman is ushered through the hotel doors. As we shall see, the hotel functions as something of a temporary sanctuary from the brutalising social relations outside the hotel. Inevitably, however, the hotel itself is constituted by those relations and must finally expel those seeking sanctuary back out into the world beyond its doors.

The hotel is in fact one of the key characters in the programme. Apart from a few brief scenes, it is the site of almost all the action. There are economic determinants at work in this textual characteristic. As executive producer Anthony Root explains:

It's always a series that is going to be circumscribed by its budget. It was invented precisely to be a low-budget show. So the stories are always played out within the context of the Grand Hotel and the sets we have there and one or two occasional other sets. It's shot extremely fast, as well. It's shot at eight and half days for each episode. That's about two or three days shorter than other people would try and make a 50-minute drama in.[21]

It clearly makes sense to have the hotel as the main site of action given the temporal and financial resources available (the budget for each episode is £340,000 instead of the £500,000 a comparable drama series might expect).[22] One of the features which differentiates this setting from a series like *Upstairs Downstairs* is that the latter, as Anthony Root points out, 'was exclusively a family with their servants. *The Grand* is a commercial operation, it's not about a household in quite the same way.'[23] As with the single location and intertwining of private and public, personal and business transactions in *Country*, the setting of *The Grand* signifies a social *totality*. For Lukács, the figuring of the extensive social totality outside the work of art requires an internal composition: 'the circumscribed and self-contained ordering of those factors which objectively are of decisive significance for the portion of life depicted'.[24] In this case, the totality figures the intra- and inter-relations between employers and employees – or the bourgeoisie and labour at the service sector end of the economy. The first two decades of the twentieth century saw a gradual expansion of the number of women working in the service sector.[25] Thus *The Grand* both speaks to that particular historical moment while also being a very suitable dramatic scenario for 1990s Britain, where manufacturing is on the decline and the service sector constitutes our growth industry, recruiting de-skilled, non-unionised, low-waged, part-time and short-term contracted labour, which is increasingly female.[26]

The series begins with the Grand Hotel being reopened by John Bannerman, who has inherited it from his deceased father. Almost immediately, however, a financial crisis forces Bannerman to invite his brother Marcus to invest in and become a part-owner of the business. Each holds 49 per cent of the business, while John's wife Sarah plays the role of final arbiter in any policy conflicts by owning 2 per cent of the hotel. Marcus Bannerman, played by Mark McGann, is the more intriguing character of the two brothers. A ruthless operator and shady businessman, he simultaneously functions as a critic of the hypocrisy and moral confusions of his peers. He occasionally makes helpful interventions, for example, reclaiming the savings of Mr Collins, the head steward, who in one episode is the victim of a sting operation. However, this is not a predictable attempt to humanise a thoroughly unpleasant character, for Marcus has an ulterior motive. Such interventions are part of his elaborate seduction of his brother's wife, Sarah. Marcus hopes to present himself to her as an enigma, a rich ambiguous puzzle: one that she may find attractive in comparison to her honest but rather bland husband. Marcus is a strikingly contemporary figure, but he is not a Thatcherite for he has none of the New Right's investment in certain ideological constructs. His contemporaneity lies elsewhere. Marcus's insistence on his own self-generated morality, the crafted aesthetics of his seduction of Sarah, his very public disdain for his own fiancee, Ruth, his delight in unmasking the material interests which are concealed by the moral values of his own class; all this has strong Nietzschean resonances.[27]

One of the reasons why Nietzschean ideas re-emerged so widely in the 1980s is that they seemed to strike a chord with the relativising effects which the expansion of market principles has had in Britain. Like Nietzschean perspectivism, the logic of commodity relations is to act as a dissolvent on the transcendental and metaphysical values in which bourgeois society has invested so much. As Marx noted in *The Communist Manifesto*, capitalism transforms 'all that is solid into air', The more they are enmeshed in commodity relations, the more mutable institutions, practices and values become. This contradiction between base and superstructure is an enduring one, but the last 15 years or so has seen the tensions become very acute.[28] Marcus Bannerman is very much a typical figure in the Lukácsian sense.[29] For Lukács typicality is neither the statistical average, mired in mundanity, slipping beneath the register of history's dynamic forces, nor the extraordinary character transcending their context, where cause and effect are reduced to individual will – the twin failures of naturalistic characters and Hollywood-style heroes, respectively. Rather, Bannerman is typical in the way that he is a nodal point for some of the key socioeconomic forces which have been at play in our era.

Again, Bannerman's contemporaneity is routed through a representation of the past, specifically a period in which Nietzschean discourses might flourish. For underpinning Nietzsche's sceptical stripping away of bourgeois morality was his delight and pessimism that with the death of God, the master signifier, European civilisation's self-deceptions and illusions would be brutally exposed in the near future. Given that 'the whole of our European morality' was based on the Christian God, Nietzsche can only contemplate,

[the] long plenitude and sequence of breakdown, destruction, ruin, and cataclysm that is now impending ... an eclipse of the sun whose like has probably never yet occurred on earth.[30]

It is this prophetic breakdown, in the shape of the First World War, which Marcus Bannerman has lived through. He connects with our own context, not directly, but via his relationship to his own historical moment where 'breakdown, destruction, ruin' has undermined, as marketisation has in our own time,[31] appeals to transcendental values.

Another key character through whom the aftermath of the war is played out is Stephen, John Bannerman's son. A soldier in the First World War, his time in the army has damaged his ability or desire to integrate back into the hotel as a manager or as a member of the family. He comes close to suicide, before taking refuge in drink. However, the key disruption which he represents is conveyed through his attraction to Kate Morris, one of the maids, as someone who he can 'talk to'. His attraction to Kate causes a disruption of the class hierarchy from above while his frank admission of impaired masculinity disrupts the gender order as well. However, while Kate is the object of Bannerman's affections, she herself is extremely wary of crossing the class divide. Kate's sober assessment of the risks and pitfalls of attempting upward class mobility stands in stark contrast to her friend and 'new girl' Monica Jones.

Monica represents a similar force of change, of historical alteration, to Stephen Bannerman – except where he is damaged by the war, she appears ready to seize an historic opportunity. She has aspirations to leave the service class and become 'a lady'. As she tells Kate, 'chances are up for grabs with half the men buried in France'. She makes an alliance with Esme Harkness (played by Susan Hampshire), the semi-retired courtesan who represents one of the few ways of being an 'independent' woman in the nineteenth century. Esme advises Monica that 'Its a different world now, the men are falling from their pedestal.' Both however underestimate the extent to which society and the hotel remain rigidly demarcated by boundaries of class, gender and social values. To cross those boundaries, to be physically and ideologically in those places where one should not be, risks drawing a brutal retort from the dominant power relations.

In the first episode, a wide-eyed Monica, curiosity having got the better of her, wanders through the hotel's reception area – a place where she definitely should not be. She meets John Bannerman, returning from a bruising meeting with the bank, and when she talks back to him, he promptly fires her. Kate will intercede on her behalf; Bannerman shows generosity and Monica is reinstated. This however is a false reprieve since her aspirations will lead to a fatal conclusion in the last episode. However, this theme of the dangers of crossing physical and moral boundaries, of occupying spaces and demonstrating values which contravene bourgeois social relations is developed further in the second episode to which we now turn.

The Individual and Society

The second episode foregrounds two issues that have dominated political discourses in our own contemporary period: homelessness and the related question of the nature and extent of welfare structures to support people in times of need. While the trajectory of some characters plays up this issue of crisis and how existing social structures impact detrimentally on individuals, for other characters the crisis in social structures appears to hold out the prospect of individual opportunities of both a social and sexual kind. Thus the text conforms to Lukács' observation that realism requires the selection of typical events and actions. The typical is here again understood not as the mean average, but as phenomena in which there is an accumulation of socially significant forces.

The episode begins with a characteristic stress on the economic pressures constantly at work on the hotel. Marcus sweeps into the foyer with a band of auditors to check the books. In order to invest in the hotel Marcus sold his slum housing and applied to the bank for a bridging loan. The interest rates on the loan are high and Marcus is looking to increase profits. He hits upon the idea of turning the forty staff beds into eight new guestrooms. John and Sarah protest, using a discourse similar to Labour exhortations for business to invest in human capital. Marcus however insists that, 'If it makes money, it makes sense.'

This narrative strand is paralleled and thematically twinned with the storyline concerning Janet Brady, an ex-service girl with the hotel. She is seven months pregnant, on her own and has been made homeless. Her pregnancy, an affront to bourgeois values, is compounded by a second transgression, this time economic in character. She enters – as Monica did before her – a forbidden space (forbidden, that is, if you cannot pay for it): an empty bedroom in the hotel. These two narrative strands are run together. Once rumours of Marcus's plans start to circulate, the simmering discontent of the staff, the prospect of unionising and striking is played off against the individual fate of Janet Brady. Running two causally separate but thematically cross-referenced narrative strands together in this way is one of television's distinctive contributions to narrative storytelling. It is, for example, structural to the soap drama. What it allows for is a degree of complexity in exploring a particular subject from a variety of angles or in different manifestations. However, while the soap drama tends to leave the various strands of a theme (e.g. the self-destructive tendencies of masculinity) as merely the properties of individuals, *The Grand* relates individual lives back to structures, in this case the question of property relations. Janet's trajectory, for example, is directly connected to the fate of the hotel. For she had been living in the ironically named Jericho Lane, the slum housing formerly owned by Marcus Bannerman, but sold by him to save the hotel from bankruptcy. Thus the lives of both the staff as workers and Janet as citizen have been shaped by capital flows in a manner all too resonant with the contemporary period. What has happened to Janet and what could happen to the staff underlines the precariousness of any security, the thin line between belonging to society and destitution.

This conceptual interlinking of separate narratives by the structure of the text is further underpinned by the dialogue which is unusually politicised for such a mainstream production. When Kate Morris finds Janet in the bedroom, she tells Janet that her employers will call the police. Janet's response identifies the class relations which underpin that threat. 'Oh, yeah?' she asks, 'and where's the police when your home's been taken away?' Kate allows her to stay overnight, but returns the next day and pleads with her to leave. It is in this scene that we discover how truly alone Janet is. Whereas she had suggested that she was waiting for her brother to be demobbed and that he had plans to set up a shop and look after her, she now confesses that her brother died in the war. With immediate familial support structures sacrificed in the trenches, the consequent dialogue maps out the choices left for a women in Janet's condition.

> There's only the workhouse, if I go to the workhouse they'll take my child .... Even the army of God will take my child. And they won't have finished with me. There's an asylum waiting for women like me ... they'll lock me away because I'm filthy, shameful and diseased. Because I've dared to give birth.

There are no support/welfare structures awaiting Janet beyond the temporary sanctuary of the hotel. Instead Janet describes to the 'good but naive' Kate, an institutional network of punishment, pathologisation and discipline that Foucault would have recognised.[32] The text is here drawing on popular memory in a complex articulation with the present. The coercive apparatus awaiting Kate symbolises the betrayal of the promises of social justice – a land fit for heroes – which followed the First World War. The election of the Labour Government in 1945 and the establishment of the welfare state was in no small part a response to that betrayal and its culmination in the hardships of the 1930s. Now, at the end of the millennium we see the welfare state being steadily stripped back down to the coercive apparatus it was designed to replace.

If Kate's class position effectively frustrates the spectator's desire to see a causal agent resolve Janet's dilemma, the audience might hope to find in Sarah Bannerman a character with both the empathy and the power to help. Such expectations are so ingrained in popular culture that this seems precisely to be the point of Sarah's confrontation with Marcus over the staff rooms. Marcus is in fine Nietzschean form, observing that she has 'come to speak on behalf of the downtrodden masses'. He reminds her however that as a result of his investing in the hotel by selling Jericho Lane, she is already complicit with making a large number of people homeless. Having disarmed her social conscience, he then makes clear how constraining he sees her own personal investment in bourgeois institutions. 'If you could lose the chains of wife and mother, think what we could achieve,' he urges her. Sarah baulks, but this candidness reveals how the apostle of Nietzsche is operating in a world whose fundamental values have been sapped and eroded by the war.

The episode now builds towards its conclusion. The final scenes intercut Marcus's announcement to the staff with the discovery of Janet in a guestroom. Gathering the staff together and distributing champagne, Marcus toasts their efforts and squashes the rumour that they are about to be deprived of accommodation. The financial pressures on him have been resolved for the moment by a deal he has struck with the city's theatres to put up visiting performers, thus ensuring the hotel is running at maximum capacity. His connections with the art world are significant, of course, since the resolution is itself part of Marcus's constant reinvention of himself, a perpetual performance whose most important audience is the watching Sarah.

As for Janet, her fate has been precipitated by Monica. It was she who in a more minor form transgressed in the previous episode by being in the wrong space and demonstrating the wrong demeanour to her employer. Seeking to ingratiate herself with her employers, she tells the hotel management about Janet. Sarah arrives in the bedroom where Janet is about to be expelled by the staff (whose own accommodation is now safe). Realising that Janet is a victim of Marcus's relocated investments, it appears that she may offer the 'charity' (a key ideologically charged word since Thatcherism) which Janet is pleading for. Instead she promises to write a letter to the 'Institute' explaining Janet's circumstances. 'A hundred rooms and you can't give me one?' exclaims Janet, to which Sarah, obviously flustered, replies, 'I can't, I just can't.' As Janet is dragged from the room, the camera cuts to Sarah's point-of-view of Janet. She lurches forward and spits at the camera/Sarah. It's an extraordinarily uncompromising scene. Once again we see the refusal of closure and the mapping-out of Janet's trajectory once she is expelled from the hotel. The episode also demonstrates the linkage between the open-ended series structure with the serial, as the story for that episode ties into the longer-running story of the relationship between Sarah and Marcus. With Janet gone, Marcus enters the room and the episode concludes with the same shot/reverse-shot between two characters discussed in the episode concerning the incestuous rape of a young woman.

Embedded in that final shot/reverse-shot (so different from its naturalistic use in the soap where it individualises problems) is a complex argument concerning the parameters and limitations of individual actions. Sarah's complicity with the objective social relations in which she is enmeshed would have been familiar to Lukács, with his combination of Marxism and humanism. Her tragedy is that she has a conscience, but the reality is that it is social being not conscience which determines her actions. As Terry Eagleton has noted, Nietzsche represents that highly risky alternative possibility for bourgeois society, of generating one's morality up from one's social base and discarding the fictions and facade of an imposed superstructure.[33] It is this opportunity which Marcus holds out to Sarah. As we have seen, this becomes a possibility only at a time when the superstructure, in both its state and civil society components, has been massively racked by change and crisis. In 1920 the crisis stems from the aftermath of the war. In the 1990s the crisis stems from the general commodification of society which Thatcherism initiated, but which has eroded the very social institutions (particularly the family) which Thatcherism valorised.

Conclusion

We can understand *The Grand*'s return to a 'classical' aesthetic against the background of social fragmentation wrought by Thatcherism. The classical aesthetic testifies to a palpable hunger for a return to a politics that admits that the social, with all its interconnections and reciprocal dynamics, still exists. However, *The Grand* is no apologia to One Nation rhetoric, insisting as it does on the deep divisions that remain within the social order. I have suggested that *The Grand* represents these divisions through a complex interplay between past and present: a dual focalisation. The former is not unknowable, merely the screen on which we project our own anxieties and/or comforts. Rather, we inherit the past with all the accumulated and polysemic meanings that have become attached to it. Those meanings themselves have passed through and been shaped by concrete historical contexts and struggles. If the voices of the exploited and the oppressed have achieved any purchase on that inheritance, then it is up to progressives in *their* present to activate and rework those voices in their own new contexts. The historical dialogue which *The Grand* sets up around class and gender divisions are summarised in Figure 3.1.

The diagram maps out how both Stephen and Marcus are the subjects of desire – that is, they are subjects who desire and whose desires cross class boundaries. Sarah and Kate are in a familiar position: they are the objects of desire, but what is interesting is that the question as to whether to reciprocate, to become subjects of desire themselves, is constantly raised. However, if they are to become subjects, it means crossing class boundaries (inter-class boundaries in the case of Kate and Stephen; the values of decency and propriety of their own class in the case of Marcus and Sarah); it also means, simply by virtue of becoming subjects of desire, crossing gender boundaries. The risks involved in moving into these forbidden spaces are illustrated by Monica Jones who, as a desiring woman, crosses gender boundaries and in her aspirations to become 'a lady' crosses class boundaries. This results in her being raped, killing a man in self-defence and then being hung by the state. This, it should be stressed, is not a punishment which the text metes out to Monica; its

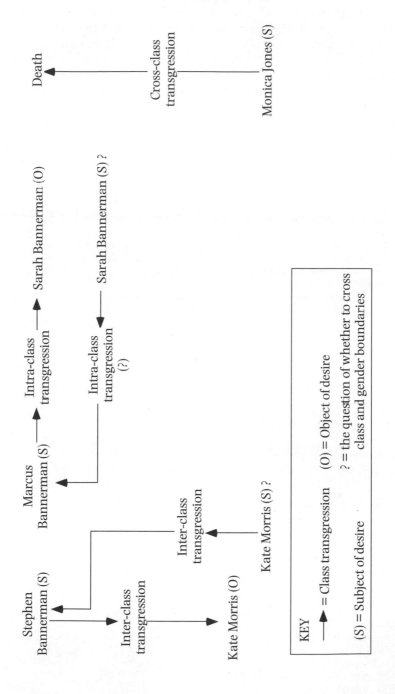

Fig. 3.1   Class and Gender Dynamics in *The Grand*

narrational voice is clearly appalled. The distinction Lukács made between critical realism and socialist realism is relevant here. *The Grand* is an example of critical realism, presenting the violence and contradictions of bourgeois society, but unable to identify the social forces working to transform it. It would be churlish however to see this as primarily a flaw in the text given the commercial and political context it is operating in. It is more productive, surely, to conclude by linking *The Grand* to the kind of historiography that Walter Benjamin advocated: the idea of 'constellating' two historical moments, bringing past and present into a dynamic configuration, seizing hold of a memory 'as it flashes up at a moment of danger'.[34]

Notes

1   This chapter deals only with the first series of *The Grand*. A second series ran during the first months of 1998 but was, in my opinion, a disappointing follow up.
2   Anthony Wood, producer for *The Grand*, interviewed by the author, 11 November 1997.
3   Colin MacCabe, 'Realism and the Cinema: Notes on some Brechtian Theses', in *Screen*, vol. 15, no. 2 (1974).
4   Colin McArthur's reservations concerning MacCabe's arguments are in *Screen*, vol. 16, no. 4 (1975/76).
5   Bertold Brecht, 'Against Georg Lukács' in R. Taylor and F. Jameson, (eds) *Aesthetics and Politics* (Verso, 1980), p. 75.
6   Georg Lukács, 'Realism in the Balance' in Taylor and Jameson *Aesthetics and Politics*, pp. 28–59.
7   John Caughie, 'Progressive Television and Documentary Drama', in Tony Bennett, Susan Boyd-Bowman, Colin Mercer and Janet Woollacott (eds) *Popular Film and Television* (OUP/BFI, 1981), pp. 327–52.
8   Brecht, 'Against Georg Lukács' (1980), p. 70.
9   Fredric Jameson, *The Political Unconscious: Narrative as a Socially Symbolic Act* (Routledge, 1989), p. 31.
10   Ibid., p. 35.
11   See, for example, Chris Norris, *Uncritical Theory: Postmodernism, Intellectuals and the Gulf War* (Lawrence and Wishart, 1992) and Bill Nichols, *Representing Reality* (Indiana University Press, 1991).
12   Terry Lovell, *Pictures of Reality, Aesthetics, Politics and Pleasure* (BFI, 1983), p. 51. Lovell points out how comparsons with the real/history are inevitable if any knowledge about texts is to be generated. Such comparisons are 'perfectly proper and necessary'. The problems start when those who reject realism smuggle such comparisons into their analysis covertly. See pp. 88–92.
13   Kenneth O. Morgan, *The People's Peace: British History 1945–1990*, 'The Facade of Unity', pp. 3–28.
14   Roland Barthes, *Mythologies* (Paladin/Grafton Books, 1986), p. 143.
15   Geoff Hurd (ed.), *National Fictions: World War Two in British Films and Television* (BFI, 1984).
16   John Hess, '*Godfather II*: A deal Coppola couldn't refuse', in B. Nichols (ed.) *Movies and Methods*, vol. 1(University of California Press, 1976), pp. 81–90.
17   V. I. Lenin, *Imperialism: The Highest Stage of Capitalism* (Junius/Pluto Press, 1996). Introduced by N. Lewis and J. Malone.

18   Chris Wrigley, *Lloyd George and the Challenge of Labour* (Harvester Wheatsheaf, 1990), p. 15.
19   Anthony Wood, interview, 11 November 1997.
20   For example, the Prime Minister Tony Blair told delegates at the 1997 TUC conference that he had no intention of abandoning the 'flexibility of the present labour market'. Larry Elliott, *Guardian*, 11 September 1997, p. 7.
21   Anthony Root, interviewed by the author, 2 November 1997.
22   Wood, interview, November 1997.
23   Root, interview, November 1997.
24   Georg Lukács, 'Art and Objective Truth', in *Writer and Critic* (Merlin Press, 1978), p. 38.
25   Noreen Branson, *Britain in the Nineteen Twenties* (Weidenfeld and Nicolson, 1975), p. 209.
26   John Clarke, *New Times and Old Enemies: Essays on Cultural Studies and America* (Harper Collins/Academic, 1991), p. 105.
27   See Friedrich Nietzsche, *The Gay Science* (translated by W. Kaufman) (Vintage Books, 1974); also, Julian Young, *Nietzsche's philosophy of art* (Cambridge University Press, 1995), and Terry Eagleton, *The Ideology of the Aesthetic* (Basil Blackwell, 1990), pp. 234–61.
28   Terry Eagleton, 'The Crisis of Contemporary Culture', in *New Left Review* 196, Nov/Dec 1992, p. 33.
29   Georg Lukács, 'The Intellectual Physiognomy in Characterization', in *Writer and Critic* (Merlin Press, 1978), pp. 154–8.
30   Nietzsche, *The Gay Science*, p. 279.
31   The term 'marketisation' was popularised by Will Hutton, to describe the restructuring of social institutions by market imperatives. See *The State We're In* (Jonathan Cape, 1995).
32   Michel Foucault, *Discipline and Punish: the birth of the prison* (Allen Lane, 1977).
33   Eagleton, 'The Crisis of Contemporary Culture', 1992.
34   Walter Benjamin, 'Thesis on the Philosophy of History' in *Illuminations* (Fontana Press, 1992), p. 254.

4

Kenneth MacKinnon

Bare Necessities and Naked Luxuries: The 1990s Male as Erotic Object

The male object of the gaze appears to be established on 1990s television, as in 1990s movies, advertising and magazines. Years of Levis 501 commercials, with their emphasis on half-stripped male bodies sinking voluptuously into baths or on fully stripped backwoodsmen skinny-dipping in rural lakes, provide evidence for this statement. There are the men's cologne and aftershave ads, with their solitary, self-regarding, 'unthreatening' male models, partly or fully stripped. Yet, even if the commercials permit the surmise that the male object of the erotic gaze is ubiquitous, caution is required. That object keeps disguising itself, explaining itself as something else: dressing itself up in a version of equal opportunities, whereby the putative demands of the female gaze are respected; in laddish humour; or justified as a matter of economic necessity. Thus, the man who exhibits himself, or allows himself to be exhibited, on television entertainment is doing women a favour, helping to compensate them for centuries of erotic objectification; or he needs the money so desperately that he has little choice in the matter. It seems that, in an age when men are objectified in TV soaps, and when entire game shows are created around male attention-seeking, mainstream television denies any awareness of the phenomenon, by resolutely refusing to take it seriously. Although it happens all the time, it is only for a laugh. In effect, men don't really want to exhibit themselves, whether or not women want to gaze at them.

To find evidence that beautiful male objects are not to be laughed or explained away, *Playgirl* proves invaluable. *Playgirl* professes upfront attitudes of approval to decorative men and to male nudity. It focuses attention on television actors in terms of their physical appeal to its imagined 'liberated' women readership. In doing so, it seems to refuse any disavowal of their object status which might be maintained by recourse to explanations of, say, narrative exigency. (On the other hand, by its very title, the magazine disavows its male readership as clearly as the British *For Women*. The writer of 'Nude Reviews', Vivian Holland, has a usefully androgynous forename, while the entire name recalls that of Oscar Wilde's son.) The looks and sex appeal of actors, particularly actors in American daytime soaps, are discussed frankly. They are questioned as to their personal and sexual lives in such regular features as 'The Probe (*Playgirl*'s Inside Scoop on All Things Hot)' or 'The Celebrity Interview'. In the present relation, its monthly 'Soap Stud Update' is specially noteworthy.

To accompany interviews which stress the sexual aspect of their subjects' personal lives, there are photographs which usually bare their bodies to some extent.[1] This is particularly true of the Diego Serrano interview,[2] where his photographs are decidedly in the pin-up style, divided between 'active' (soccer practice for one, it seems) and 'passive' (undressed, holding glass of red wine, in Latin-lover mode). It may be this coverage which prompts him to plead in words reminiscent of 1960s (female) starlets: 'I don't want to be just a sex symbol; I want people to know me for my work. There are a lot of pretty faces out there, but beauty can't buy talent.'[3]

Soap actors are expected to be aware of and capable of discussing their object status. Several react cautiously or favourably to their identification as sex symbol. Even Diego Serrano finally admits, 'If you have it, why not use it?'[4] Some attempt to explain their status in terms of the medium and the genre. Thus, Joseph C. Phillips of *General Hospital* discusses the difference between movie and TV stardom: 'You're a little bit smaller and you come into their homes – which makes you more familiar. You're like somebody they know.'[5] Or somebody they so want to know that they resort to stalking their prey![6] Soaps are special in this respect, perhaps – one actor suggests[7] – because the writers of soaps are often female. Austin Peck, of NBC's *Days of Our Lives*, both acknowledges object status and defends it in now traditional 'equal opportunities' manner, when he answers, on women objectifying men,

> I'm all for it. Women have had it done to them forever, and they've been told to suppress their sexuality for eons. It's great when a woman can set herself free sexually without caring what other people think.[8]

While Stuart Dade claims that British soaps have upgraded the sexual element in storylines in the 1990s, he locates the reason in 'realism'.[9] Peck's view has greater currency: that male objectification is, if not vociferously demanded by women, at least virtuous in relation to women.

It is not only actors in daytime soaps that are featured and questioned in the pages of *Playgirl*. There is star gossip about, for example, Jason

Priestley of *Beverly Hills 90210*,[10] Chad Allen of *Dr Quinn, Medicine Woman*,[11] David Charvet of *Baywatch*,[12] George Clooney of *ER*,[13] John Stamos of *Full House*,[14] Geraint Wyn Davies of *Forever Knight*[15] and Richard Biggs of *Babylon 5*.[16] There is a Celebrity Interview with Jason Simmons of *Baywatch* notable for photographs of Simmons which are almost indistinguishable in their male pin-up style from more upfront 'hunk' photographs;[17] these are immediately followed by a 'Surf, Sand and Surrender' nude layout featuring one woman and two men, which is very reminiscent of the less explicit *Baywatch*. There are others, similar in terms of personal probing and pin-up visuals, with David Faustino of *Married ... With Children*[18] and Corey Feldman of the forthcoming *Bordello of Blood*.[19]

The most 'in your face' feature of *Playgirl* is its 'Nude Reviews'. Movie stars are usually centred on, but David Duchovny of *The X-Files*, perhaps because of his crossover celebrity, seems to be an actor of special interest. We are told that his penis appears in two films 'that he coyly neglected to mention in his *Playgirl* April '95 interview',[20] that he appears to be a 'compulsive nudist' – that he has stripped in nearly all his feature films – and that his 'prick' is 'big, swarthy and circumcised'. The candour of the terminology is rare, but it expresses the underlying reason for interest in all the actors mentioned above: their physical appeal. Whether or not virtuously choosing to right wrongs inflicted on women, each actor may be understood to be identified as an erotic object of the TV audience's gaze or, in the discourse of *Playgirl*, as a sex symbol.

Awareness of the tendency manifest in the 1990s, whereby men not only receive erotic attention but seek it out, informs the 'Beautiful Men' programme in BBC2's *Modern Times* documentary series. 'Beautiful Men' concerned the eclipse of the Miss World contest, pioneered by Eric and Julia Morley, by the present-day Mr UK competition created by the Morleys. The documentary centres on regional heats and national final of Mr UK, with contributions from, for example, former Miss Worlds as well as the contemporary male aspirants to the Mr UK title.

The BBC televised Miss World from the 1950s until 1980, whereafter it was taken on by ITV, who abandoned it in 1988, ostensibly because it was degrading to women. Despite its international popularity, the show is to be seen only on satellite today. This brief history of the female competition offered by the programme raises obvious questions, principally why a similar-seeming competition is not seen as degrading to men, or, if it is, by what strategies that potential degradation is negotiated.

Several of the competitors deny any sense of exploitation. Only one, a quantity surveyor, opines that 'strutting about in trunks' is demeaning, but he insists that the emphasis is on evening wear and 'upper class' accoutrements. Eric Morley himself falls back on the 'virtuous' explanation of the event: 'Everybody's been on about equality, so we thought, if we give men the same opportunities as women, there can never be that statement again ... there can never be a statement that women are being exploited in a competition.' (It has to be borne in mind at this point that there is a Miss UK competition running alongside Mr UK.)

Men's enthusiasm for the competition can be gauged by the soundtrack statistic, that more than 3,000 men between the ages of 17 and 25 entered for it. Male dedication to augmentation of their beauty is indicated on the programme by protagonist Simon Peat's near-mummification 'to tighten up fatty tissue' and the finalists' visit to Moss Bros. Female spectators' delight in the parade of male objects for their gaze is indicated by the visuals of women pointing and grinning, and in the soundtrack by whoops and cheers. Their approval extends, apparently, to the losers, who are appraised positively by 'backstage' women. This female enjoyment of male spectacle is partly explained by a beauty therapist, who claims that women want more today from men, particularly that they should look good. A newspaper commentator on the programme suggests that modern TV advertisements are filled with male images, such as that of the hunky Diet Coke builder, to which women expect their men to shape up.[21]

The fact of the contestants' objectification is clearly signalled in the documentary by the invitation to them to appraise themselves in terms of what they most and least like about themselves. Visuals also fragment the men's bodies in the style that was once commonplace for photography of the female equivalent. A striking example of the tendency to suggest narcissism, and to criticise it, as explanation for the phenomenon is in the use of Bing Crosby's version of 'Beautiful Dreamer' on the soundtrack as ironic commentary in the coverage of one contestant's 'magic act'. He describes himself as a 'magician with muscle', a 'cross between David Copperfield and a Chippendale'. His self-description is accompanied by images of his nipple and then his back. (Some 'justification' for the Crosby song is discoverable in his approving quotation of Eleanor Roosevelt's dictum: 'The future belongs to those who believe in the beauty and power of their own dreams.') A possible disjuncture between self-image and actuality is tentatively suggested too by the inclusion on two occasions of 'television shots' of the contestants juxtaposed with 'realistic' views of them performing.

Yet, the potential destabilisation of traditional male/female images suggested as a possibility by the competition itself as well as by the more 'audacious' sequences in the documentary is constantly contained, the hints of radical change in the sexuality of men dispelled, by several recuperative devices, whether these be part of the competition's own armoury of reassurances or of the programme, which cannot resist, it seems, poking sly fun at its beautiful men.

That there would have to be some form of disavowal behind the bravado of the competition could be guessed from its being sponsored by the *Sun*. The tabloid does feature a 'Page 8 Mate', but whenever it appears to eroticise a young male, the *Sun* takes care to specify a female spectator and a laddish 'fella' getting his kit off for a laugh. Eric Morley says of the competition that nobody would have entered five to fifteen years ago, and then nervously qualifies this by claiming that it would have been for 'a certain kind of person, whether it be bodybuilders or anyone else'.

Homophobia, in its root sense of *fear*, stalks the competition and is vigorously exorcised. Heterosexual 'normality' is repeatedly asserted, or signalled when verbal language breaks down, as it does surprisingly often. Julia Morley, for example, claims that it has 'evolved' that it is 'quite normal for a guy to have a go'. Her husband would like mothers to be proud to have the winner as their son. Simon Peat's grandmother, with whom he lives for a time, declares that she likes helping him and hopes that he wins. In one sequence Simon is shown walking in the outdoors; tellingly, the extradiegetic music chosen has the Bee Gees singing 'You can tell by the way I use my walk I'm a woman's man.' Asked to talk of his hobbies, one competitor launches into macho overdrive, claiming that he likes girls – 'big boobs, little boobs, anything'. Nervous about the (it is declared) erroneous conception that the competition is for 'gays', competitor Craig attempts to stave off the implication by camping it up for the TV camera in the company of the competitor with whom he has to share not only a hotel bedroom but a bed. Simon, at the final, apparently cannot resist flirting with the female MC. ('They don't call you Sparky for nothing,' she quips.) The traditional sort of masculinity guaranteed in the competitors is one explanation for their extraordinary lack of verbal skills. So poor is Simon in this area that he keeps losing heats, he believes, because of that section of the competition, and so he substitutes the photographic heat for it. One fireman competitor declares his hobbies to be 'rescuing cats out of trees', while another, a builder, offers 'Drinking, basically.' The documentary cruelly includes the moment where the muscled magician says, of the judging of verbal skills, 'I think they are looking for articulation.' The banality of utterance received adverse comment from a number of television critics. Surely, though, this infelicity is a mark of a certain kind of machismo, and fits well with the competitors' need to reassert their 'normality' and unperturbed masculinity.

The need to assert traditional masculinity seems to be more keenly felt by male judges and male spectators than by the competitors. Thus, the judges have to be carefully instructed on what to consider (looks, physique, how they walk and act onstage – the list is hardly surprising). Michael Winner, as one of the judges, comments, very reasonably in this context, that there is a fear that men assessing other men will make them 'seem gay and effeminate. Frank Warren is adamant that he has no idea what to look for in an attractive male, and that he had to keep asking the two women beside him what they thought. Male spectators of the competition, when faced with brief questioning of their part in the show, become embarrassed and tongue-tied, feeling evident relief when they hit upon the explanation that they can't talk about the competitors' looks because they are 'not that way inclined'. A friend of one claims that he does not wish to show too much interest lest he be thought vain or to be interested in men. The most that any will admit to is jealousy. As David Thomas puts it, '... for an average bloke, there is ... something extremely unnerving about watching handsome, well-built, scantily clad men'.[22]

All this posturing only helps to delay the inevitable question. If exhibiting, judging, spectating of the male body is so suspect that it has constantly to be disavowed, why then do these young men *choose* to put their beauty on show? The answer, the only one permissible apart from the equal-opportunities rationalisation, is that this is a matter, not of straightforward choice, but of economic necessity. The explanation that the competition, though 'just fun', is also the chance to be launched into another career is offered by judges Frank Warren and Judith Chalmers. Simon in particular feels this need and believes in this opportunity. He is an electrician 'just for money', but he wants a career in television. Former Miss World Anne Sidney recognises that plumbers and electricians want the better life they believe others already have. The fireman Phil Cooke notes with some bitterness that those who play firemen in *London's Burning* are better paid than the real thing. He wants, he claims, to be famous, to get into 'any kind of acting'. Clearly, he thinks that through Mr UK he has a chance of realising these ambitions. The programme's producer/director Helena Appio seems to see career opportunity as the only reason for entry into the competition: 'If you were gorgeous and earning a fortune in the City, I don't think you'd bother.'[23] A sociologist and market researcher also understands the phenomenon in terms of unqualified men having to rely on their looks for economic survival.[24] The chance to succeed by exhibiting their bodies is so eagerly embraced by the competitors that there is no need for the castrating stare that Richard Dyer generally detects in male pin-ups purveyed to the female spectator.[25] These young men are expected to face their viewers without need for excuse. The competitors in the Derby regional heat are instructed, 'Eye contact with the audience at all times, please.'

Among the male-exhibiting game shows popular on current British television are LWT's *Man O' Man* and Carlton's *God's Gift*, the former a bigger-budget version of the latter.[26] Both shows feature a large, female, audience. Those of *Gift* seem generally younger (late teenage) and stand throughout the competition, while *Man*'s women spectators sit in groups at what seem like night-club tables. While *Gift*'s female spectators have a female MC (Davina McCall) who guides and sometimes initiates their responses, the slightly more mature women of *Man* have a chorus of 'glamorous', thoroughly fetishised, female dancers who execute the results of the spectators' computer votes by throwing the eliminated into a large swimming pool and kissing the survivors on the cheek. The MC is male, Chris Tarrant, while the offscreen voice occasionally heard on the programme is female; the offscreen voice frequently heard on *Gift* is recognisably that of Stuart Hall, who at the start of the programme announces himself as 'God'. While the relationship of the female MC to the spectators is clarified by her conduct and comments to them, the very title sequence of *Man* instructs new watchers that the chorus stands in for the female spectators – in that young men offer themselves or their acts directly to the women of the chorus. (On stage, the competitors keep their backs to the chorus when the latter is assembled above them surveying the computer screen for voting results. Their performances are for the spectators only.) During the same credit sequence, the chorus sings, 'Girls, what are we looking for? I said, Girls, what are we searching for?' It is a question both shows raise, perhaps inadvertently. The chorus moves into initiatory mode when the words become 'Sometimes you kiss them, sometimes you dump them.' This is to be a show where women are explicitly invited by Chris Tarrant to be cruel. The ridicule heaped on some performers in *Gift* for their puny physiques or their inadequate talents is more direct. At these points, Davina may intervene to reprove the spectators for not recognising the courage it takes to enter a contest of this sort. Yet, earlier in the programme, she assiduously sets up the competitors for ridicule, by acting sincerity and admiration to them but turning aside to the spectators to criticise. The theme, of female mockery of male parading of masculinity, was established before the show itself began on 13 June. Both before and after the commercial break preceding it, a female announcer used a clearly ironic tone to promise displays of virility in the programme.

Tarrant's function as male MC appears to be as a guarantee of heterosexual 'normality', in that he assures the women of the show's audience that he is 'absolutely pathetic at this competition', being 'a bloke'. He can also function in the same capacity to reassure other 'blokes'. He would never enter the competition, it is made clear, since he is 'a coward'. Tongue in cheek, he first comments, 'This isn't a studio. It's a Roman amphitheatre, where men get eaten alive by 300 breathtakingly beautiful women.' As the show proceeds, his matiness with the women grows, until he refers to them as the Lorena Bobbitt Appreciation Society, and as Pan's Grannies. The female MC of *Gift* seems more definitely on the side of the females, whom she assures at one point are more attractive than the men on show.

Yet, the split in the albeit 'entertaining' and, in Tarrant's case, ingratiating attitude of the host's mindset (admiring or cruelly destructive), exactly mirrors the split in the concepts of both shows. Both of them seem daring. However, both revert to the thoroughly old-fashioned and traditional, perhaps to counteract the daring of inviting men to exhibit 'talents' and, finally, physiques to critical, and (obviously, since there is a winner) approving women. Both seem to deal with female arousal at male exhibitionism, but at the same time to deny that arousal by making great efforts to render the male displays – especially the more explicit – ridiculous.

Gift at first sight is less traditional as an entertainment, and yet it seems to be very much after the fashion of ITV and Channel 4 'youth programming', with its large, comparatively bare studio space, its air of disorganisation, the noise level and general 'rudeness' of the MC and her incitement of the spectators to rudeness, as well as the lack of resentment at this treatment by the exhibits. It distances itself from the more mainstream shows, such as Cilla Black's *Blind Date*, by aping it and yet repudiating it. Thus, couples are permitted to meet suddenly, if not exactly 'blind', and there is a spoof report on the previous week's date. Instead of the far-flung holiday destinations of *Blind Date*, there may be an outing to a bingo hall, for example. By this means, the show both toys with the possibility of romance arising from the winner's choice of a girl from the audience, but also denies the seriousness of that possibility. As with so much of this entertainment, the show tries to have its cake and, let alone eat it, in determinedly 'youthful' fashion, denies that it would want it at all.

Gift's males, at the show's climax, take off their shirts individually and their trousers communally for the squealing delight of the audience within the show. Yet not one of them is left with a shred of sexual credibility, however determined the bid to be sexually arousing. Paradoxically, in fact, the more a competitor strives to exhibit sexually, the more the show combats his display, the more it reduces his bared bottom, for example, to a visual joke. When it is not in itself funny, the MC places a square of cardboard over the 'offending part' and claims that she does not know where to look! This on a show which positively demands that the entrants to the competition should mimic the sexuality of TV commercials and get their kit off in the final stages. At another point, they are invited to confess some dark happening in their past. To their face, Davina shows or calls for a measure of compassion. Immediately after, turning to the spectators, she will invite reproach and censure. In the same way, she encourages the competitors to be as sexy as possible, but when they are she invites ridicule for their efforts. If there is any restraint on the part of the audience, then Hall's soundtrack laughter insistently mediates the spectacle. He seems to be cast as more 'on the side of' the young men, but he will desert them as rapidly as Davina, though with less venom and with no assumption that he speaks for the young women on the sidelines. The title of the programme says it all, it appears. If even the winner can be described as 'God's gift', then what is targeted presumably is male vanity, in thinking that men, however attractive, can be anything but conceited. Their exhibiting becomes a matter of playing for laughs.

Man's competitors seem keen to please and to enter gamely into whatever is demanded of them, and not just in terms of providing a physical exhibition. The women of the audience seem in some instances genuinely excited and approving. Nevertheless, the programme works to deny the importance of that in preference to the need to puncture male pomposity. There is a constant struggle between new ideas and conduct and the overpowering force of the tried and tested ways of the past. To ensure that the contestants, however physically attractive, are rendered absurd in their pretensions to attractiveness, a 'real' muscleman, Kevin, confronts them with his oiled, Nautilus-trained body and makes them attempt gymnastic routines in which he is accomplished but in which they must look awkward and puny. Kevin it is who takes their robes from them as they expose their bodies to the laughter cued by Chris Tarrant, and it is he who enters the audience to receive adulation and to bestow a kiss here and there. The three contestants are kept in their place to emphasise their not sharing the freedom of movement and impressiveness of the real thing.

The insistence in the format of the show that it is just another 'entertainment' with the traditional values still intact is aided by frequent intertextual references to other entertainments. Approaching one woman, Tarrant says, after describing the programme as silly, 'You were expecting *Panorama*, weren't you, madam?' She claims that she expected *Question Time*. As the contestants prepare for their very own question time, Tarrant remarks, 'Just a small handful of men being interrogated by a whole army of women. It's a bit like *Tenko* in reverse ....' This sort of intertextuality could be comforting for an audience which might otherwise find female gazers and male objects of the gaze, too disorienting to contemplate seriously for long. 'Seriously' may be the operative word. If the viewers can be reminded constantly that this is a joke, there is less danger of exception being taken. That may be why the sort of innuendo that found its greatest welcome in the *Carry On* series is revivified for both shows. One of the *Man* contestants labours his self-introduction; 'I'm a student with a big, big ... heart.' The professionals on the programme might have delivered the line with greater aplomb, but it would not otherwise be out of place in their patter. *Gift* in particular seems to revel in the laboured *double entendre*. Davina says of a contestant who had his hands down his trousers, 'It's too early for that ... Mustn't peak too soon, must he, Stuart?' 'Winsome wenches, manipulate your maracas', sounds as if it were written for Frankie Howerd. It is uttered here by Stuart Hall, who proceeds, in reference to one competitor, 'He has a groin strain, but he'll do something magical now with his pencil with its big lead in it.' To loud female applause, he makes a wand arise from a bottle. 'He could certainly make it rise, that's for sure,' Hall remarks.

More is going on here than meets the eye, or ear. *Gift* has had a set of gay male spectators, and even the girls'-night-out programme on 13 June had an advertisement for a Gay Chatline in its commercial break. Nevertheless the closure of these shows recuperates any of the subversive potential encountered earlier. One winner runs around the female audience, with the applause and admiration usually reserved for Kevin, but this male has won on (appropriately) winning personality and unassuming charm. The other is able to enjoy a date with a female spectator of his choice. He must politely gain her assent in traditional manner.

Laura Mulvey, in detailing the visual pleasures open to narrative cinema's spectators, dismissed the possibility of a male object: 'Man is reluctant to gaze at his exhibitionist like.'[27] It is untrue, either in cinema or on television, that there is any dearth of male objects. What remains true is that male erotic looking at males is taboo. Hence the emphasis throughout all male exhibitions on TV that this is for the benefit of women who are ravenous for male objects to gaze upon. Even this, though, is accompanied by incessant need for disavowal. (It's only a joke, for God's sake. Who wants to see a bloke without his clothes unless it's for a bit of a laugh?)

The current importance of male stripping and the strength of the concomitant need to disguise that very importance in jokiness and po-faced sociological explanation are both well attested by Ken Blakeson's comedy drama for Granada *The Bare Necessities*. This was shown on ITV on 13 January 1996 at 9 p.m.

One way of understanding the play's broad structure is to see it as establishing traditional male/female working-class relations, then explaining drastic change in both gender relations and working practices by reference to new (broadly Thatcherite) economics, but also establishing that normality and tradition continue in a different, adapted form, appearances to the contrary.

The men of Debbington, backed by their wives, have just lost the battle to keep their pit open. After impersonating male strippers so as not to disappoint the womenfolk who were promised a male strip show, economic circumstances encourage them to look at the activity as possible wage-earning work. 'The Bare Necessities' troupe is born with the reluctant acceptance of the males involved, and the gradual acquiescence and approval of their wives.

From the early scenes, it is established that these miners are regular blokes. They make the usual sexist jokes, and one of them treats women to smacks on the backside. This is the way that at least the older women of Debbington seem to want. The classic relations of male and female, gazer and gazed-at, are established in the Social Club: Steve (Joe Duttine), overhearing a dance instructress give advice to her female pupils, remarks, 'If I were a judge, I'd give you all 10 out of 10 before you started dancing.' The teacher is not amused. Undeterred, he flirts with one of the girls: 'Ello, love. I might buy you a drink later if your Mam's not looking.' Classic relations are still more succinctly suggested by the next sequence, in which a bare-chested young man catches sight of a young woman in a window opposite removing her top and black brassiere, while she stares knowingly at him all the while. He is nearly caught by his mother, but spins his head away from the desired sight in time. When he turns back to it, the exhibitor pulls the curtains. The 'normality' of this future male stripper is signalled by the footballing photos on his walls, the female pin-up on his door, and his frustration at the woman's denial of further gazing satisfaction.

In the first half of the drama, the camera seems further to assert traditional roles. It ogles Sonia (Caroline Loncq) in leotards and particularly her thrust-out backside ('Movement's my speciality,' she proudly informs her male admirer). When the men begin to train seriously to perform stripping, they are surprised by two little girls who exclaim in amazement, 'Uncle Ralph, why have you got no knickers on?'

One of the means by which stripping as a job is 'naturalised' within the drama is by pointing up the resemblances to the old job of mining from which the men are now debarred. Immediately after the credit sequence, which features male strippers under club lights, the next lights in the darkness look like further stage lighting but turn out to be shed by the flashlights held by now redundant miners leaving the darkness of underground. Mining involves showering and naked intimacy among the men. In the showers, one older man scrubbing a younger one claims, 'I'll say one thing for this pit. I won't have to scrub your scabby back again.' When, later, the men are due to leave in their van intent on their new work as strippers, one woman looks as if she is running out of the house to provide them with sandwiches. Instead, it is to give the youngest a knitted posing pouch. When one of their number does not appear among the troupe onstage, Sonia makes reference to their previous conditions of work when she reproves them for thinking of joining the absentee: 'One out, all out, you mean? National Union of Strippers? That's a really good idea. Worked a lot for you in the past, didn't it?'

As the men take up stripping full time, there are some jolts to tradition. They encounter gay male spectators and their own prejudices. They have to come to terms too with the fact that women find male spectacle entertaining. (This is emphasised by having the mining women peeping at the lads changing without the latter's knowledge. One stalwart of the community comes upon them in voyeuristic mood. 'So – this is what's happened to the Debbington Women Against Pit Closures!' she comments. The women look crestfallen and confused. Suddenly, her expression changes. 'Get out of the way – let's have a look.')

None the less, these jolts to tradition are made more imperceptible than might seem possible within such a narrative. Much stress is placed, for example, on the need for the men to be *taught* to strip, by a woman. One of them takes to it with ease, but the most macho character fights against the teaching and the notion of the new job until Sonia challenges him to a press-up competition, and wins. They suddenly take to stripping at their first real gig. It is as if their natural talent for it takes them, and Sonia too, by surprise, as if they have suddenly developed a properly masculine pride in an activity which might once have been dismissed by them as 'queer'.

This achievement makes full sense as 'masculine' within this narrative only when it is clearly established that there is no other form of employment possible for the men. The contempt of the former miner Vinnie (John Forgeham) for men who still talk in terms of scabs distresses the men whose pit has been closed. But, what really irks them is his air of affluence, his economic buoyancy when they are facing straitened times. Ralph (Eamon Boland) does find work, but elsewhere, and cannot manage without his family around him. Steve takes to gambling but loses more than he wins. Stripping is an economic lifeline for these men. 'It's money, Ralph, and it's a job,' Sonia points out. When he finally hands the first earnings over to his wife, Ralph is told, '... you'd better do as many gigs as possible before your body goes, hadn't you?'

Ultimately, public nudity becomes, paradoxically, a mark of achievement for these men. This surely is the meaning of the near-final sequence in which Vinnie is forced to march naked from the disused mine in the sight of the former miners and their wives. He has up till now made light of their union principles and taken personal pleasure in their defeat, with the subsequent filling-in of the mine to make way for a shopping and leisure complex. In an attempt to belittle the transmogrification of the miners into strippers, he holds his hands aloft from his naked body. 'You see? You're not the only lads who can do it.' Ralph replies, 'We'd love to take you on, Vinnie. But I don't think you've got the equipment.' The remark is a means of bringing the men together and asserting their pride in their survival through stripping. Their women wave them a loving goodbye as Sonia drives them off to their next gig.

This play evinces a tension between admiration for the resilience of the former miners, their adaptation to new circumstances in a way that would have gladdened Margaret Thatcher's heart, and a suppressed sense that the virility of the unionised miners has somehow been sapped by their transition into a job as strippers. It is presumably symptomatic of that tension that there is such a rush to re-establish 'normal relations' towards the end of the narrative. The young man who once admired the bra-less young woman in an opposite window suddenly ends up with her, kissing and laughing. The women return to the site of the mine, as at the beginning, but instead of seeing their men emerge defeated they see the boss-figure Vinnie humiliated by the newly optimistic, wage-earning ex-miners.

Giving particular expression to a sense of economic exploitation survived is Spuggy (Paul Rider) whose alleged admiration for Aboriginal culture explains his loincloth and white-painted body and face, his resorting to playing the didgeridoo, to dancing tribal dances or chanting at times of oppression. He begins by emerging, defeated, from the mine still in Aboriginal body make-up and clutching the didgeridoo. He reverts to the guise when Vinnie seems to mock the strippers by making them perform in the very club that he owns. After kidnapping Vinnie and subjecting him in the abandoned mine to promises of spectacular death when the pit is filled in to create his shopping mall, Spuggy allows him to emerge naked from his ordeal. He himself is still in tribal costume. For Spuggy, miners are a tribe, with their own rituals and customs. When Vinnie is humiliated by being rejected as insufficiently equipped to be one of The Bare Necessities, Spuggy mounts the van, still in his loincloth and holding his didgeridoo, glad to rejoin the lads. This ending seems to say that the miners have not been defeated, but have turned privation into new opportunity by sticking together. Stripping, in this narrative, is a worthwhile activity for miners. It allows them to feed their families and to be independent, free of the immoralities of gambling, and no longer subjected to taunts from scabs who rejected union solidarity for the privileges of being boss.

In various ways television has exploited the apparent demand for male erotic objectification evidenced by, for example, the soaps and their most loyal audiences. It has made it the subject of documentaries, game shows, even drama. Yet what it offers is reassurance that, appearances to the contrary, men are still in their appointed place, women in theirs. What all the game shows and dramatic narratives refuse to acknowledge is male exhibitionism, male *pleasure* in self-display. What is highlighted, as compensation and explanation, is female voyeurism. Exhibitionism and maleness are somehow opposed in these entertainments. Male exhibitions are explained as a politically conscious nod to female need and as recompense for objectificatory harms done to women for centuries, or, with less complication, as merely a laddish joke. If it is to be taken seriously at all, it can only be as a matter of economic necessity. Mainstream TV entertainment can cope easily, it seems, with the representation of bare necessities. What it cannot begin to countenance, on this evidence, is either frank admission that the male is commodified alongside the female in late consumer capitalism or, still less, that self-objectification may be explained in relation to satisfaction of the long-denied male pleasure of exhibitionism. It cannot be allowed to be an enjoyable luxury in its own right.

Notes

1   Proof of these statements may be found in the verbal and visual treatment of, for example, Eddie Cibrian (*Playgirl*, October 1995, p. 11), Nathan Fillon (*Playgirl*, November 1995, p. 11), Timothy Gibbs (*Playgirl*, December 1995, p. 11) and Austin Peck (*Playgirl*, January 1996, p. 11).
2   *Playgirl*, October 1995, pp. 42–5.
3   Ibid., p. 44.
4.   Ibid., p. 45.

5   *Playgirl*, September 1995, p. 11.
6   Ibid., p. 9.
7   Matt Ashford states: 'Many of the shows' writers are women, so naturally some of what the male characters say might not be typical of men' (*Playgirl*, March 1996, p. 11).
8   *Playgirl*, January 1996, p. 11.
9   S. Dade, 'I do it 22 times a week ...', *For Women*, August 1996, p. 37.
10 *Playgirl*, October 1995, p. 11.
11 Ibid., pp. 8–9.
12 *Playgirl*, December 1995, p. 6.
13 *Playgirl*, November 1995, p. 7.
14 Ibid.
15 *Playgirl*, November 1995, pp. 8–9.
16 *Playgirl*, March 1996, pp. 8–9.
17 *Playgirl*, September 1995, pp. 30–4.
18 *Playgirl*, November 1995, pp. 30ff.
19 *Playgirl*, March 1996, pp. 44ff.
20 *Playgirl*, September 1995, p. 9.
21 D. Thomas, 'Living Proof of Men's Vanity', *Daily Express*, Tuesday, 26 March 1966, p. 23.
22 Ibid.
23 A. Jivani, 'Where's the Beefcake?', *Time Out*, 27 March–3 April 1996, p. 157.
24 Thomas, 'Living Proof', p. 23.
25 R. Dyer, 'Don't Look Now: The Male Pin-Up', *Screen* (ed.), *The Sexual Subject: A Screen Reader in Sexuality* (Routledge, 1992) p. 269.
26 I am indebted to one of my male students for this observation, and for his other remark that *Man O' Man* seems squarely aimed at blokes. Both of these comments seem easily justified.
27 L. Mulvey, *Visual and Other Pleasures* (Macmillan, 1989), p. 20.

5

Deborah Philips and Garry Whannel

'The Fierce Light': The Royal Romance with Television

... kings have a superhuman essence, and when they temporarily borrow certain forms of democratic life, it can only be through an incarnation which goes against nature, made possible through condescension alone. To flaunt the fact that kings are capapable of prosaic actions is to recognise that this status is no more natural to them than angelism to common mortals, it is to acknowledge that the king is still king by divine right.

Roland Barthes, 'The Blue Blood Cruise'[1]

Whether one is a royalist or not, the events of the Royal Family mark one's own personal history; the major events in the lives of the different generations of the Royal Family – births, schooling, courtship, marriage, separation, divorce, illness, injury and death – seem to parallel our own trajectories as British citizens and as subjects of the Queen. As prominent as major politicians, the Royal Family have been around for far longer. During the reign of Queen Elizabeth II there have been ten Prime Ministers; politicians come and go according to the fortunes of their party, while the Royal Family are ever present as emblems of national identity. And that iconic status has become even more inscribed in the television era, the parallels are marked more firmly, as the events of the Family enter our homes through the television set.

The First British Family are of ideological importance not only in their status as an image of Britishness (or, more accurately, Englishness), but also because, as John Ellis pointed out in 1982, the nuclear family is so central to an institutional construction of both television and its audience:

Broadcast TV, its institutions and many of its practitioners alike assume that its domestic audience takes the form of families. 'The home' and 'the family' are terms which have become tangled together in the commercial culture of the twentieth century. ... the family is held to consist of a particular unit of parents and children: broadcast TV assumes that this is the basis and the heart of its audience ... .The particular ideological notion of the nuclear family in its domestic setting provided the overarching conception within which broadcast TV operates.[2]

If this is still the case (and, with the exception of Channel 4 – established in its charter as an alternative and innovative television channel, it remains largely true), then the Royal Family and its representation as an ideal and idealised British family is central to the discourses of television. Television programmes, and the institutions of the BBC and the IBA, construct their audiences as a consensual nation, and the representation of the Royal Family has become a crucial instrument in that construction of audience and of nationhood. Royal events and celebrations become a signifier of national consensus, and schedules are cleared accordingly, prioritising royal marriages and deaths in news reports and programming over almost any other civic or national events. The Royal Family, the family of the nation and individual families, are articulated together in an apparently natural and cohesive link between the aristocracy and commoners, the people and the nation, the ordinary and the extraordinary. As Rosalind Brunt has suggested:

> The Royal family's capacity to offer this kind of magical transcendence derives from the roles they play in Britain's pageant of Living History. The story of the monarchy is commonly understood to parallel that of 'our island race', whereby the genius of both the British and their monarchy is said to lie in their particular ability to be adaptable and stable at the same time.[3]

The BBC is, in its very formation, a monarchist institution: it was established by Royal Charter in 1927. The annual Christmas message from the monarch (inherited from radio) and the organisation of schedules around important royal events, weddings, funerals and investitures clearly proclaim the institutions and programming of television as royalist. Even the parodies of the Queen's Speech on Channel 4 are less 'alternative' than that they are an affectionate confirmation of the televised Christmas Speech as a fixed and central national event.

The BBC as an institution, like the Royal Family, has always had the implicit ideological role of producing a unity out of the diverse elements of the British state, in which three subordinate nations have become incorporated under English dominance. The state that the Royal Family has to represent is named the United Kingdom, and although the Prince of Wales may be no more Welsh than the Duke of Edinburgh is Scottish, major royal occasions do attempt to draw in and incorporate the component parts of a 'United' Kingdom. The BBC faces a similar task, and so it is inevitable that in the ideological work of imposing unity on diversity, the institutions of broadcasting and royalty have found themselves working together. From the beginnings of the broadcast media, royal broadcasts were employed in a project of knitting together the Royal Family, listening families, the 'family' of the nation, and the 'family' of the Empire.

It was the BBC who took the early initiatives; Reith first suggested a royal Christmas message in 1927, and the King finally agreed in 1932.[4] The first BBC radio broadcast by the King and the Prince of Wales was produced from the Empire Exhibition at Wembley on 23 April 1924.[5] In 1934 the King addressed his listeners in his Christmas message as 'all the members of our world-wide family'. According to Paddy Scannell:

> The Christmas Day broadcasts unobtrusively underwrote a particular version of society; of Britain as a nation of families, fundamentally all alike and bound together from top to bottom by a newly familiar monarchy as its focus and epitome.[6]

The Royal broadcasts on Christmas Day were preceded by an elaborate feature programme which aimed to link nation and empire in a common celebration of the family and Christian festival.[7] Royal occasions, through radio, became 'ritual expressions of a corporate national life'.[8] Broadcasting forged links between the pomp and ceremony of royal occasions and the lived cultures of everyday life. During the 1935 Jubilee celebrations, the radio transmission provided a focal point for street parties, and for the Coronation of 1937, according to Pegg, 'the day revolved around the radio set: chapels and churches changed their ceremonies to suit broadcasting times'.[9]

Radio broadcasters established clear conventions of respect and deference for the Royal Family, and were complicit with them in the preservation of a royal mystique. Scannell writes of the new dilemmas of social etiquette that royal broadcasts posed; was it permissible to eat or write or read during a regal broadcast? Should the broadcasters stand during the National Anthem?[10] Once television images were on the agenda, it became the policy of the corporation not to show the Queen in close-up throughout the playing of the National Anthem, and the Queen was always informed in advance about camera positions.[11] There is an unwritten law that members of the Royal Family should never be shown at prayer and ITV later decreed that 'nothing disrespectful to the Royal Family' should be broadcast.[12] These conventions were reinforced by statutes – among them the prohibiting of ITV from transmitting advertisements within two minutes of any appearance by a member of the Royal Family.[13]

Television, in adding a visual dimension to broadcasting, reinforced the power of the media to construct the royal spectacles in ways that mobilised a de-politicised national consensuality. In 1949 Norman Collins, then controller of BBC Television, wrote lyrically of the possibilities of the new medium for the representation of royal events:

> ... with nation-wide television, when the King leaves Buckingham Palace the Mall will extend as far as the Royal Mile and the King will ride simultaneously through the four Kingdoms. A Royal Wedding will be a nation's wedding. On Remembrance Day the shadow of the Cenotaph will fall across the whole country and on great rejoicings the fireworks of Hyde Park will burst and sparkle at every fireside.[14]

From the beginnings of television, the BBC did far more than relay such events, but was actively interventionist in framing them. When George VI died in 1952, the BBC revised its schedules, and issued a free special supplement to the *Radio Times* to all newsagents and booksellers.[15]

Television was in many ways the making of the modern Royal Family. The 1953 Coronation features large in histories of television, as the moment at which, for the first time, television had a bigger audience than radio; in the words of a 1953 advertisement for Shell (May 1953): 'Neighbours with Television are relying on their sets to bring them the majesty and splendour of the year's great occasions.' Eleven million listened on radio, but 20 million saw the event on television, and the broadcast marked the moment at which television outstripped radio as the major national medium. As the *Radio Times* itself recognised at the time:

> ... it is possible to regard the Service as one which by the marvels of modern science, broadcasting, television and film – is of world-wide significance, and of which the full meaning, with all its implications, has only been fully realised within the last fifty years and perhaps not even yet.[16]

But if, as Ros Coward has argued, it is television that has led the way in the spinning of the contemporary royal narrative,[17] television could also be seen as instrumental in its unravelling. A sequence of *anni horribilii* have challenged broadcasters and programmers in the once fixed and accepted conventions for the representation of royalty, and have also disrupted a once relatively secure and comfortable relationship between television broadcasting and the monarchy.

The new technologies of the print and broadcasting media, the range of national and international broadcasting, telephoto lenses, and the speed of information exchange have now made it possible to scrutinise the finer details of royal life in ways that the once deferential and distanced reporting could not have imagined. And the royals themselves have colluded in that scrutiny. Close-ups, which Ellis has cited as 'a central feature of TV production',[18] became, after the long-distance and deferential reportage of the Coronation, an increasingly familiar mode of representation for members of the Royal Family, and was to become a disquietingly fierce gaze upon particular individuals (most notably Charles and Diana), and, eventually, on the institution of monarchy itself.

The current Royal Family are more media creatures than any previous generation; the monarch's position is now brought to a wider public and is subject to more media scrutiny than ever before. Television had been a presence at the 1937 Coronation, but in a very different way from that of the Queen's coronation; it was 'a humble supplicant, knocking at the door of Westminster Abbey and being allowed in to watch discreetly from the loft ...'.[19] The 1953 Coronation was in effect the first royal television spectacle; it brought the monarchy into the daily lives of the nation in a way that was markedly different from the entirely deferential representations of the print media; television institutions and broadcasters were no less respectful than their newspaper counterparts, but the medium of television in itself presented viewers with a new kind of picture of the individuals and institution of the monarchy.

The Coronation was a significant moment in television, not only because it gave the first reason for many in Britain to watch television, but also because it was a broadcast on a greater international scale than ever before. Described in the *Radio Times* as 'The biggest sound and television operation ever carried out by the BBC', it was technically a breakthrough in the possibilities for broadcasting. As the *Radio Times* proudly pointed out:

> To appreciate the significance of broadcasting the Coronation it is worth recalling that all through the ages there can never have been more than four thousand people able to see the actual service and ceremonial. ... The real significant advance of 1937 was not the admission of film cameras to the Abbey but the broadcasting by the BBC of the Coronation service. At a single stride the congregation participating in the service had risen from four thousand to untold millions .... Now in 1953 comes a second stride forward. Her Majesty's subjects in Great Britain will be able to take part in the service by eye as well as by ear. ... a live television programme will for the first time be shared by four different countries. ... Thus will the Coronation of Queen Elizabeth II be seen and heard throughout the world.[20]

The Coronation was flagged in the *Radio Times* for weeks beforehand, with 'special Coronation broadcasts'. Viewers were prepared with three special Coronation films in the weeks before the event 'designed to provide a background to the Coronation'.[21] The Special Coronation number of the *Radio Times* in May 1953 contained the Order of Service, a map of the Coronation route and an address by the Archbishop of Canterbury. The screening of the ceremony and procession was accompanied by a series of programmes prompted by the Coronation, among them: 'Our Concern is the Future' – in which six young people were invited to discuss 'the problems and possibilities of the new Elizabethan age'.[22]

The new availability of the monarchy through broadcasting is one which even at the moment of celebration of the Coronation was to cause some disconcertion. An editorial headlined 'Long Live the Queen' argued, in recognition of potential dissent:

> There may be cynics here and there who will murmur that the glowing brilliant backcloth that has been devised for the drama of the Queen's crowning is all antiquated mummery and foolishness. To such people there is an irrefutable answer. If this transformation scene be foolishness, so is all literature and painting, all sculpture and music, everything that brings mystery and poetry and colour into the life of man.[23]

Nonetheless, there is no question for the BBC that the impending Queen was assumed to be a nationally 'beloved Princess';[24] the *Radio Times* reader is addressed in its Coronation editorial as among 'those of us who are now the Queen's people'.

The great success of the Coronation and its televising was linked by many commentators (both at the time and since) to other symbols of national well-being. Peter Black, television critic of the *Daily Mail*, later wrote:

> That year, what with Hillary and Tensing climbing Everest, England regaining the Ashes and Gordon Richards winning the Derby, it really did seem for a time that some benevolent force was trying to cheer us all up.[25]

The BBC commentator for the Coronation, Richard Dimbleby (who also produced a book in the same year in celebration of the Queen),[26] made explicit the links between the occasion, tradition, and national self-image: 'I believe that we as a nation have done ourselves a profound service by showing to the world how unchanging are the traditions and pride which are our foundations.'[27]

The growing confidence of broadcasting professionalism had enabled it to enter into the details of the planning for royal spectacle that had hitherto been the province of the aristocracy; BBC producer Dimmock did not like a march specially written for the Coronation and persuaded the Duke of Norfolk to substitute a piece by Elgar.[28] The *Radio Times* exhibited a disconcerted awareness that the BBC's role in the event heralded a new relationship between the public and the monarchy:

> Literally as well as figuratively, the eyes of millions will be upon her – for the marvel of television will annihilate distance and range far-off

multitudes with the congregation in the Abbey. The 'fierce light which beat upon a throne' is fiercer by far in our age than it was in Tennyson's.[29]

The fierce light of television that was first seen in the Coronation broadcast was to become fiercer and fiercer as the Queen's reign progressed, and not least because members of the Royal family themselves chose to embrace it. By the end of the decade, television had become a routinised and active element in the management of royal representation. For the Queen's first Christmas message in 1957 she was rehearsed by the BBC in every detail with precise care, the BBC made her a training film in which announcer Sylvia Peters demonstrated ways of delivering a speech. By the time of the wedding of Princess Margaret and Antony Snowdon in 1960, their balcony appearance was brought forward in order to avoid a post-procession hiatus without any interesting television pictures.[30] In just a decade, the BBC had moved from humble supplicant to active collaborator in the production of spectacles of the Royal Family.

The BBC maintained a dominant position as the corporation linked with major royal and state occasions, and refused ITV's requests for alternating the televising of royal events.[31] ITV was unable to shake its viewers' habit of 'reverting to the establishment channel for establishment occasions'.[32] However, a rare collaboration came in 1969 when the monarchy granted unprecedented access for 'behind the scenes' filming of their lives and work. *The Royal Family*, which used *cinema-vérité* to humanise the Queen at work[33] was a joint production by the BBC and Independent Television; a commemorative book *Royal Family* marked the event as a 'Historic Documentary Film'. Access to filming and editing were tightly controlled by the Palace (the Duke of Edinburgh was a member of the Advisory Committee) but the programme did represent a royal recognition of the power and importance of television. The programme portrayed formal and informal royal events throughout the year, and marked a shift in the representation of royalty, in showing the family in relatively informal poses, breakfasting at Buckingham Palace, and barbecuing at Balmoral. As Crisell puts it:

It was not until 1969 that Royalty decided to make some concession to the democratizing effects of the new medium of television by allowing itself to be seen in a more intimate and less formal light. The result was Richard Cawston's documentary in which the Queen apppeared in a happy domestic setting and thus inaugurated a honeymoon period in Royalty's relations with television.[34]

The tone of both programme and souvenir book were similarly insistent that the monarch and her family were a repository of heritage and tradition and, at the same time, a modern family; that they could manage to be simultaneously like and unlike us, the Queen's subjects:

Britain's Royal Family is unique. Its traditions stretch back over a thousand years. At its head is a Queen who is directly descended from the grandfather of King Alfred the Great. . . . She is occupied each day with the business of being a Queen, involving all kinds of duties on a grand scale. At the same time she is a wife and mother bringing up a family, with a sense of humour and fun as well as a strong sense of duty.[35]

The royal year is constructed in the programme and in the souvenir book as at once historically extraordinary and reassuringly familiar:

For the Queen and Prince Philip and their four children, Christmas at Windsor, with presents round the tree, is a seasonal family event. It is also a reminder of their remarkable family history. The first Windsor Castle was built here nine hundred years ago by William the Conqueror ...[36]

In 1969 the paradox that Barthes had cited in the 1950s as integral to the mystique of monarchy could still be upheld:

Thus the neutral gestures of daily life have taken, ... an exorbitantly bold character, like those creative fantasies in which Nature violates its own kingdoms: kings shave themselves! This touch was reported by our national press as an act of incredible singularity, as if in doing so kings consented to risk the whole of their Royal status, making thereby, incidentally, a profession of faith in its indestructible nature .... All this gives us, antiphrastically, information on a certain ideal of daily life: to wear cuffs, to be shaved by a flunkey, to get up late. By renouncing these privileges, kings make them recede into the heaven of dream: their (very temporary) sacrifice determines and eternalizes the signs of daily bliss.[37]

If the Queen was to be seen barbecuing in *Royal Family*, rather than shaving, nonetheless the effect of seeing the Royal Family engaged in doing ordinary things had much the same effect as the newspaper and magazine reports of the royal cruise that Barthes was discussing. But, there was something qualitatively different in the televisual representation of the royals at play – they could not only be seen to be doing ordinary things, they could also be heard. And they, as a family, did not sound 'ordinary' at all. If a pictorial representation confirmed and externalised the monarchic principle, a television recording made their temporary entrée into ordinary life seem precisely temporary and artificial. No longer protected by the formal rituals of a coronation or wedding ceremony, the notion of the Royal Family as a representative British family became less easy to sustain.

As Crisell points out, and as Lord Mountbatten had warned, in opening their domestic lives to television, the Royal Family had cast off some of its mystique:

> ... television is always a dangerous guest to admit since it ends up hosting the party. As members of the Royal Family were seen more and more often on TV, their magic began to wane and popular reverence to diminish. They came to seem unremarkable, even a little dull.[38]

The Investiture of Prince Charles as the Prince of Wales reconfirmed the remarkable position of the Royal Family. It was the first such Investiture for 58 years, and therefore the first to be televised. Flagged in the *Radio Times* as 'The most difficult and massive Outside Broadcast operation since the Coronation and the biggest colour operation ever',[39] this was also the first major royal occasion to have been primarily designed as a television event.

The Investiture signalled an attempt to return to the formal pomp and ceremony of royal ritual, and its purpose was to establish Charles as a worthy inheritor of royal tradition. Like *Royal Family* in the same year, the television construction of its individual member, Prince Charles, framed him as a modern individual inhabiting and taking up a position of heritage, simultaneously contemporary and traditional. Prince Charles made himself available for an interview and gave his views on 'Welsh Nationalism, his stay at University College, Aberystwyth, his education generally, his leisure interests and several day-to-day aspects of his life'.[40] *The Prince of Wales* was the first programme in a week of programming dedicated to the event, and told a 'story spanning 1000 years of Welsh and English history ... [which] looks at some of the fascinating men, both Welsh and English, who have held it [the title]'.[41] A Special Souvenir issue of the *Radio Times* outlined a programming schedule in which the Investiture itself was shown for almost three hours on both channels of the BBC, with highlights repeated on both channels in the evening.[42]

In fact, the Investiture was an event entirely constructed for television. A new crown (the first to be made for over 600 years) is the only indication in the *Radio Times* and the programming that this ceremony was an invented tradition. Insistently, the Investiture was televised as a 'historic ceremony',[43] and presented as supported by the great and the good of television and other institutions. The President of the University College of Wales, assorted Welsh mayors and the BBC Welsh Orchestra were among those corralled into lending the occasion an air of authenticity and of historic significance. Caernarvon Castle was restored and altered for television spectacle, with theatrical designer Carl Toms responsible for the design, and the canopy above the dais was made transparent so that television cameras could see through it.[44] Cliff Michelmore took over the role of royal reporter from Richard Dimbleby, and the event was given a stature not seen since the 1953 Coronation. And so Wales was coerced into the consensual monarchism of the BBC; as the *Radio Times* expressed it, having established some tangential Welsh connections for Charles: 'And so His Royal Highness is a link between contemporary Wales and its historic past, a symbol of the unbroken monarchical tradition of an ancient people.'[45]

Further attempts were made to evoke this 'unbroken monarchical tradition' in 1977 with the Jubilee celebrations. The celebrations were staged in the middle of a period in which a postwar welfare state consensus was breaking up, at the moment of the formation of Thatcherism as a political and ideological force. The rise of the National Front, the anarchic challenge of punk rock, and a high level of trade union dispute; all suggested a society characterised by contestation. In such a context, the royal celebrations represented a rather flimsy attempt to mask political conflict with images of tradition and unity; like television, the Royal Family was one of a diminishing number of British institutions admired abroad.[46] The Jubilee evoked and marshalled nostalgia for the Coronation. It represented resistance to national and imperial decline; an attempt to persuade, by pomp and circumstance, that no such decline had really taken place, or to argue that, even if it had, it did not really matter.[47]

The presence of the Sex Pistols record 'God Save the Queen' high in the charts in Jubilee week, however, suggested at angers and resentments not easily subsumed by tradition and nostalgia. Yet the combination of the Royal Family and broadcasting proved to be extraordinarily resilient; the ability of the partnership to constantly generate new consensual spectacles has become a major prop in ensuring royal popularity.

Throughout the decade of the 1980s, this popularity seemed firmly established. Rosalind Brunt could still confidently assert in 1992:

> In world terms, hereditary monarchies are a declining breed – variously exiled, assassinated, or nicely pensioned off throughout the twentieth century. But in Britain, far from disappearing, the monarchy has never been so popular .... The British monarchy's popularity is frequently attested in both public surveys and personal testimony .... When most of the rest of the world has long gone republican, there is no anti-royalist movement of any signficant size in Britain and the abolition of the monarchy appears as neither an important nor even an achievable demand of any progressive party manifesto.[48]

The popularity of the Royal Family was at its height when the long period of speculation about a bride for Charles culminated in the Royal Wedding of 1981. The 'fairytale wedding' marked another high point in the public popularity of the royals, in which the basis for a new generation was established and the family seemed once again to have managed the delicate balance of tradition and adaptation. The event was again marked by a Royal Wedding Souvenir issue of the *Radio Times*. As for the Investiture, the event was preceded by a series of programmes celebrating the Prince of Wales, and also by a broadcast of the Royal Fireworks the night before. Prince Charles, unlike his mother on the event of her Coronation, granted an exclusive interview, and the Order of Service and a map of the wedding route were included in the *Radio Times*. The morning programme schedules for BBC1 and BBC2 were cleared to broadcast the event to a worldwide audience of a billion people.

However, the shifting definitions between the public and the private, in the lives of the Royal Family and in broadcasting, and the willingness of journalists to exploit new media technologies, meant that this popularity was increasingly threatened. A less rigid commitment to royal protocol amongst some of the younger royals, particularly those who were royal by marriage, meant that the process of induction of a new generation of the Royal Family was anything but smooth. Indeed, the seeds of crisis were already sown. From the mid-1980s, media representations of the Royal Family suggest a growing destabilisation of image in which a satisfactory balance between remoteness and accessibililty, formality and informality, becomes ever more elusive.

The 1987 *It's a Royal Knockout* in which Princess Anne, Prince Edward, Prince Andrew and Sarah Ferguson, the Duchess of York, led teams in a games show, has been described by Ben Pimlott as 'toe-curling', and indeed it was.[49] According to Pimlott, the participation of the young royals in a popular television games show represented a new shift in the relationship between the monarchy and television: 'Floodgates opened ... It was an age of greater accessibility, as the younger Royals responded to media interest with frequent appearances on chat shows.'[50]

This greater accessibility and the informality had actually already been established in the 1969 *Royal Family*. Nonetheless, *It's a Royal Knockout* did establish a new precedent for the coverage of royalty, and for the ways in which some of the new generation of the Royal Family were prepared to be represented. Moreover, these younger royals had come of age in a television era, and were open to television appearances and interviews in a way that the previous generation had not been.

The programme foregrounded the benevolence and sportsmanship of the young royals. They were billed in the *Radio Times* as

> Royal Champions: Four members of the Royal Family bestow their favours on their chosen charities as they lead their teams into the 'Grand Knockout tournament' ... .[51] It's all for fun and funds ... . Follow the Royal leaders: the four team captains who set a high standard of sportsmanship for their celebrity squads.[52]

However, this attempt to link charitable work with an informal display of the younger royals in the context of a slapstick games show produced a spectacle that was cringingly embarrassing in its home movie amateurishness. Star appeal has always depended on a combination of the familiarity of an image with a degree of mystique and remoteness. *It's a Royal Knockout*, rooted in informality without dignity, merely undermined any royal mystique its participants may have had.

This period of television's new informality and intimacy with royalty coincided with the entry into the family of the young women who were to strain the relationship between the royals and television to its limit, Diana Spencer and Sarah Ferguson. The *Radio Times* at the time of the Royal Wedding described Diana as 'the woman who will have more influence on [Charles] than anyone else',[53] but could not have envisaged the extent of that influence, not only on Charles but on the institution of monarchy itself.

The appearance of Diana on television news and in the tabloid press initially operated to the advantage of the Royal Family. As a commoner, marrying into the royals, she at once combined aspects of the 'girl next door' (at least, if you lived in Kensington) with a glamour unattainable by most members of the public and of the Royal Family, in a 'double dialectic of likeness and unlikeness'.[54]

The royals also benefited from the limited popularity of Margaret Thatcher during the 1980s. Whilst winning elections, her divisive and controversial politics and personal style ensured a substantial degree of public hostility, and at times the Church and the monarchy became the bearers of consensus politics. ITV's *Spitting Image* had a running gag in which the Queen was shown attempting to oust the Prime Minister. As Brunt points out, in this 'the Queen, along with Prince Charles, was being viewed in the role of champion of her people; a member of the establishment, of course, and admittedly one of them, but somehow on the side of us'.[55]

In 1988, the year of his fortieth birthday, as a king-in-waiting still, Prince Charles appeared in two significant BBC programmes. The first was the flagship current affairs programme, *Panorama* in a special report: *Prince of Conscience*, an indication of the particular role Charles has chosen for himself as heir to the throne. He manifested this conscience again in a programme which he wrote and presented for *Omnibus, A Vision of Britain*, in which he pondered on architecture and demonstrated himself to be a serious and worthy inheritor of the throne. If such representations of the Prince and other royals on television remained fundamentally benign and deferential, those images were read alongside a very different discourse in the tabloid press. Rumours of marital discord between Charles and Diana grew throughout the late 1980s, culminating in the publication of transcripts of private phone conversations between Charles and his alleged mistress Camilla and between Diana and a then unidentified man with whom she was clearly on intimate terms.

From the beginning of the 1970s, the British tabloid press had been transformed by the impact of the republican and Australian Rupert Murdoch's ownership and relaunch of the *Sun*. The hallmarks of the new tabloid style were a heightened dramatisation and personalisation of stories, a greater prominence of gossip and scandal, and a willingness to expose matters hitherto regarded as part of the private sphere. The *Sun* expressed a degree of hostility to some of the pillars of the corporate state establishment – the professions, the civil service, trade unions and the Royal Family – that paralleled and augmented the rise of Thatcherism. The Murdoch-led destruction of the power of the print unions at the start of the 1980s ushered in a second tabloid revolution. The introduction of computerised layouts and new print technologies allowed for more flexible page layouts and the use of colour. Headlines and photographs ceased to be a mere illustration to the body text, and instead became the main focus of the message, in a process which heightened the sensational impact of major stories. In the late 1980s and early 1990s the gradual public unravelling of the marriage of Charles and Diana (and later of the Duke and Duchess of York) became a standard feature of the 'red-top' press, and a central focus of the tabloid wars.

While television was far more circumspect about the relaying of gossip and rumour, and retained something of the culture of deference, its images of royalty could not but be consumed in conjunction with tabloid rumour, scandal and sensation. In such a climate, Diana, Charles, and their supporters were drawn into a battle of image manipulation, in a struggle to win a war of representation in the press, and eventually on television. As Crisell acknowledges, the combination of tabloid journalism and television had come to constitute a major problem for the image of the royals:

> ... with the revelations of matrimonial breakdowns and sexual adventures, notably those of Prince Charles and Princess Diana, royalty began to acquire a negative, more tawdry kind of glamour.
>
> It has to be said that television was not the only, perhaps not even the primary cause of this change. Its news programmes simply echoed stories which had invariably originated in the tabloids – and even then, only when they had become so sensational that they could no longer be ignored. But television clearly gave them a wider currency, and its pictures fleshed out and made us all too familiar with those about whom they were written.[56]

Television news programmes did not however 'simply echo' tabloid journalism; they could and did add a new dimension to those stories and made the monarchy vulnerable in ways that the print press could not. The divorce of Charles and Diana, announced by then Prime Minister John Major on the television news, acquired the status of national news. This transformation of speculation, rumour and innuendo into established 'fact' gave the events an official status; as Crisell put it: 'By the 1990s [television] was a monstrous dictator before whom a prince and princess would come to justify their private lives.'[57]

Charles's and Diana's competing television interviews in 1996, on rival television channels, represented a real shift in what the royals were prepared to say on television. If the interviewing style was still respectful, the revelations confirmed tabloid speculation. Television animated the tabloid icons, and it gave them a soundtrack; Charles and Diana were seen and they were heard, and they chose a confessional form of self-presentation. Although Diana's interview was not marked even by a programme description in the *Radio Times*, and if she herself was no republican, it represented the most dissenting voice against the monarchy that television had ever allowed. In her *Panorama* interview Diana became, as many broadsheet feminist columnists articulated, 'one of us'. Despite the formal editing and *mise-en-scène* of the interview, in her story of infidelity, eating disorders and therapy, Diana's discourse was that of the talk shows of Oprah Winfrey or Ricki Lake. She became 'like us' in a way that Charles (as a man, an admitted adulterer and as the inheritor of the monarchy) could not.

Diana claimed in her interview that she wanted to be the 'Queen of Hearts'. Her death, at a moment when her relationship with Dodi Fayed had become the principal romance narrative of the royal soap opera, confirmed that that is indeed what she became. Just before Diana's death Channel 5 had shown a sympathetic documentary about Camilla, Charles's mistress, widely reported (and cited implicitly in both Charles's and Diana's interviews) to have been the cause of the end of the marriage. Diana's death in 1997 put an end to any sympathy for Camilla and Charles; in the public sanctification of her memory, she altered the map. And in that transformation the other royals, constructed in their difference from Diana, became more remote and unlike us. Ironically, the very absence of Diana herself, far from freeing the monarchy of the burden of having to handle a maverick, has increased pressure on them to be more like Diana. It is striking that Charles's recent public appearances have featured walkabouts, meeting the people, and the appearance of a greater accessibility. The agenda of 'caring' established by Diana has thrown the spotlight on Charles's role as a father; it is clear that he will be judged through his parenting of the young Princes and in his faithfulness to Diana's legacy, and that his relationship with his sons is now more foregrounded.

Public resentment against the Royal Family was expressed as an anger that they had not appeared publicly (on television) to acknowledge the impact of Diana's death. The Queen was, in effect, forced onto television to respond to demands that the Royal Family be seen to express their grief. The Royal Family were no longer able to draw a discreet veil over their private affairs; their expectation of national rejoicing over the televising of formal royal celebrations such as weddings, coronations and the Investiture now required a television appearance at a moment of crisis.

It was television itself that made possible the extraordinary public response to Diana's death. On the morning that her death was announced, all terrestrial channels but Channel 4 cleared their schedules for the entire day. The 'floral revolution' was fuelled by television pictures of early visitors to Buckingham and Kensington Palaces, and it was selected television images that promoted Diana as the patron saint of a diverse and multicultural Britain. She became indeed the 'People's Princess' (in Prime Minister Tony Blair's term) as repeated footage of young black and Asian and gay male mourners were shown on news reports and on tribute programmes throughout the day of her death and continuously until her funeral. This cultural and ethnic mix of mourners was offered as a representation of the cultural diversity of the nation, in an inclusive assumption that all mourned Diana and that to be profoundly affected by the monarchy was to mark one's Britishness.

Diana's funeral became a public television event on a scale probably not witnessed since the Coronation, and its extraordinary aftermath could not have taken the form that it did without television. The televised cortège brought people out onto the streets along its route, prompted by the significance of the event as television spectacle. Television reporters were attacked (on screen) at Kensington and Buckingham Palaces, where some mourners saw them as agents of the media, which they perceived to be the cause of Diana's death. Both in its actuality and in its televising, the funeral embodied the tension between populist demands and royal protocol. While the public claimed Diana as a 'People's Princess', it was simultaneously expected that she be buried with all the ceremony befitting a member of the Royal Family.

Earl Spencer's funeral oration was hardly a republican voice, but it was nonetheless dissident in his implied attack on the Royal Family (as individuals rather than as an institution). His poignant tribute to his sister in the formal setting of Westminster Abbey was dramatic enough, but the real impact of what he had to say came not from inside Westminster Abbey, but from the crowds in Hyde Park, whose applause, prompted by a relay of the telecast of the service on huge screens, circulated and swelled into the formal service. The broadcasting and relaying of the service and its impact on the formal ceremony, the impossibility of separating the actual ceremony and the broadcast, made the event a simulacrum.

Baudrillard has asserted that:

... the common illusion about the media is that they are used by those in power to manipulate, seduce and alienate the masses ... the more subtle version, the ironic version is precisely the opposite. It is that, through the media, it is the masses who manipulate those in power.[58]

While we would not accept this as a general proposition, we would suggest that in the case of Diana's funeral, the 'people's voice', as articulated through television and the press, has acted as a powerful pressure on the Royal Family to conform more to public expectation.

At a period in which there has been extensive discussion of a 'crisis of the family', the Royal Family have become a site for competing discourses about family values, marriage and parenting. Representations of Princess Diana, on television and in the print media, in particular, became a point of articulation around which critical and dissenting discourses about royalty, authority, personal morality and femininity could cluster.

Benedict Anderson has argued that:

... monarchy lies transverse to all modern conceptions of political life. Kingship organises everything around a high centre. Its legitimacy derives from divinity, not from populations, who, after all, are subjects, not citizens.[59]

In Britain, the monarchy has come to recognise that it must become modernised in order to reproduce this legitimacy, and to do so in a form that does not seem anachronistic. In the era of television and tabloid journalism, the complex balance of familiarity and separateness that this legitimacy requires has become a conjuring trick that is increasingly harder to pull off.

Barthes argued in the 1950s that:

... this mythical character of our kings is nowadays secularised, though not in the least exorcised ... . Kings are defined by the purity of their race (Blue Blood) like puppies, and the ship, the privileged locus of any 'closure' is a kind of modern Ark where the main variations of the monarchic species are preserved.[60]

If the mythical character of our contemporary kings has undoubtedly been secularised, it is now in doubt whether it can be sustained at all. The preservation of the monarchic species is no longer unquestioned, and television has had a great deal to do with challenging the neat 'closure' that the Royal Family believed they could effect. There are popular hints of a republicanism in the 1990s, and an acknowledgement of these on television that was unthinkable at the time of the Coronation. The popularity of the Queen herself has dropped; her Christmas message was watched by 28 million in 1984; ten years later, it was almost half that figure.[61]

The Royal Family have themselves embarked on a process of re-branding and image transformation; they have followed the model of the Blairite reconstruction of the Labour Party in establishing the 'Way Ahead Group', dedicated to the modernising of the monarchy and have recently announced that they are to appoint a spin doctor.[62] This is in response to the first reports from focus groups, which suggest that the Royal Family is seen as out of touch, remote and poor value for money.[63] All those involved in these focus groups will know the royals largely through their television representations, and the Royal Family no longer have the control of that representation in the way that they once did. Even while the legal and cultural restraints on what television can broadcast about the Royal Family remain in place, the Palace can no longer exert control over their representation, there is a constant slippage of meanings that have escaped those controls. The royals are currently more reactive and less proactive than they have ever been.

The institutions of television itself do not permit a space for a republican voice. But the tensions and contradictions of the institution of the monarchy have in the late twentieth century made themselves felt nonetheless. Even while the monarch controlled her own representation on television and the Palace exercised powerful controls over what could and could not be shown of footage of the Royal Family,[64] the medium itself is one which has revealed the cracks in the delicate balance between remoteness and accessibility. The fierce light of television has made the mystique of royal protocol seem arcane, while the attempts at royal accessibility through television has exposed too much to sustain the myth of monarchy.

Notes

1   Roland Barthes, *Mythologies* (Paladin, 1973), p. 33.
2   John Ellis, *Visible Fictions* (RKP, 1982), pp. 113–15.
3   Rosalind Brunt, 'A divine gift to inspire? Popular cultural representation, nationhood and the British monarchy', in D. Strinati and S. Wagg (eds), *Come on Down: Popular Media Culture in Post-war Britain* (Routledge, 1992), p. 290.
4   Asa Briggs, *The Golden Age of Wireless* (OUP, 1965), p. 112.
5   Mark Pegg, *Broadcasting and Society 1918–1939* (Croom Helm, 1983), p. 191.
6   Paddy Scannell and David Cardiff, *A Social History of British Broadcasting, vol. 1, 1922–39* (Basil Blackwell, 1991), p. 282–3.
7   Ibid., p. 286.
8   David Cardiff and Paddy Scannell, *The Social Foundations of British Broadcasting* (OU, 1981). NB A different version of this paper, without the cited quote, appeared in B. Waites, T. Bennett and G. Martin, *Popular Culture: Past and Present* (Croom Helm, 1982).
9   Pegg, *Broadcasting and Society* (1983), p. 192.
10   Scannell and Cardiff, *A Social History of British Broadcasting* (1991), p. 284.
11   Gordon Ross, *TV Jubilee*, (W H Allan, 1961), pp. 141–3.

12   Bernard Sendall, *Independent Television in Britain, vol. 1: 1946–62* (Macmillan, 1982), p. 23.
13   Ibid., p. 100.
14   Norman Collins, *BBC Quarterly,* vol. 4, no. 1, April 1949, p. 31.
15   Ross, *TV Jubilee* (1961), p. 89.
16   *Radio Times,* 29 May 1953, p. 5.
17   Rosalind Coward, *Female Desire: Women's Sexuality Today* (Paladin, 1984), p. 164.
18   Ellis, *Visible Fictions* (1982), p. 181.
19   Andrew Crisell, *An Introductory History of British Broadcasting* (Routledge, 1997), p. 272.
20   *Radio Times,* 15 May 1953, p. 5.
21   *Radio Times,* 8 May 1953, p. 15.
22   *Radio Times* Special Coronation Issue, 22 May 1953.
23   *Radio Times,* 29 May 1953, p. 3.
24   *Radio Times,* 22 May 1953.
25   Peter Black, *The Biggest Aspidistra in the World* (BBC, 1972), p. 169.
26   Richard Dimbleby, *Elizabeth Our Queen* (University of London, 1953).
27   Leonard R. Miall (ed.), *Richard Dimbleby, Broadcaster* (BBC, 1966) p. 85.
28   Black, *The Biggest Aspidistra* (1972), p. 169.
29   *Radio Times,* 29 May 1953, p. 3.
30   Ross, *TV Jubilee* (1961), pp. 142–3.
31   Bernard Sendall, *Independent Television In Britain, vol. 2: 1958–68* (Macmillan, 1983), p. 158.
32   Jeremy Potter, *Independent Television in Britain, vol. 4: Companies and programmes 1968–80,* (Macmillan, 1990), p. 107.
33   Ben Pimlott, 'My Husband and I', in *Radio Times,* November 1997, pp. 23–6.
34   Crisell, *An Introductory History of British Broaddcasting* (1997), p. 174.
35   *Royal Family: A Historic Documentary Film* (The Hamlyn Group, 1969), p. 2.
36   Ibid., p. 23.
37   Barthes, *Mythologies* (1973), pp. 32–3.
38   Crisell, *An Introductory History of British Broadcasting* (1997), pp. 174.
39   *Radio Times,* 26 June 1969, p. 30.
40   Ibid., p. 12.
41   Ibid.
42   Ibid., p.19.
43   Ibid., p. 25.
44   David Cannadine, 'The context, performance and meaning of ritual: The British Monarchy and the "Invention of Tradition" *c.* 1820–1977', in Eric Hobsbawm and Terence Ranger (eds), *The Invention of Tradition* (Cambridge University Press, 1983), p. 159.
45   *Radio Times,* 26 June 1969, p. 33.
46   Jeremy Potter, *Independent Television in Britain, vol. 3: Politics and Control 1968–80,* (Macmillan, 1989), p. 12.
47   Cannadine, 'The context, performance and meaning of ritual' (1983), p. 160.
48   Brunt, 'A divine gift to inspire?' (1992), pp. 285–6.
49   *Radio Times,* 15 November 1997, p. 25.
50   Ibid.
51   *Radio Times,* 13 June 1987, p. 3.
52   Ibid., p. 5.
53   *Radio Times,* 26 July 1981.
54   Brunt, 'A divine gift to inspire?' (1992), p. 293.
55   Ibid., p. 300.
56   Crisell, *An Introductory History of British Broadcasting* (1997), p. 174.

57   Ibid., p. 173.
58   Jean Baudrillard, 'The end of the millenium or the countdown', in *Theory Culture and Society*, vol. 5, no. 1 (Sage, 1998), p. 8.
59   Benedict Anderson, *Imagined Communities* (Verso, 1983), p. 19.
60   Roland Barthes, 'The Blue Blood Cruise', in *Mythologies* (1973), p. 33.
61   Crisell, *An Introductory History of British Broadcasting* (1997), p. 175.
62   See *Guardian*, 23 February 1998.
63   *Sunday Times*, 22 February 1998.
64   See *The Media Show*, Wall to Wall for Channel 4, 1991.

6

David Butler

'Progressive' Television Documentary and Northern Ireland – The Films of Michael Grigsby in a 'Postcolonial' Context

every cultural form is radically, quintessentially hybrid ... So vast and yet so detailed is imperialism as an experience with crucial cultural dimensions, that we must speak of overlapping territories, intertwined histories common to men and women, whites and non-whites, dwellers in the metropolis and on the peripheries, past as well as present and future; these territories can only be seen from the perspective of the whole of secular human history.[1]

The Trouble With 'Progressiveness'

Historiographical studies of politics and society in Ireland (constitutional history, economic history and so forth) generally divide writers and readers into opposing paradigms. It should be no surprise that studies of representation have tended to do the same. Marxism is a common core to most media studies writings in relation to NI. Despite this, the dominant 'anti-imperialist' purview appears to have been quarantined from trends commonplace elsewhere in the discourse of contemporary cultural studies. Specifically, at a time when 'anti-essentialism' and the 'politics of difference' are colonising all before them – around a consensus that *all* subjectivities and social identities of a racial, gendered, national and/or 'other' variety are indubitably 'constructed', a matter of 'invention'[2] – the proponents of anti-imperialist media studies appear to rely on bluntly absolutist distinctions: as between the legitimate/praiseworthy/heroic status of oppressed *native* interests and the illegitimate/damnable/villainous status of *settler* interests. To argue, without qualification, as Liz Curtis and David Miller each have done, in support of a 'troops out' diagnosis is to reduce non- and anti-nationalist mentalities to a clientist 'false consciousness' (a model of ideology owed to Connolly rather than Gramsci). Miller speculates:

> Perhaps the most perplexing question is why the British have remained in Northern Ireland for so long. The simple truth is that it is easier to stay than to go ... . There is no 'objective necessity' for British forces to remain in Ireland ... But this is only to say that the monolithic inertia of the British state is moved in new directions only when the interests of the state are seen to override the difficulties of a change in policy or when opposition is unstoppable ... . It seems likely ... that the impetus for a British withdrawal will only become strong enough when the cost ... becomes great enough to worry an insecure government. [3]

On this view Northern Irish unionists cannot conceivably be what they *know* themselves to be, that is, British. To speak of 'the British' and 'withdrawal' in this 'green Marxist' [4] manner presupposes that nothing about the economy, employment, education, material culture and lifestyles in NI is or can be genuinely British because the local inhabitants are the descendants of colonialists, 'planters' so to speak, and thus their preferences may be disregarded as reactionary and irrelevant to the dispute between the historical principals – the British state and the 'nationalist people' of Ireland. Reasoning of this kind does not permit that national belonging may be determined on a civic and elective basis. Whether critics of this kind have thought through the implications or not, in effect they are making common cause with irredentist and ethnicist conceptions of cultural purity and impurity. No room here for mulatto or creolised British identities. My own perspective on the question of social identity is that these are made, not simply found; fluid, not fixed, and that the process of identity formation is greatly influenced by the discursive authority of representation. The third of these items points to the 'effects' of the media of public communication, especially their capacity to contribute to, affirm and reproduce commonly held ideas and beliefs in circulation in society – notably ideas about history and beliefs about cultural similarities and differences.

Putting Method in Perspective

It is a truism of film studies that 'how' is 'what'. [5] The grammar of film is meaningful – the story structure, the look of the film, etc. – and must be understood as such. Grouped by author, genre, or theme, film is generally studied in a formalist manner. Styles of reading follow primary theoretic and disciplinary sources. From pre-origins in Saussure, Marx, Freud – semiology, ideology critique, psychoanalysis – film studies, an elementary part of emergent media studies programmes (variously situated in literary studies, history, social science, arts, education and other institutional contexts) developed in and through combinations of textualist and/or sociological approaches. Not mutually exclusive by any means, it follows that the formation of 'media and cultural studies' programmes in a social science as compared to an Arts or Adult Education context, influenced styles of critical engagement in particular ways.

For a number of good reasons television is more usually interpreted in political rather than stylistic terms. The institutions of broadcast television are closely related to the conditions of political society in a way that cinema is not. The limits of television representation tend not to deviate far from the norms of leading opinion in the state and economy in any given period. Television is particularly vulnerable to political 'controversy' – i.e. to the criticisms of senior politicians and vested cultural authorities. By the same token, the idiomatic features of television cannot be reduced to a function or effect of supra-determining structures. TV-texts do possess meaning-making specificity. The critical value of the concepts of 'flow', of television's 'bardic function' and its typically 'segmental' form (introduced in Williams's *Television: Technology and Cultural Form*, Fiske and Hartley's *Reading Television* and Ellis's *Visible Fictions*) was that these recognised and attempted to develop understanding of the 'effectivity' of televisual material in ways traditional social science methods were not equipped to calculate.[6]

Intended to amend the reductive reasoning of preceding sociological studies – where orthodox coverage of political violence was explained as not much more than iteration of the 'dominant ideology' – Schlesinger, Murdock and Elliot's *Televising Terrorism* analysed television programmes according to an index of 'relatively closed' through to 'relatively open' outlooks.[7] By the former they had in mind the expression of attitudes 'mainly or wholly within the terms of reference set by the official perspective'. In this way news bulletins may be seen to correspond naturally to dominant interests. And by the latter designation they meant categories of representation, 'open in the sense that they provide spaces in which the core assumptions of the official perspective can be interrogated and contested and in which other perspectives can be presented and examined'. The single-play and feature documentaries were identified as liable to permit expression of alternative and, on occasion, oppositional voices. Further, to factor in the significance of how elements within programmes are arranged and presented, Schlesinger *et al.* made critical distinction as between 'tight' formats, 'in which the images, arguments and evidence ... are organised to converge upon a single preferred interpretation and where other possible conclusions are marginalised or closed off', in contrast to comparatively 'loose' programme formats, 'where the ambiguities, contradictions and loose ends generated within the programme are never fully resolved'.[8]

Televising Terrorism was a key work in the development of media studies approaches, not least because its analytic formula moved the debate beyond simplistic reliance on the instrumental 'ruling ideas/ruling class' coda of marxist sociology hitherto. And yet the functionalism of their method produces a mechanistic relation between the style of the programme under scrutiny and the attitude said to inform its authorship. Schlesinger *et al.* evidently preferred open/loose to closed/tight formats on the grounds, presumably, that pluralism is intellectually enlightened and politically inclusive where univocal forms retard reasoned argument. Contrary to their stated aim, however, the methodology of *Televising Terrorism* restricts the activity of formal analysis to a schematic inventory of programme types, thereupon prescribing specific mentalities to specific formats. What John Corner says of nonfiction is equally true of fiction forms:

> basic questions about ... documentary discourse do not easily and directly correlate with particular forms. For instance, a commentary film, ostensibly a traditional closed form in which discursive management is direct and often continuous, can be constructed in such a way in relation to the various other voices it uses, and in its combination with visuals, as to present viewers with a thoughtful and questioning viewing experience. On the other hand, a fly-on-the-wall programme, despite its apparent openness, can work with a very tightly managed sense of the significance of what is going on.[9]

For in order to mount a coherent and suasive thesis, 'oppositional' film-makers are as likely to employ tight and closed approaches as are mainstream film-makers. Indeed, as oppositionalities, arguably it makes sense that the few opportunities presented be made use of in as disciplined and single-minded (and univocal) a way as possible. By indicating that oppositional perspectives incline towards openness and officialdom closedness, the critical language of *Televising Terrorism* suggests anti-statist perspectives are progressive as a rule. This is, to say the least, a politically problematic conclusion – and not only in the context of NI. First, as argued, in analysing film and television texts, there is and can be no one-to-one affinity between progressive politics and progressive forms of representation such as Schlesinger *et al.* imply. Secondly, although the semantics of their book equate progressiveness with openness, in fact by oppositional they meant contra-official perspectives. These may or may not be pluralist and may or may not be politically progressive. Thirdly, the study is ahistorical and fourthly, it follows, inaccurate in its diagnosis of the conflict in NI. On the last point, the misunderstanding is in no small part due to the *Britishness* of their theory and methods. This is not to insist on Irish solutions to Irish problems only, recalling Lenin's critical remarks on 'the national question', to prefer concrete analysis of concrete situations:

> The categorical requirement of Marxist theory in investigating any social question is that it be examined within definite historical limits and that if it refers to a particular country ... account be taken of the specific features distinguishing that country from others in the same historical epoch.[10]

Ordinarily, centrist and left studies of Ireland have been focused through a lens of British definitions, reflecting the contradictions of *their* national politics and histories more than those of the circumstance represented. A 'contextual poetic' of the sort advocated here requires a method of study adjusted, in appropriate magnitude, to the formal and conceptual specifics of the texts under review. It requires, furthermore, that the interpretations produced be situated in historical knowledge of the context studied.

Victims and Villains

'My driving force in documentary has been trying to find a way to give voice to the voiceless',[11] says Michael Grigsby. In 30 years of independent film-making Grigsby has revisited a number of favoured causes: among them, the social conditions of the British working classes and the commonality of experience between fishing, agricultural and industrial communities; the conditions of postcolonial societies, notably of Vietnam and Ireland. He is a practised exponent of naturalist technique. Where possible Grigsby will choose steady, medium- and long-distance perspectives and lengthy, single takes, preferring panning and travelling shots to the cropped framing and ceaseless cutting of the television aesthetic. Using available light when he can, his films privilege 'ordinary people' speaking unhindered, and shows others like them, in-shot, listening sympathetically. Grigsby doesn't generally use name captions, so we may take it that the subjects of his films are emblematic of collective identities. He dislikes current affairs-style interlocution and voiceover commentaries, instead linking and integrating testimony/discussion sequences by means of symphonic sound/image montages.

The Time of Our Lives (1993) is a confessional 'mass observation' of the values of five generations of an East End London-Irish family, descendants of immigrant Richard Harris, the celebrations around whose eighty-fifth birthday provide the fulcrum for Grigsby's text. Commissioned for the BBC2 *Fine Cut* series, at an early point in the film, on the day in question, Grigsby's subjective camera meets then follows a woman of late middle-age years. A warden, presumably, she walks, carrying keys and blankets, along neat corridors, into a lift and up, through fire-doors, etc. (in what looks like sheltered accommodation), to the old man's apartment and his bedroom (a crucifix prominent on the wall above his bed), where he lies, hardly visible, peaceful, asleep. The journey, shot in real time, occupies two and half minutes on-screen. Over these pictures Grigsby segues memorable political soundbites, reversing through the decades to the mid-30s (when Harris first travelled from Limerick to London in search of employment): the *News at Ten* chimes cuts into Neil Kinnock's eve of election oration, '[i]f Margaret Thatcher is returned on Thursday ... I warn you not to ...'; to Norman Tebbit's 'got on his bike ... and looked for work' conference speech; reportage of nationwide power cuts merge with an apocalyptic broadcast by Prime Minister Heath, circa 1974; orchestral mixed with British beat music dissolves into 'they think it's all over', England World Cup, 1966, and to Harold Wilson's 'white heat' speech; the BBC Home Service signature tune; Macmillan, 'never had it so good'; populist hubbub at the time of the coronation of Elizabeth II, 1953; and on finally, to a stiff-collared radio talk by Beveridge outlining plans for social security provision to the accompaniment of a big band in waltz time ....

Counter to the mannered stylelessness of institutional (aka current affairs) documentaries, where the fetish for neutrality requires the elimination of evocative technique, most of Grigsby's films are laced with lyrical notations of the sort just described. These act something like a zip-pan and/or the auditory equivalent of a 'montage of attractions' (Eisenstein), to precis conjunctural shifts and/or 'quicken' (Barthes) major themes. They are, as we shall see, especially significant in filmwork that is otherwise observational in approach – which is to say, that aims to permit unstructured access to pro-filmic material. Grigsby's method is distinguished by a comity of naturalist and formalist strategies. In this, as with much else of his approach, he is faithful to the aesthetic lineage of the British documentary film movement. Retrospectively cast as incompatibles, the liaison of modernist and realist film technique – apparent, for instance, in Jennings's peerless *Listen to Britain* (1942) – was in no sense illicit in the context of their formal co-development in the interwar period. Suspicion of formalism followed from the founding of a calvinist 'anti-aesthetic'[12] as the operational orthodoxy of television nonfiction. At any rate, as a consequence of the predominance of utilitarian formats and the conformity of current affairs programming to centrist opinion, 'controversial' and/or 'poetic' documentary features (i.e. those expressing other than centrist views in ways not restricted to the *balanced* formality of current affairs) are nowadays confined mostly to the margins of the schedule.

Alan Lovell describes *Drifters* (1929), the Ur-Griersonian text, as characteristically conjoining 'an approach derived from Flaherty, editing techniques suggested by Soviet films, and Grierson's own interest in social process'.[13] The elements identified, of naturalism, associative cutting, and an ethos of left-collectivism, fairly well sums up the poetics and politics of Michael Grigsby's documentary studies also – with the important caveat that Grigsby (like Jennings and other of the film-makers under commission in the GPO/Crown period) is further to the left than Grierson. The stylistic trace of 1930s experiments in non-naturalistic dubbing and of overlapping auditory-visual montage, where sound and image tracks are set in discontinuous arrangement, feature strongly in Grigsby's commanding film style. He acknowledges the debt to Jennings in particular. Intellectually, too, a film like *Living on the Edge* (1987) self-consciously refers back to the political idealism of the era of 'The Road to 1945'[14] in acute contrast to the dystopia of Thatcher's Britain. Made in the darkest of dark times as an exposition of the state of nation, *Living on the Edge* was transmitted in a 'Viewpoint '87' slot on the ITV network. It is a social history of disappointment from the point of view of four marginalised groups and areas: a Devonshire dairy farming family gone bust as a result of the recession; redundant residents of a housing estate in Birkenhead; a South Wales mining community; a party of young and unemployed Glaswegian men. Sketched across a broad historical canvas, from the Jarrow Marches to the privatisation and de-industrialisation policies of the 1980s, as with *The Time of Our Lives*, affidavits are contextualised through a generational perspective, connected and thematised by figurative montage sequences – motifs of derelict heavy machinery, the venality and indecency of consumer society, Britain's vassal relationship to US imperialism, recur in narrational cycles. Popular music signals mood. 'In the thirties people had principles. Now they've got mortgages and cars'; 'togetherness'; 'the roots have gone'; 'a life sentence without a crime'; 'loss of cohesion'; 'Stand up and scream ... Is anyone listening?': the declamations of the subjects of this film are for the most part plaintive and nostalgic for organic, vertically integrated communities of bygone industrial Britain and the defeated values of working-class solidarity, full employment, and the enabling, social democratic state.

Examined in relation to the grammar of conventional interview set-ups (i.e. as punctuated by classical point-of-view editing – over-the-shoulder shooting, to and fro fixed camera positions and static, mostly medium close-up framing – and the structuring formality of questions asked and answers given), the syntax of Grigsby's filmed interviews appear loose and vernacular in style. Signifying non-intervention, it would be truer to say the inferential frame around the testimony sequences is not visible in the finished text – as if questions and quotation marks have been erased, seeming to leave verbatim transcriptions to *speak for themselves*. The discursive unanimity of *Living on the Edge* and *The Time of Our Lives* suggest an old-time socialist imagining. Both films look back sentimentally to the productivist verities of unified class identities and a clear divide between the interests of Capital and organised Labour, to a time before the corrupting allure of consumerism.

It maybe worth re-emphasising at this stage that the *neutral* styles of institutional documentary programmes are not at all neutral. Knowing the ideological complicity of Griersonian, public service forms with dominant interests, but aware also that in naturalist discourse how is what, Grigsby adroitly works the codes of naturalist transparency *in support of* partisan socialist-humanist ends *and against* the bogus objectivity of official coverage of current affairs. Requiring a certain professional judgement to conceal in order to reveal, the cognitive impact of this mastery of documentary form is to present powerfully empathetic identification with the subjects of the texts. Michael Grigsby is no 'naive realist'.[15] His habit is to conduct ostensibly multivalent voices to an unequivocal point of closure, as prefigured in the allegoric montage sequences. The constructed unconstuctedness of his dissident naturalism is thus a formalism of kinds (a variety of modernist naturalism). But nor is Grigsby a 'post-Griersonian' documentarist. Though rejecting the contract with orthodoxy and anti-formalism, his aims are consistent with the pedagogic purpose of conventionally *British* documentary films, whose corporate project, Brian Winston reminds us, has been to 'look like evidence inviting judgement', while in truth being 'ruthless in their positioning of the spectator'.[16]

Grigsby's Irish films combine faultless artistry with flawed politics. *Too Long A Sacrifice* (1984) and *The Silent War* (1990) are skilful impressions of British involvement in Ireland underwritten by an anti-imperialist romanticism. Founded on a logic of blame and virtue of oppressor and oppressed, *The Silent War* favours an externalising narrative which attributes responsibility for all ills – emigration, economic hardship, etc. – to unwarranted occupation by the British state. With two consequences. Internal divisions are elided and structural similarities between the experience and character of native and settler communities stressed. The second of these strategies infers that the antagonism of unionist culture to reunification is an effect of misguided loyalty to the colonial power.

The Silent War concentrates on the detailed evidence of a Catholic and Republican family – not explicitly identified as such, but a fair conclusion based on their language and suppositions. Testifying to the daily reductions imposed on them by the British Army, they speak in a commonsense way of the absolute necessity of ending 'British' occupation. Amongst other material cited, their primary accounts are supported by a series of secondary witness statements as to the intrusiveness, inconvenience and harassments of living under military surveillance. As far as it possible to tell, of the second group all are non-Catholic – as indicated on the same basis as before, they speak of 'soldiers' where the principal subjects routinely use the language of 'Brits'. But where the former express a fairly wide range of political views and recollections, the opinions of the latter are confined to detailing the negative effects of military infringement in their daily lives. In this way, the contributions of the non-Republican respondents appear to concur with the thrust of the film's anti-imperialist diagnosis. Their views on the constitutional status of NI – as to whether NI *is* and might remain British – are nowhere manifest in the text. Perhaps the questions were not asked. More likely, by means of seamless occlusion, Grigsby permits only one meaning of the recorded material to become visible. Dissenting voices to the 'troops out' rationale – that the best solution is withdrawal in the interests of achieving a unitary state – are not raised.

About a third of the way through the film, Grigsby uses the common 'documentarist fiction'[17] of an arranged meeting between the Catholic and the Protestant women in a city-centre pub to stress commonality of interest. Immediately following it, a straight-to-camera march past by Orange flute bands segues, after a few moments' silence (the duration of an establishing shot), from the lingering Orange tune on the soundtrack to the sound of a single player, who, it is soon disclosed, is the adolescent son of the principal family, practising in his bedroom. The ironic coincidence of instruments and tunes is of course striking. Grigsby, like others of a cultural nationalist persuasion, wants to encourage recognition of the perceptible sameness of Loyalist and 'indigenous' custom and practice. Within the film as a whole, this sequence stresses the mistaken character of Loyalist faith in their 'Britishness', suggesting further that when the colonialist chimera is finally shaken off, self-acknowledgement of the Irish essence of Orangeism will follow naturally. And in the mean time, according to anti-imperialist logic, the basis of political opposition to an all-Ireland outcome may be discounted as a kind of false affinity syndrome.

To be explicit on this point, the thesis advanced is that understanding the terms and conditions of Ulster unionist affiliation to Britain will not ultimately be aided by telling them they've imagined the whole thing. The Britishness of NI is, of course, an imperial legacy. To say so, however, does not delegitimise the integrity of the 'lived experience' of *being* British in NI, any more than saying that contemporary Australia is less than truly Australian because it was once a British dominion. The racialism infecting present-day Australia and the sectarianism ingrained in the NI economy and polity are true expressions of the contradictions of postcoloniality – in a way that popular support for the jingoism of the British tabloid press may also be understood as a feature of an imperialist past.

Demonstrating that film techniques are neither orthodox or oppositional, Grigsby has perfected a style of associative editing derived from wartime propaganda films. *Listen to Britain* is a quite extraordinary evocation of social harmony and national belonging. Rooted to and routed through symbols of kith and kin, Jennings binds the home front, by means of intellectual montage, to the land and to the cultural and industrial life of the community at war. Without aid of verbal commentary, one sequence moves from:

1   the calm picture and sound of wind in a mature tree:
2   (overlapped now by piano music) cut to a closely framed interior in which a young woman prepares high-tea; she turns and looks from her window:

3   to long shot of a country schoolyard where children play a
    choreographed game:
4   cut back to the interior; side-on, she looks out at the scene:
5   to the exterior, closer this time; a girl's voice is heard, 'Mammie!', above
    the piano music to which the children skip and clap in time, in a large
    circle, in pairs:
6   to the interior again; cutaway from her (the mother) to framed
    photograph of absent soldier (the father), this shot held in big close-
    up (clapping hands and piano continue on the soundtrack):
7   to exterior scene, closer than before, children facing one another,
    arms raised, slapping left hand on right and then ducking into the centre
    etc.; one girl (the daughter) miscoordinates her step (before the next
    cut, a heavy rumbling is heard):
8   to an army convoy passing through narrow Elizabethan village
    streets ....

There are two components to this series of transitions I want to highlight
in illustration of Grigsby's film rhetoric (7 and 8). First, the connotative
connection of women-and-children to the reassuring presence of the
military is achieved by the disjoining of image and picture to create an
aural anticipation, which is to say, by means of prolepsis: the loudness
of jeeps and tanks precedes their sighting, thus sealing a relationship of
security with the earlier scenes *in advance of* the latter's appearance. A clean
cut from one scene to the next could not have made such a strong
association. Secondly, above all it is the haphazardness of the child's
mistimed step which verifies pro-filmic authenticity and thus demonstrates
the documentary truth of the sequence.[18]

Associative editing of the kind described is a trademark of the pioneering
films of the British documentary movement. Grigsby has emulated and
extended the semiological range of these techniques. To establish the
disharmony of British military presence on Irish soil, *Too Long A Sacrifice*
opens on a scene of a tranquil hillside, into which, on the soundtrack, comes
the proleptic crunch of a soldiering boot *ahead of* the appearance of a
wary foot patrol. It is the first of many such devices in this and the later
work. *The Silent War* contains a sequence resonant of the *Listen to Britain*
passage quoted above, but constructed to diametrically opposite
interpretative ends:

1   two tableaux shots (duration 30 seconds): (a) a raw panorama, set
    against a threatening sky, the frame filled from fore to background by
    long grass, through which the wind whistles and (b) (the sound carries
    over) a distant sloping hillside with grazing cattle:
2   from a position mounted on top of an army jeep, a soldier's visored
    profile occupies the left half of the frame, he holds a rifle raised to
    shoulder-height, above the turret in which he stands, trained outward

(from a static position the camera, in effect, looks out through the gun-sights for the duration of the shot) as the jeep travels (for 90 seconds) through an inner-city Republican area (signified by generously graffitoed gable-ends), past rubble and derelict dwellings into and along comparatively tidy terraced streets. Beginning with the cackle of on-board short-wave radio, in aural accompaniment (throughout 2), Grigsby intersperses routine British sounds, heard above the noise of gear changes, etc., as the jeep drives: at intervals, the chimes of Big Ben; announcement of 'BBC News at Six O'Clock. Good Evening'; an ice cream van; the *EastEnders* signature tune ....

Towards the close of this travelling shot, as the vehicle corners, a small boy comes into view. In the fraction of time he is visible, he 'gives the fingers' to the Land Rover as it passes. The transparency of this pro-filmic moment encapsulates the anti-colonial truth of the entire passage. The sequence is bookended by stories of blindness caused by the malicious discharge of a baton round and, at the other end, details of routine disruptions resulting from army patrols. Pinpointing the disturbing effects these have on the children of the household, that the latter story is told by a non-Republican mother fastens the message of shared experience of military oppression.

Michael Grigsby is not alone on the left in opting to prioritise political commitment over analytic complexity. The reasons are understandable and of course perfectly defensible, on the grounds, not least, that while academics may interpret the world in various ways, the point, presumably, is to change it. The critical matter must be how best to mobilise opinion against systemic injustices. Affecting and valuable as evidence of crushing asymmetries in contemporary society, my view is that his filmworks incline nonetheless to diminish elaborate and contradictory social histories to disconsolate narratives of victims and villains.

Speaking up for Others

Cultural theories and political movements have appeared and passed by while the 'dreary steeples' of the NI conflict persist in view. One legacy of crumbling empire none of us can easily avoid is the increasingly creolised character of the modern world. These polyvalent trends create pressures on the monocultural boundaries of the nation-state which, for the most part, chauvinistic national elites do their best to resist. Constant, but subject to revision, allegories of national identification remain the most forceful political rhetoric around. Whatever else is new, we plainly do not yet live in post-nationalist times.

Silencing as well as remembering, identity is always a question of producing in the future an account of the past, that is to say it is always about narrative, the stories which cultures tell themselves about who they are and where they came from.[19]

Each and every national identity develops out of overlapping histories of hybridisation; most emphatically where the trauma of colonial encounter informs emergent narratives of self and nationhood. Together with the common institutional bequest of colonialism (the economic, social and political structures of the era of colonial rule tend, inevitably, to condition the institutional forms of postcolonial state and society), Hall is here highlighting the ideological formation of national consciousness in relation to the cultural residue of foreign suzerainty. He is, in other words, stressing the significance of and connection between material *and* immaterial forces (notably, the definitional authority of representation) in the construction of cultural imaginings. In differing ways, both states of Ireland are postcolonial. But this is not to imply that struggle for 'national liberation' in NI is the same as occurred in Algeria or South Africa or that the incidence of communal disturbances in NI are analogous to those in Rwanda or the Balkans. Political comparisons with Wales or Poland, for example, bear a certain likeness in their relations with the imperial power, but none of these, remembering Lenin, is equivalent in its concrete historical circumstances.[20]

Traditionally, on the metropolitan left, the test of a nationalist cause has depended on internationalist, anti-imperialist credentials. Using Michael Grigsby's films as symptomatic of a species of reasoning and engagement on the British left, my contention has been that his attitude to Ireland demonstrably misrepresents the basis of division by regarding the problem as one of a valorous native culture under siege from an imperialist invader. The mindset in question is fairly typical of the 'cultural imperialism' thesis, characterised by David Morley as presuming 'the existence of a pure, internally homogenous, authentic, indigenous culture, which then becomes subverted or corrupted by foreign influence'.[21] Grigsby's approach to understanding contemporary Vietnam, as shown in his film *Thoi Noi* (Central Television, 1993), has marked stylistic and conceptual similarities with *The Silent War*. For him these would appear to be equivalent instances.

Contrary to the current vogue for 'identity politics' – where the claims of gendered and racial definition (amid a plurality of other interests) are said to be crowding out the ageing discourses of class and nation – it is all too evident that the historic forces of the national ideal are not in decline. Even 'the new politics, and its narratives', Michael Billig remarks,

typically take the nation-state for granted. What is often at stake is not an argument against nationhood, but an argument about the nature of the nation and who should be taken as representing the nation.[22]

Grigsby's representations of the political nation in Britain are humane and persuasive in their defence of the civic values of postwar social democracy. In these studies of Britishness, it is in the interests of *traditional* industrial working-class communities and values on whose behalf he speaks. Whole communities betrayed and deracinated, rarely heard or seen other than in caricatural terms, their lives indeed merit sympathetic narration. In Michael Grigsby *they* have found an eloquent advocate and reporter. These are fine films; intellectually and emotionally engaging, a rich source of evidence for socialist debate, reminding us of the absolute centrality of class and capitalism in the reproduction of systematic social imbalance. And all the more so, in my view, for the rarity of their lucid, filmic quality.

Michael Grigsby cannot be held responsible for what else he might have done. The preferred meanings of the films discussed are the ones that matter to him. (For to underscore a point made earlier, notwithstanding the mannered naturalist transparency of Grigsby's empathetic representations of subordinated subjects, the authorial voice is, finally, his. In this, of course, Grigsby is not unlike most other documentary realist film makers.) But outside the texts, considering their political reception, what of the 'voiceless' interests in contemporary, 'postcolonialised' Britain whose interests are not described by a Labour 'history from below' account? What of immigrant cultures of diaspora and 'becoming',[23] from origins more distant and mixed than Ireland? And more generally, too, in the articulation of counter-hegemonic narratives, is there not a danger, if only by unintended inference, that the non-appearance (invisibility) of *other* marginalised categories within 'progressive' studies of community risks reinforcing dominant perceptions of these as somehow inauthentic and exogenous to the conditions of the British working class? Irrelevant and unfair if the texts are offered and judged only as a defence of *particular* communities, questions of this kind become politically relevant if their narratives are taken as *national* allegory. In relation to racialised identities in Britain, Avtar Brah writes:

[T]here are several similarities in the social experience of the Irish and black groups in Britain. Both sets of people have a history of being colonised by Britain, their migration patterns share common features, both groups occupy predominantly working-class positions within the British class structure, and they both have been subjected to racism. But anti-black and anti-Irish racism situates these groups differently within British society. As white Europeans, the great majority of Irish people are placed in a dominant position *vis-à-vis* black people in and through the discourses of anti-black racism, even when the two groups share a similar class location. In other words, we assume different subject positions within various racisms. Analysis of the interconnections between racism, class, gender and sexuality must take account of the *positionality* of different racisms with respect to one another.[24]

Unionist and Loyalist interests have not been particularly oppressed. Nor have they been subjected to a history of material reduction and unrelenting social inferiorisation in the way that racialised identities in Britain have. What they share with black British subjects is an historically irregular position, when situated in relation to the norms of Britishness. As it happens they also share a good deal of their cultural history and identity with the British working-class subjects Grigsby is elsewhere concerned to represent sympathetically. The argument against Grigsby, as a case study of a fairly common view on the left in Britain, is that his agitational documentary features reduce a multiplicity of factors to an evangelical dichotomy of oppressor/oppressed. Relationships between 'things' in NI and the 'words' used to define them are not usually that straightforward.

Notes

1   Edward W. Said, *Culture and Imperialism* (Chatto and Windus, 1993), pp. 63 and 72.
2   Edward W. Said: 'The construction of identity – for identity, whether of Orient or Occident, France or Britain ... is finally a construction – involves establishing opposites and "others" whose actuality is always subject to the continuous interpretation and re-interpretation of their differences from "us". Each age and society re-creates its "Others".' *Orientalism* (Penguin, new edition with Afterword, 1995), p. 332; Eric Hobsbawm and Terence Ranger (eds), *The Invention of Tradition* (Cambridge University Press, 1983).
3   David Miller, *Don't Mention the War* (Pluto Press, 1994), p. 10.
4   John McGarry and Brendan O'Leary, *Explaining Northern Ireland* (Blackwell, 1995), p. 76.
5   V. F. Perkins, *Film as Film* (Penguin, 1972), pp. 116–33.
6   Raymond Williams, *Television: Technology and Cultural Form*, 2nd edition, Ederyn Williams (ed.) (Routledge, 1990); John Fiske and John Hartley, *Reading Television* (Routledge, 1989); John Ellis, *Visible Fictions: cinema, television, video* (Routledge, 1992).
7   Philip Schlesinger, Graham Murdock, Philip Elliot, *Televising Terrorism* (Comedia, 1983). For a booklength analysis of relationships between the British state and the broadcast media in Britain with reference to 'news & current affairs' and documentary studies of the NI conflict see my *The Trouble With Reporting Northern Ireland* (Avebury, 1995).
8   Schlesinger *et al.*, *Televising Terrorism* (1983), p. 32.
9   John Corner, *Television Form and Public Address* (Edward Arnold, 1995), p. 103.
10   V. I. Lenin (1914), 'The Right of Nations to Self-determination', in *Lenin: Collected Works* vol. 20 (Lawrence and Wishart, 1962), pp. 400–1. And, in the same volume:

>   the Marxist fully recognises the historical legitimacy of national movements. But to prevent this recognition from becoming an apologia of nationalism, it must be strictly limited to what is progressive in such movements, in order that this recognition may not lead to bourgeois ideology obscuring proletarian consciousness.

'Critical Remarks on the National Question' (1913), ibid., p. 34.

11   Quoted in Kevin Macdonald and Mark Cousins (eds), *Imagining Reality: the Faber Book of Documentary* (Faber, 1996), p. 370.

12

> Documentary was from the beginning – when we first separated our public purpose theories from those of Flaherty – an 'anti-aesthetic' movement. We have all, I suppose, sacrificed some personal capacity in 'art' and the pleasant vanity that goes with it.

> 'The Documentary Idea' (1942), in *Grierson on Documentary*. Edited with an Introduction by Forsyth Hardy (Faber, 1979), p. 112.

13   Alan Lovell and Jim Hillier, *Studies in Documentary* (Secker & Warburg/BFI, 1972), p. 12.

14   The title of Paul Addison's valediction to the postwar settlement, *The Road to 1945* (Jonathan Cape, 1975).

15   Williams, 'Introduction' to Christopher Williams (ed.), *Realism and the Cinema* (RKP/BFI, 1980), p. 10.

16   Brian Winston, *Claiming the Real* (BFI, 1995), p. 246.

17   John Corner, *The Art of Record* (Manchester University Press, 1996), p. 118. The phrase is used in relation to Grigsby's *Living on the Edge* (see pp. 108–24).

18   Annette Kuhn writes that the 'non-fiction film is one which declares that a profilmic event has not been constructed or arranged for the purposes of producing a film'. 'The Camera I: Observations on Documentary', *Screen*, vol. 19, no. 2 (Summer 1978), p. 71. Critically, the inclusion of unplanned, haphazard, narratively redundant material in a documentary film signifies a sense of 'unconstructedness' – i.e. faithful to the event 'as it happened' – and thus tends to convey an impression of 'authenticity'.

19   Stuart Hall, 'Negotiating Caribbean Identities', in *New Left Review*, no. 209 (January/February 1995), p. 5.

20   For an indictment of cultural relativist varieties of 'post-colonial studies', see Ella Shohat/Robert Stam:

> Positioning Australia and India in a similar 'colonial' relation to an imperial center, for example, equates the situation of European settlers with that of indigenous populations colonized by Europeans, as if both groups broke away from the 'center' in the same way. The crucial differences between Europe's genocidal oppression of indigenous peoples, on the one hand, and Europe's domination of European 'creole' elites on the other, are leveled with an easy stroke of the 'post.' *Unthinking Eurocentrism* (Routledge, 1994), p. 38

> See also, Aijaz Ahmad, 'The Politics of Literary Postcoloniality', in *Race and Class*, vol. 36, no. 3, 1995.

21   David Morley, 'EurAm, modernity, reason and alterity: or, postmodernism, the highest stage of cultural imperialism?', in David Morley and Kuan-Hsing Chen (eds) *Stuart Hall: Critical Debates* (Routledge, 1996), p. 330. See also John Tomlinson, *Cultural Imperialism* (Pinter, 1991).

22   Michael Billig, *Banal Nationalism* (Sage, 1995), p. 146.

23

> Cultural identity ... is a matter of 'becoming' as well as being. It belongs to the future as much as to the past. It is not something which already exists, transcending place, time, history, and culture. Cultural identities come from somewhere, have histories. But, like everything else which is historical, they undergo constant transformation. Far from being eternally fixed in some essentialized past, they are subject to the continuous 'play' of history, culture and power. Far from being grounded in a mere 'recovery' of the past, which is waiting to be found, and which, when found, will secure our sense of ourselves into eternity, identities are the names

we give to the different ways we are positioned by, and position ourselves within, the narratives of the past. Stuart Hall: 'Cultural Identity and Diaspora' in Jonathan Rutherford (ed.) *Identity* (Lawrence and Wishart, 1990), p. 225

24   Avtar Brah, 'Difference, diversity and differentiation', in James Donald and Ali Rattansi (eds) *'Race', Culture and Difference* (Sage/Open University, 1992), p. 133. See also note 20, above.

7

Colin McArthur

The Exquisite Corpse of
Rab(Elais) C(opernicus) Nesbitt

What happened in Scotland in the 1960s and the 1970s and what laid
the foundation for the enormous creative achievements of the 1980s
was the liberation of the voice. The Scottish voice declared its
independence ... The liberation of the voice was at first an acceptance
of and an assertion of the vernacular ... But the real liberation of the
voice came not from the assertion of the rights of the vernacular itself,
but from the assertion of the right to move without boundaries *between*
the vernacular and standard English, between the demotic and the
literary ....[1]

In the Beginning was the Word ...

Despite eliciting praise from most *English* television reviewers and
achieving some sort of cult status, BBC Scotland's networked sitcom, *Rab
C. Nesbitt*, has also provoked a strong sense of otherness from the same
source, a response which emphasises the series' linguistic difficulty for
non-Scots. Thus:

> Apart from the impenetrability of the Govan Glasgow accents, given
> the operatic level of violence and caricature on which *Rab C. Nesbitt* is
> pitched, subtitles would be helpful to English speakers ... [M]ost viewers
> will be still tangling with the dipthongs of that preliminary to most
> conversations, 'Si yiewe' ('See you' or perhaps 'Now look here, my
> good man') ....[2]

> Many viewers still complain that they can't understand a word of the
> broad dialect and need subtitles.[3]

... virtually incomprehensible to anyone born south of Berwick-upon-Tweed.[4]

There are problems with the show for Southerners ... Heaven knows what the Ceefax subtitler manages to make of lines which often seem to have the phonetic structure 'Ochty baster nachty blooin'.[5]

... [S]urely the filthiest and most disgusting character on television, I am convinced hat he is broadcast in England only because the censors cannot understand his Gorbals accent – in the same way that Rab Burns has always been printed because he wrote in Lallans ....[6]

One reviewer helpfully provided a glossary of 'Rabspeak':

SWALLY an alcoholic beverage
STOATING most agreeable
TO RIP THE PISH OOT O' to take a rise out of
A RAN DAN NIGHT a hugely enjoyable evening[7]

In general, the metropolitan British press's observations about the linguistic difficulty of *Rab C. Nesbitt* are good-humoured enough but, as in jokes about 'wogs', 'niggers' and 'paddies', the underlying discourse of power may be revealed in all its imperial arrogance and viciousness in other linguistic situations relating to Scotland, as in Booker Prize judge Rabbi Julia Neuberger's publicly dissociating herself from the decision, of the panel on which she served, to award the prize to Glasgow writer James Kelman's novel *How late it was, how late*. Rabbi Neuberger described herself as 'implacably opposed to the book. It is not a book which is publicly accessible'.[8]

Kelman has himself described the experience (a common one for Scots as for other peripheral peoples) of being on the sharp end of this Standard English imperium, of seeking vainly in English literature for any adequate representation of the inner life of Glaswegians like himself:

How do you recognize a Glaswegian in English literature? ... [H]e's the cut-out figure who wields a razor-blade, gets morocolous drunk and never has a single, solitary 'thought' in his entire life. He beats his wife and beats his kids and beats his next door neighbour. And another striking thing: everybody from a Glaswegian or working-class background, everybody in fact from any regional part of Britain – none of them knew how to talk! ... unlike the nice stalwart upperclass English hero ... whose words on the page were always absolutely splendidly proper and pure and pristinely accurate whether in dialogue or without ... Most interesting of all, for myself as a writer, the narrative belonged to them and them alone. They owned it. The place where thought and spiritual life exists ....[9]

When Kelman talks of 'the narrative belonging to them and them alone', he echoes Frantz Fanon and Edward Said in their accounts of how imperial power not only expropriates the material life of the colonised, but their mental life as well, causing them to think of their own identities within categories fashioned by their oppressors.[10] The Scots are perhaps particularly schizophrenic in this respect. At a material level, they are a First World people, the beneficiaries of being what Tom Nairn has described as the junior partners in a highly profitable imperial enterprise. Inside their heads, however, Scots are (have been?) a Third World people, their identities shaped by images and discourses (English literature, Hollywood movies) articulated elsewhere but, chillingly, increasingly lived within by Scots themselves.[11] As the quotation which heads this essay suggests, it has been the profound political as well as artistic achievement of novelists such as James Kelman and Irvine Welsh, and poets such as Edwin Morgan, Tom Leonard and Liz Lochead, to have fashioned a distinctively Scottish voice, one homologous with Scots' interior life and experience of the world.

This is a claim I would make also for *Rab C. Nesbitt*. Indeed, I see the emergence and consolidation of the series over the last half decade as being part of the 'revolution of the word', a phrase used by Colin MacCabe in the context of Ireland and James Joyce[12] but entirely in line with the process described by Cairns Craig above, even though the mix of internationalist modernism and 'parochial' vernacular differs in the two examples. What is often not grasped by outsiders is that Scotland is a tri-lingual society comprising Gaelic, English and Scots, it being part of the imperialism of Standard English that it regards Scots as an inferior version of itself rather than as a separate language, a fate suffered by diverse 'creoles' and 'pidgins' throughout the colonised world. The language spoken by the central characters of *Rab C. Nesbitt*, particularly Rab himself, is that of working-class Glasgow, a vernacular variant of Standard English heavily laced with Scots words such as *jaicket* (jacket), *wean* (child), *merrit* (married), *shilpit* (puny), *fears* (afraid) *keech* (shit) and *glaikit* (stupid).

In 1969 the French film journal *Cahiers du cinéma*, exploring the relationship between films and ideology, offered a seven-category classification which was to become very influential in British film theory of the 1970s.[13] Far and away the greatest interest was stimulated by category 'E', those films which at first sight appear wholly within the dominant ideology but which, in fact, dismantle or, at least, critique it from within by the nature of their 'writing', by which *Cahiers* meant primarily *mise-en-scène*. The *Cahiers* classification, in these postmodern times, has fallen from favour as being irretrievably bound up with the marxist 'grand narrative' and, as such, too monolithic to account for the diversity of meanings generated by films in their passage from production through to consumption. Nevertheless, one of the other *Cahiers* categories can, if stretched somewhat, offer a useful model of how *Rab C. Nesbitt* is operating ideologically within the fault lines between metropolitan British culture and Scottish culture and between the metropolitan BBC and BBC Scotland. *Cahiers* defined its category 'C' as those films in which 'the content is not explicitly political, but in some way becomes so by the criticism practiced on it through its form'.[14] This formulation seems to me to be very close to what *Rab C. Nesbitt* is doing by foregrounding the Scottish vernacular voice, although – as will be seen – the series becomes increasingly 'political' in the more direct sense. In order to heighten the 'vernacularity' of the central characters – Rab (Gregor Fisher), Cotter (Tony Roper), Mary (Elaine C. Smith), and Ella (Barbara Rafferty); Rab and Mary's two sons Gash (Andrew Fairlie) and Burney (Eric Cullen); and Rab's other two friends Andra (Brian Pettifer) and Dodie (Iain McColl) – the series operates non-naturalistically by having many of the authority figures, even the working-class ones such as policemen, DSS clerks, social workers, shopkeepers and licensees, speak with (sometimes) rather posh, Received Pronunciation-based Scottish accents. The nature of the Word is the central political terrain of *Rab C. Nesbitt*.

The turn to the vernacular, in any culture, carries with it certain dangers, most notably the adopting of a whining, nostalgic, sentimental, self-congratulatory, 'here's tae us, wha's like us' tone. *Rab C. Nesbitt* substantially avoids this, primarily on account of its corrosively satirical stance, often towards those very institutions more nostalgic vernaculars celebrate, of which more presently. The series' virtues, in this regard, are writ large when compared with two other examples of the turn to the Scots vernacular, the poetry of Adam McNaughtan and the plays and television films of Bill Bryden. Here is an extract from a McNaughtan poem about the changes which have come about in his native city:

> Oh where is the Glasgow where I used to stey,
> The white wally closes done up wi' pipe cley;
> Where you knew every neighbour free first floor tae third,
> And to keep your door locked was considered absurd.[15]

Ian Spring, in his book *Phantom Village: the Myth of the New Glasgow*, has accurately described McNaughtan's work as '"stairheid" nostalgia *par excellence*'.[16] Bill Bryden, a native of Port Glasgow, has achieved a well-deserved international reputation as a theatre director. A brilliant theatrical technician and *metteur-en-scène*, his exploitation of the resources of theatre and, in particular, his movement of large ensembles through theatrical space is often breathtaking. However, as a writer, his turn to the Scots vernacular in plays and TV films such as *Willie Rough*, *Benny Lynch*, *Ill Fares the Land*, *The Ship* and *The Big Picnic* reveals a sensibility suffused with a coarsely sentimental populism. There is a joke which circulates within Scottish culture to the effect that Bryden cannot write anything with a Scottish setting which does not include at least one funeral, preferably that of a child. This may reflect the power, within the Scottish vernacular tradition, of one particular strand of Victorian sentimental literature, the Kailyard school, the best known exemplar of which is J. M. Barrie. It should be said that the extent of its power within Scottish culture is contested,[17] but a 'worst case scenario' would be that it has irretrievably damaged the sensibilities of several generations of Scottish writers. However, the possibility is that in consequence of the tough-mindedness of *Rab C. Nesbitt*'s key creative personnel (writer Ian Pattison and producer/director Colin Gilbert) the series may have bodyswerved past 'urban Kailyard' to connect with those older, more scabrous traditions of Scots vernacular explored below ('Where extremes meet').

Is There Such a Thing as Scottish Screen Acting?

Clearly, *Rab C. Nesbitt* marks a significant advance for the local vernacular on Scottish and, due to its being networked, British television. There is a sense, therefore, in which the question is redundant. Manifestly, Scottish actors, deploying vernacular voices, throng Scottish screens and are significantly present in British television and beyond. An actor like Richard Wilson (Victor Meldrew in *One Foot in the Grave*), although born in the West of Scotland, has built his reputation mainly by playing within Received Pronunciation, but others such as Bill Paterson, Robbie Coltrane and, above all, Sean Connery, have tended to 'Scotticise' verbally any roles they have played (though this is less true of Coltrane who is particularly adept at accents). So the answer to the above question, if confined solely to questions of *voice*, is assuredly 'Yes'. At the same time, it is less certain that the same affirmative answer would be given if the question were posed in relation to *gesture* and *body language*. There is a dearth of work in this area, so the following argument should be regarded as impressionistic and provisional.

James Naremore's pre-eminent book on screen acting, *Acting in the Cinema*, to the extent that it discusses acting and ethnicity, does so primarily in relation to *voice*.[18] I first began thinking about the 'problem' of Scottish screen acting while watching newsreel footage of the Upper Clyde Shipbuilders 'work-in' of 1972 in which, in an inspirational act of working-class industrial tactics, the workforce, threatened with the closure of their yard, occupied it. The charismatic workers' leader, Jimmy Reid, addressed the workers and urged them to behave with dignity and self-discipline. He then proposed a series of prohibitions on certain kinds of behaviour, expressed with that superb sense of public rhetoric Reid displayed throughout the affair, and couched within the recurring trope 'There will be no ...'. When he reached his ultimate prohibition 'There will be no *bevvying*', as he hit the operative word, he threw his torso forward and moved his head slightly to right and left in a piece of body language as distinctive to the West of Scotland as is the dismissive hand gesture deployed by a New York Jew telling you 'I don't want any of that stuff' or the peculiar head toss of South India which can carry a variety of meanings according to context. I am struck by the extent to which such geographically rooted pieces of body language seem to have been 'ironed out' of the screen performances of Scots actors. Much more work would have to be done to confirm or refute this, but my sense is that those Scots actors like Connery who appear to maintain a Scots vernacular in their performances do so solely at the level of voice and that gesturally their performances have become subsumed within the classic, naturalistic screen acting style that is so heavily influenced by Stanislavskian ideas as filtered through the practice of Lee Strasberg and the Actors' Studio. To the extent that geographically and culturally rooted gesture and body language survive into the performances of Scots screen actors, my impression is that they are to be found principally in *Rab C. Nesbitt*. For example, in the programme in which he takes his pet canary out for a walk on a lead, Rab, exclaiming 'Go on, ya beauty!', kicks his leg across his body in a very specific piece of West of Scotland body language. In short, the series asserts, brings to public view, not only the West of Scotland vernacular *voice*, but the West of Scotland vernacular *style* as well.

I would appear to be in something of a cleft stick over this. Back in 1982, in a work substantially traducing stereotypical screen representations of the Scots and the extent to which they had, among other things, impoverished Scottish screen acting, I praised the Group Three film *The Brave Don't Cry* (1952) precisely for the opportunity it gave Scots actors formerly confined to stereotypical roles to display their talents within the tradition of naturalistic screen acting.[19] However, I think the contradiction is more apparent than real. By calling for the visibility of Scottish vernacular gesture and body language on screen, the last thing I want to see is a return to the demeaning thespian rhetoric of, for example, *Rob Roy: the Highland Rogue* (1953) and *Rockets Galore* (1958). Rather, my argument is that genuinely culturally rooted Scottish gestures and body languages have never yet been seen on screen, with the possible exception of *Rab C. Nesbitt*.[20]

This celebration of the foregrounding of vernacular voice, gesture and body language in *Rab C. Nesbitt* as important political as well as aesthetic advances should not be misread as an all-out call for parochialism and naturalism on Scottish screens. There are powerful forces at work in Scottish moving image culture which seek to deracinate the screen representations coming out of Scotland so that they become more assimilable by the world audio-visual market, which basically means the American market.[21] The chimera which such forces chase is films which, like *Four Weddings and a Funeral* (1994), made a financial killing in the American market. The recent discussion over the extent to which *Trainspotting* (1996) requires redubbing for its American release will doubtless encourage these forces to advocate such commercially motivated self-censorship at the production stage, rather as one prominent British producer, contemplating a film about the interwar 'bodyline' tour of Australia by the English cricket team, instructed the screenwriter not to have players getting out lbw. as this would not be understood by the Americans. In my view, such forces, happy to go along with the historical and continuing hegemony of Hollywood, are having a reductive, impoverishing effect on Scottish screen acting which a series such as *Rab C. Nesbitt* to some extent counteracts by setting down markers of the possible. Those forces in Scottish moving image culture are choking off a rich source of performativity by turning their backs on the Scottish vernacular, are seeking to elide a 'natural' process of development of the national moving image culture before it has even arrived. Think of the incredibly expressive boost given to American cinema by the arrival on screen, in the 1930s, of (whatever their *actual* backgrounds) the ethnic/proletarian styles of James Cagney, Humphrey Bogart and John Garfield.[22] In short, Scottish cinema and television need to go through a period in which *mimetic* theories of acting are stressed and the country's vernacular resources of voice, gesture and movement are exploited. That said, acting as *mimesis* should not be fetishised. It has been argued, correctly in my view, that the dominance of the Strasbergian version of Stanislavski's method has had a profoundly impoverishing effect on American acting.[23] There are other traditions from which Scottish acting can learn much and which, it has to be recognised, are designed precisely to deracinate, to universalise, the acting process. The post-Poor Theatre work of Jerzy Grotowski is a case in point, with his discussion of the extent to which hunters in every culture in every continent adopt the same posture and body movement.[24] However, the particular conjuncture in Scotland, both in terms of its body politic and the level of development of its screen industries, requires that acting as mimesis be foregrounded. No better example of this than *Rab C. Nesbitt* exists.

Where Extremes Meet

Alongside English television reviewers' preoccupation with *Rab C. Nesbitt's* linguistic difficulty, there is another curious feature about their accounts of the series: their recurring description of Rab himself as 'philosopher' – 'a lone drunken philosopher raging briefly and incoherently into the ether',[25] 'the ranting, Glaswegian street philosopher',[26] ' ... philosopher, drunk and general Glaswegian bauchle'.[27]

On the face of it, 'philosopher' is a strange description and not one which has been applied to those other great television ranters, Alf Garnett and Victor Meldrew. However, the reviewers may be on to something more than they are altogether aware of. As Cairns Craig has observed in another context:

> To the extent that much of Scottish middle class society models itself on English values, distinctively Scottish culture has more affinity with the working classes than English culture ... [T]o the extent that the element of the middle classes who are active in Scottish culture are professionals – legal, religious, educational – the tonality of Scottish culture is much more abstract and philosophical than in England. ... Scotland has retained links with the traditions of European intellectual debate in a way that England, locked into a conception of philosophy as description rather than criticism, has not .... Scottish writers are both more working class and more philosophical than is normal in English culture ....[28]

Such an inheritance has meant that what T. S. Eliot called the 'dissociation of sensibility', that dire separation of thought from feeling which Eliot purported to find in post-Metaphysical Poets English literature, never took hold north of the border and there remained in Scottish culture a peculiar, perhaps unique melding of the most disparate elements from what might be called High Culture and (often the most scurrilous) Low Culture.

This mixture is well conveyed in Hugh MacDiarmid's poem of 1935 *Glasgow 1960*, despite the fact that he was being ironic and thought of Glasgow as a cultural wilderness. The narrator of the poem has returned to Glasgow 'after long exile' and is amazed to find that the buses and trams packed with people heading towards the Ibrox stadium are on their way to a philosophical debate rather than to watch football. Meanwhile, the news boys shout the headlines, 'Special! Turkish Poet's Abstruse New Song .../ and, holy snakes,/ I saw the edition sell like hot cakes.'

The mix of the vernacular and the abstruse or, more generally, High Culture and Low Culture, is central to *Rab C. Nesbitt*, very often within Rab's monologues and asides to camera. Rab's description of himself as 'Govan's Renaissance Man', of his children as 'the fruit of my loins', and of Govan humour as 'the Laughter of Cruelty'; and his references to MacDiarmid's *A Drunk Man Looks at the Thistle*, to Eliot's 'birth, copulation and death'. to Aleister Crowley and to 'wee Frankie Kafka' have worried certain reviewers who, misreading the series as a wholly naturalistic sitcom, have complained that such High Art allusions would be beyond the frame of reference of such as Rab. They are more comfortable with the Low Culture side of the equation, as in Mary's observation to Rab that 'I wouldnae rattle a stick in a shite pail for you' or the likelihood that, should you have a cup of tea at the Nesbitts', you are liable to be served 'an impetigo scab for a biscuit'. The undissociated sensibility of *Rab C. Nesbitt* is beautifully conveyed in Rab's description of his son Gash as 'seventeen year old and so anal retentive he's still shiting rusks'.

This conjoining of the entire spectrum of human experience and cultural reference is evident in 'serious' Scottish writing, for example the poetry of Edwin Morgan or the novels of William McIlvanney. It is another joke within the Scottish cultural community that the latter cannot pen one of his novels of Scottish working-class life without also referring to the Spanish philosopher Miguel de Unamuno. But, as with *Rab C. Nesbitt*, the undissociated sensibility is present also in Scottish popular cultural forms, most notably in the work of the 1940s/1950s Glasgow newspaper cartoonist Bud Neill which, as well as covering a similar vernacular linguistic range to *Rab C. Nesbitt* also makes extensive reference to, among others, Freud, Shakespeare, Tolstoy, Dickens and Matisse.[29] This extends backwards in Scottish history to Burns and beyond. Robert Burns, still popularly thought of as, in Henry Mackenzie's words, 'this Heaven-taught ploughman', a kind of eighteenth-century noble savage, was in fact extremely well educated in philosophy, science and the humanities.[30]

Even Rab's much commented upon verbal aggression, punctuated by such phrases as 'ye bastard' and 'ye swine', might be linked with the ancient Scottish rhetorical form of *flyting* as described by Edwin Morgan:

Fantasy, catalogues, and a far more grotesque pullulation of images characterize the extreme and peculiarly Scottish kind of satire called the flyting .... The flyting, as a contest in virtuosity of vituperation, has some antecedents or analogues in other poetic traditions, including especially Gaelic tradition, and in part at least it may be regarded as a ritualized, aestheticized survival of the belief in bardic power, anciently shown in superstitious conviction that an enemy could be 'rhymed to death'. Something of this dark power remains in the Scottish flytings ... yet the fact that the abuse has been ritualized has not removed, but rather heightened the unease, the sense of nightmare which the performance produces in us.[31]

'Virtuosity of vituperation' and 'abuse ... ritualized' could stand as highly appropriate rubrics for *Rab C. Nesbitt* generally, achieving glorious local realisation in, for example, the moment when Cotter, returned after a night on the 'ran-dan', has his testicles seized by Ella. As he writhes in her vice-like grip she warns him about his future conduct and about the dire consequences of his backsliding: 'You'd better hope there's somebody oot there wi' a bollock donor card, pal, for you're gonny need it.'

The holding together of High Culture and Low Culture is, to some extent, at odds with another powerful current in Scottish life. Edwin Morgan has observed that:

in a country where life tended to be harder, and people poorer, than in England, uppishness and pretentiousness were ready targets for mockery, and the well-known and not always very amiable Scottish 'reductive idiom' makes its appearance, lying in wait to bring down every climbing hypocrisy and puncture every vain aspiration .... How far does this bespeak some worry about the national psyche, the national identity?[32]

Successful Scots, particularly those who have achieved acceptance furth of Scotland (Billy Connolly would be a good example) constantly complain about the tendency of their fellow-Scots to 'take them down a peg'. Alexander Scott, in his poem *Scotched*, deals with a wide variety of Scots institutions in a series of brief verses. His verse headed 'Scotch Equality' reads: 'Kaa the feet free Thon big bastard'.[33] The dichotomy between the two traditions – the undissociated sensibility which regards as perfectly proper the holding together of the scurrilous and the abstruse, High Culture and Low Culture, and the 'reductive idiom' which says woe betide anyone who gets above himself – breeds a peculiar sensibility among Scots intellectuals of working-class origin, one which proclaims its commitment to ideas and 'high' culture while at the same time ironically disclaiming that commitment. This 'hedging of bets', ultimately a sign of nervousness about appearing 'uppity' to the milieu from which one has come, is a leitmotif which runs through the work of numerous Scots 'organic' intellectuals. It is present in Liz Lochead's poem *Inter-City* when she (or the female figure in the poem), menaced by hard-swearing oil-rig workers on a train, speaks of 'the artsy-fartsy magazine I'm not even pretending to read'; in singer/cultural critic Pat Kane's remark, in an interview with Elaine C. Smith (Rab's wife Mary) that 'once we agree on the minimum moral substance of *Nesbitt* ... we get down to pontification about its "meaning"'; in the suggestion of a Glasgow academic, recounted by Angus Calder, that the Glasgow version of Antonio Gramsci's concept of 'hegemony' might be 'Hey, Jimmy';[34] and not least in the writer of *Rab C. Nesbitt*, Ian Pattison's account of moving, as a child, from industrial Govan to greener Johnstone:

> There was a thing that Alasdair Gray once said which I'll paraphrase badly – that Glasgow's skies are very grey, but that there's a hint of another colour out there somewhere. And that was Johnstone: the other colour. We had a bit of wasteland across from our new house. I felt as if I could have written Dvorak's 'New World' Symphony at that time. I thought, 'Fuck! All this space!'[35]

Glasgow's Miles Better

In 1982 a local advertising agency was commissioned by the Glasgow City Council to devise a campaign aimed at improving the city's image.

The resulting slogan was 'Glasgow's Miles Better'. If anyone had thought to ask the question 'Better than what?', the answer would have been 'than the historical image of Glasgow constructed in discourse over more than a century – Glasgow as City of Dreadful Night'. Curiously, in the eighteenth century Glasgow was much praised for the quality of its air and the beauty of its ambience, the city with which it was most often compared being Oxford. It was after industrialisation that the image altered, the changes traceable through public health and housing reports, through the rising practice of photography, into interwar newspaper accounts of gang warfare and the appearance of key novels such as *No Mean City*.[36] The image of Glasgow as a bleak, tenement-dotted landscape inhabited by taciturn, hard-eyed men whose lives were bounded by football, heavy drinking, and explosive (sometimes sectarian) violence, often with cut-throat razors, was to become an Ur-narrative which beckoned any who would speak, or write, or make visual images of Glasgow. Jeremy Isaacs, addressing a conference in Edinburgh – the Athens of the North – amused his audience by telling them that he himself was from Glasgow, the Sparta of the North. I have written elsewhere about the Scottish Discursive Unconscious, that ensemble of Ur-Narratives and discourses (highland Scotland as elegy would be another component) which operates deterministically on representations of Scotland in official reports, through acts of historiography, to easel painting, imaginative literature, drama, postcards, newspaper and magazine features, photographs, films and television programmes and advertising.[37] So powerful that even the Scots themselves live within it, the ensemble forces Scotland, including Glasgow, 'out of history', to use Cairns Craig's term, with the concomitant failure or, at best, difficulty, of Scots artists to imagine the real landscapes they live within as having any transcendent meaning, any meaning that relates to a tradition, to history. This is well expressed in a much-quoted passage from Alasdair Gray's novel *Lanark*:

> 'Glasgow is a magnificent city,' said MacAlpin. 'Why do we hardly ever notice that?' 'Because nobody ever imagines living here,' said Thaw. '... think of Florence, Paris, London, New York. Nobody visiting them for the first time is a stranger because he's already visited them in paintings, novels, history books and films. But if a city hasn't been used by an artist not even the inhabitants live there imaginatively.'[38]

Gray puts too much emphasis on the conscious constructions of artists. He might also have included ostensibly 'documentary' discourses such as social reports, photographs and television documentaries, but his point is well taken.

Clearly the 'Glasgow as City of Dreadful Night' discourse and the 'Glasgow's Miles Better' discourse, with its tropes of art galleries, shopping malls and *haute cuisine*, are in contradiction, deliberately so since the latter was evolved to contest the former. So intense is the struggle between competing conceptions of the city that any film, or novel, or play, or television programme about Glasgow gets sucked into the controversy and gets judged in terms of its 'good' or 'bad' image of the city. Such has been the case par *excellence* with *Rab C. Nesbitt* which has been both traduced and lauded in readers' letters to the Scottish press, ferociously attacked by a Glasgow councillor and been the subject of a complaint (not upheld) to the Broadcasting Complaints Commission. The discursive construction of Glasgow was a topic at the recent annual conference of the Royal Geographical Society held in the city and the centrality of *Rab C. Nesbitt* as a point of reference in the debate was marked by Ian Pattison's being invited to the conference. The issue of the discursive representation of the city had, indeed, been a factor in actor Gregor Fisher's early reservations about the character of Rab and had been alluded to in the programme itself in one of Rab's rants:

> See us scum, us keech? We're havin a bloody hard time aff the shortbread set .... You know [adopts posh voice] 'Oh, look, look at that! It's stereotypes like him that give Glasgow a bad name. Give us Van Gogh.' Aaagh! Bloody Van Gogh! The best o' it is, see that Van Gogh? He was a bigger heidbanger than me. See if I met Van Gogh in the lavvy o' the Two Ways? I would dae a U-turn in case he chibbed me wi' his palette knife ....

The rant is also, of course, a good example of the melding of High and Low Culture referred to above.

Unquestionably, *Rab C. Nesbitt* deals with the same lumpen proletarian fragment of society as those other representations of the West of Scotland – the television plays of Peter MacDougall or the novels of William McIlvanney – which are most often cited when the 'bad' image of the Glasgow conurbation is talked about. As a frequent user of this kind of ideological analysis, I have to admit that it is a blunt weapon, good for broad discursive strokes but less effective when dealing with nuances and questions of quality within particular artefacts. As will have been clear from the opening section of this chapter on the linguistic aspects of *Rab C. Nesbitt*, I regard the series as extremely progressive on this front, a move into the terrain of popular television of those attempts by more 'serious' artists, the poets and the novelists, to speak with an authentically Scottish voice and to slough off the tyranny of Received Pronunciation.[39] Developing the point made above, that it is not simply the fact that *Rab C. Nesbitt* deals with a lumpen proletarian milieu but how the series handles that milieu that is important, I want now to look in greater detail at two programmes in the series which seem to me to show *Rab C. Nesbitt* at its best, artistically and ideologically.

Class and Nation in *Rab C. Nesbitt*

There are, dotted throughout the series, multiple indications that Rab, his family and friends belong to an urban underclass. There is their repeated self-denigrations as 'shite' and 'scum'; constant references to the DSS and provident cheques; repeated expressions of disbelief by judges, policemen, and assorted members of the middle classes about the way Rab and his friends conduct their lives – 'Until something turns black and drops off, they don't like to bother the doctor in Govan'; repeated spells in prison and brushes with the law (Rab: 'It's a long time since I got oot a caur withoot a blanket ower ma heid'); and, on one occasion, the taking into care of Rab's children. However, the question of class is sometimes given a more 'political' (in the widest sense of that term) turn as when Rab, watching some kids playing in the street, observes:

> Look at them, eh? The classic look of the eternal British underclass. Faces like clenched fists, eyes like the ringholes in spanners. We made them that way, you know. Nice and picturesque for the Sunday supplements so as the middle class could have a piquant seasoning of armchair pity over their breakfast croissant ....

However, class has never been more corrosively represented than in the programme entitled 'Lesson' in which Rab returns in flashback to his schooldays. Having just emerged from a spell in prison, and stumbling drunkenly past his old school, Rab concludes one of his monologues to camera with the words: 'Schooldays are the happiest days of your life. The happiest days of your life! What a lot of shite I talk! The happiest days of your life if you happen to be a sado-masochist ....' We see exactly what Rab means in the flashback. As played by the morosely estimable Scots actor James Cosmo, Rab's teacher is an upwardly mobile ('a semi in Clarkston') sadist with a withering contempt for his charges whom he keeps in order with frequent applications of his lochgelly, a length of thick, hard leather named after the town in Fife where it is manufactured. His attitude can be gleaned from his addresses to the class:

> You all know my philosophy. Children should be seen and not heard ... [looks menacingly at Rab] ... and 'free dinner' children shouldn't be seen at all [and, having belted Rab]
>
> Merely looking at you people is an affront to my sensibilities. But I'm paid to teach you and teach you I will. I will teach you respect. I will teach you the most important lesson people of your class can learn. Keep your head below the parapet and you won't get hurt. Work! Work hard and some of you may rise to the mediocre ....

Such darkly accomplished writing and playing may seem odd in what is, after all, a situation comedy, but one of the benefits of writer Ian Pattison, producer/director Colin Gilbert and the excellent ensemble cast having worked together over several series (and, indeed, previously on *Naked Television*)[40] is that they are able to take chances and extend the artistic and emotional range of particular episodes. 'Lesson' is particularly rich in this regard. As well as delivering the series' most sombre representation of class, it is remarkable in two further respects: its extending of Rab's emotional life and the richness of its *mise-en-scène*. The point of the drunken monologue with which Rab re-enters his childhood is to illustrate his realisation that he has 'merrit the wrang wummin'. The flashback, in black and white, reunites him with his childhood sweetheart Isabel. Several features of the *mise-en-scène* are worthy of note. Gregor Fisher's playing of the child Rab – at one level humorously grotesque – is as inventive as the analogous playing of children by adult actors in Dennis Potter's *Blue Remembered Hills*. Where television usually suffers in comparison with cinema is in the poverty of its *mise-en-scène*, its tendency to rely on static shot/counter-shot set-ups closely following the verbal exchanges of the actors. One of the exceptional features of the TV crime series *Hill Street Blues* (and, more recently, *ER*) was the mobility of its cameras which picked up and left diverse groups of actors within the same continuing shot. Something of the same thoughtfulness about style and narrative economy is evident in 'Lesson'. One series of shots/counter-shots shows Rab and Isabel exchanging looks, he in the body of the class, she at the blackboard. One such shot, from Rab's point of view, is interrupted when the teacher enters left of frame, runs his basilisk eye along the line of Isabel's gaze and lights on Rab. What this suggests, on the part of Colin Gilbert as director, is an attempt to go beyond the standard stylistics of television sitcom and thereby heighten dramatic effect. A similar thoughtfulness about the dramatic use of televisual space occurs at the end of 'Lesson' when Rab returns to his temporary lodging with Cotter (both have been evicted by their wives) and finds him in bed with a woman who turns out to be Isabel's sister. In a scene unusual for its emotional poignancy, she informs Rab that Isabel is dead. But the way the scene is realised is also unusual. Rab, facing the other two, is in the left foreground, the woman in the mid ground, and Cotter in the background. When she gives Rab the news of Isabel's death, Rab turns away from them, and towards the camera, to hide his grief, but the three figures, in the three planes of the shot, remain visible with their different responses. Both thematically and stylistically 'Lesson' rises above the characteristically mundane level of TV sitcom to reach something close to serious television drama.

'Country' has none of the sombreness of 'Lesson' or, indeed, its inventive *mise-en-scène*. It remains at the level of the broad, not to say gross comedy of the series as a whole, but it nonetheless says serious things about

Scottish national identity. Having first demonstrated their dubious patriotism – they have slogans such as 'Bonnie Scotland' and 'Scotland Forever' tattooed on diverse parts of their anatomy but are vague about the exact geographical location of Loch Lomond – Rab, Mary, the kids, Cotter and Ella weekend at a cottage on Loch Lomondside. Stretching the idea of the highlands somewhat, the programme indulges in some traditional lowland jokes at the expense of highlanders, referring to them as 'teuchtars' and 'anguses' and suggesting that their sexual preferences extend to dogs and sheep. It takes swipes *en passant* at the religious and political sanctimoniousness of certain Scottish rock bands; at the 'Englishing' of the highlands; at those climbers and hikers wearing boots 'that cost as much as a three piece suite'; and at Scots who ape American ways, but it directs its most venomous outbursts at two targets: the use of Scotland as a nuclear dumping ground, and tearful, breast-beating assertions of Scottishness.

The attack against the former is carried primarily in a long monologue by Rab as he searches for the lost Cotter, a monologue delivered, with appropriate irony, against a backdrop of heather-clad hills and photogenic highland sunsets:

> These are my mountains, eh? Keep the bloody things if ye want them. They're nuthin' but lids for nuclear dumps anyway. I mean, you can just see the equation in the Westminster nappers, can't ye? The Jocks! The Jocks! Hauf their industry's deid on its feet, but they'll have to pay for their giros some way. Why don't we just get a lot o' nuclear keech and dump it in their front rooms, eh? The bonny purple heather! The ******* stuff glows in the dark ....

The squawk of a moorhen, doubtless applied strategically in post-production, renders inaudible the word before 'stuff'. Continuing his rant, Rab jumps up and down on the camouflaged roof of a nuclear bunker: '[Jumps] That's for Dounreay! [Jumps] And that's for Hunterston! [Jumps] And that's for 9–3 at Wembley in 1961.' Rab wanders off, muttering, 'Well, that's Scottish history avenged.'

The programme's de(con)struction of the kind of misty-eyed Scottish patriotism that eulogises kilts, lochs and mountains and sobs into its whisky over battles lost centuries ago is carried primarily in a drunken monologue by Cotter at a *ceilidh* which he and Rab attend in grotesquely ill-fitting kilts. Elia Kazan has talked about 'the Anatolian smile', that submissive grin Armenians wore in encounters with their Turkish overlords. The Glasgow equivalent is a kind of nasal whine which proclaims to the world its owner's sense of himself as the scum of the earth.

The actor who plays Cotter, Tony Roper, deploys this magnificently. Lurching drunkenly among the dancers at the *ceilidh*, he ends up beside Rab:

I've fun' ma spiritual hame, here among the anguses, Rab. See the anguses, they're oor brothers. [Hears the band strike up *Flower of Scotland* and starts to weep] '*Floor o' Scotland*, Rab. That's oor anthem. Come on, let's hear it for the teuchtars! A struggle on your soil is a struggle on mine. [Poses dramatically] *Ich bin ein sheep-shagger*!

Appropriately, Rab's advice to Cotter is 'Stop makin' an arse of yersel.' It is, indeed, appropriate that *Rab C. Nesbitt*'s satirising of this kind of patriotism should light on *Flower of Scotland*, a song of petrifying banality, both musically and lyrically. That this 'execrable doggerel' (a phrase used by John Prebble about some of Sir Walter Scott's poetry) should be, according to opinion polls, the favoured anthem for an independent Scotland is, to some Scots, argument enough against the idea of Scotland as a separate state.

Rab's final statement on the national question is one many Scots would assent to:

See when you come doon tae it! Your country's like your own fizzer, intit? It might be a pock-marked, drink-ridden eyesore, but you're stuck with it. So you may as well try and love it.

A Structuring Absence?

Any cultural critic who encountered structuralism in the 1970s would probably agree that one of its enduring legacies is the importance it attaches to absences from, as well as presences within, texts and discourses. It is an idea which, present in Althusser,[41] Barthes[42] and Macherey,[43] is carried over into film criticism in the famous analysis of John Ford's *Young Mr Lincoln* by the editors of *Cahiers du cinéma*[44] in which, among other things, they demonstrate that, in order to fulfil its ideological project of presenting Lincoln as a mythical figure free of contradictions, the film has to repress known elements about Lincoln's politics. Macherey's view in relation to the ideological functioning of texts that 'in order to say anything, there are other things which must not be said', applied to *Rab C. Nesbitt*, suggests that its 'structuring absence' is sectarian allegiance.

In order to indicate the extent to which consciousness of sectarian difference is part of the warp and woof of the 'real' social milieu represented in *Rab C. Nesbitt*, let me be autobiographical for a moment about my own Glasgow upbringing. Although my own immediate family stood at some distance from religious bigotry – my father, as a communist, expressed nothing but withering contempt for Orangeism and freemasonry, and my mother, although several of her brothers were freemasons, regarded people who went on Orange marches as not altogether 'respectable' – despite all this we had a keen sense of ourselves as *Protestant* working class and of Catholics as Other. I can recall (when I was in my mid-teens and starting to go out on dates) my mother would not pose directly the question uttered in more rabidly Protestant homes, 'What foot does she kick with?' (a 'left-footer' being one of the local terms for a Catholic). Rather, she would pose coded questions like 'What's her name?' and 'What school did she go to?' On occasion I would wind my mother up by telling her 'Her name is Teresa Kelly and she went to St Bonaventure's's' whereupon my mother would blanche, put her hands to her head and say 'Oh, my God!' Our milieu was suffused with awareness of and jokes about sectarian affiliation. There were jokes about Catholic mothers who would not feed their children orange juice and Catholic window cleaners whose fingers were broken by the sash and, somewhat later, about Protestant men who would refuse to obey the little green man on the pedestrian crossing. When the local mass murderer Peter Manuel was executed the jokes often had a sectarian turn: that his insanity had been conclusively proved when they found a season ticket to Celtic Park in his pocket and that a pair of bloodstained boots found under his bed had belonged to Sammy Baird of Glasgow Rangers (a notorious 'hacker' of the time). In Glasgow dance halls of the 1940s and 1950s, a time when 'modern' dances like the waltz and the quickstep were interspersed with 'old time' dances, one of the latter, the Veleta, involved the dancers kicking one leg out (rather like Rab does in the example cited above). In certain halls the Protestants would shout 'Willie Waddell' (the name of a Rangers player) as they kicked, while the Catholics shouted 'Charlie Tully' (a Celtic player). On a recent conference visit to Glasgow, I went to play putting with several of the delegates, one of whom was of Glasgow-Irish ancestry and a vociferous Celtic supporter. Collecting the putters and the differently coloured balls, I made great play of giving him the orange ball. The point about this story is that the joke would have been meaningless – as indeed it was to the non-Scots in the company – without our mutual awareness of the historically deep-seated and pervasive sectarian narrative of lowland Scotland.

On the face of it, therefore, the absence of this narrative from *Rab C. Nesbitt* is inexplicable. The surnames of the central protagonists, Nesbitt and Cotter, suggest that they are Protestant, as does the absence of Catholic iconography from their homes and from the classroom in 'Lesson'. On the few occasions when Rab has had recourse to the clergy, for example in the programme entitled 'Ethics', they are dressed like Protestant clergymen. On the other hand, in the same programme Rab attempts what is clearly a confession within a confessional. Nor can the absence of the sectarian narrative be explained by its general absence from Scottish television comedy. Robbie Coltrane played the Protestant bigot Mason

Boyne in *Naked Video*, the series within which the character of Rab was born and which Ian Pattison contributed to, and Scottish Television's *Only an Excuse* has explored the close connection between sectarianism and football in Scotland. Significantly, apart from the reference in 'Country' to Scotland's 9–3 defeat by England at Wembley in 1961 (a reference to the Scottish *national* team rather than to club sides) there have been, as far as I can recall, no further references to Scottish football in the series. Could it be that religion, so closely tied up with football in lowland Scotland, is precisely a 'structuring absence', an absence which is quite literally 'unspeakable', which, if filled, would 'deform' the series, would constantly remind viewers that, even in this blackest of black comedies – as events in Ulster over the last few decades have proved – sectarianism is no laughing matter. In other words, could it be that the series could not function in precisely the way it does, implicitly addressing a unified working class and its sympathisers in other classes, if the sectarian discourse were to be uttered?

Conclusion

We now turn to the somewhat odd title of this essay.

Robert B. Ray, in his book *The Avant-Garde Finds Andy Hardy*, is blisteringly critical about the way film, and more generally cultural, criticism is practised.[45] He seeks to find new ways of writing and, indeed, new knowledge, by recourse to the *avant-garde*, particularly surrealism, which he sees as a kind of workshop of ideas and methods which might help free critical writing from its current malaise. He refers to the Exquisite Corpse, the most famous surrealist game, in which four players, each unbeknownst to the others, write down their assigned parts of speech, two players assigned nouns and two adjectives. The result is invariably a bizarre and collectively produced metaphor which reveals the new and unexpected combinations residing in language itself and releasable by automatic writing. I cannot claim that the writing in this chapter is very far removed from academic orthodoxy. Nevertheless, I hope the title moves in the direction indicated by Ray. The 'exquisite corpse' of the title points to the marvellously innovative linguistic dimension of *Rab C. Nesbitt*, at times verging on the surreal. It is widely assumed that Rab's full name is Robert, but I have chosen to think that it might be Rabelais, a name wholly in accord with the humorous (and frequently scatological) irreverence of the series. As far as I am aware, the precise meaning of Rab's initial 'C' has never been revealed. I have chosen to think that it might stand for Copernicus, a name appropriate to a figure who is ultimately as philosophically serious as he is funny.

Let's hear it for *Rab C. Nesbitt*!

Notes

1   Cairns Craig, *Out of History: Narrative Paradigms in Scottish and British Culture* (Polygon, 1996), pp. 193–4.
2   T. Patrick, 'Alien Life Forms', *The Times*, 5 May 1992, p. 3.
3   J. Kupferman, *Daily Mail*, 30 January 1993, p. 37.
4   M. Berkmann, 'Scot with a taste of Porridge', *Daily Mail*, 23 May 1992, p. 42.
5   V. Lewis-Smith 'Hail the King of Giro Valley', *Evening Standard*, 19 November 1993, p. 43.
6   Anon., 'A lout for our times', *Daily Telegraph*, 15 May 1992, p. 19.
7   S. McKay, 'Holding court with the Laird o' Giro Valley', *Mail on Sunday*, 24 May 1992, p. 22.
8   Cited in A. O'Hagan, 'The Scottish write to be different', *Guardian*, 13 October 1994, p. 22.
9   James Kelman, *Some Recent Attacks: Essays Cultural and Political* (AK Press, 1992), p. 82.
10 F. Fanon, *Black Skin, White Masks* (Pluto Press, 1986). Edward Said, *Orientalism* (Pantheon, 1978).
11 M. Chapman, *The Gaelic Vision in Scottish Culture* (Croom Helm, 1978); Colin McArthur (ed.), *Scotch Reels: Scotland in Cinema and Television* (British Film Institute, 1982) and Colin McArthur, 'The dialetic of national identity: the Glasgow Empire Exhibition of 1938', in Tony Bennet *et al.* (eds) *Popular Culture and Social Relations* (Oxford University Press, 1986).
12 Colin MacCabe, *James Joyce and the Revolution of the Word* (Macmillan, 1979).
13 J-L. Comolli and J. Narboni, 'Cinema/Ideology/Criticism', *Screen Reader 1: Cinema/Ideology/Politics* (Society for Education in Film and Television, 1977), pp. 12–35.
14 Comolli and Narboni, 'Cinema/Ideology/Criticism', (1977), p. 6.
15 Cited in Ian Spring, *Phantom Village: the Myth of the New Glasgow* (Polygon, 1990), p. 32.
16 Spring, *Phantom Village* (1990).
17 W. Donaldson, *Popular Literature in Victorian Scotland* (Aberdeen University Press, 1986).
18 J. Naremore, *Acting in the Cinema* (University of California Press, 1988).
19 McArthur, *Scotch Reels* (1982), p. 56.
20 According to research on the presence of certain gestures in particular cultures (D. Morris *et al.*, *Gestures: their origin and distribution* (Book Club Associates, 1979), Scotland (in common with other northern European countries) is gesturally weak in comparison with Mediterranean cultures. However, this may be misleading due to the methodological design of that study which was concerned with very broad gestures, such as the V-sign. My impression is that Glasgow body language is very rich and complex, but that would need to be checked out with an empirical study along the lines of Calbris (G. Calbris, *The Semiotics of French Gestures* (Indiana University Press, 1990)) which examines, from a semiotic perspective, the entire range of French gestures. There remains, however, the separate problem of the extent to which the gestures and body language of any culture connect with that culture's acting styles.
21 Colin McArthur, 'The Cultural Necessity of a Poor Celtic Cinema', in J. Hill *et al.* (eds) *Border Crossing: Film in Ireland, Britain and Europe* (British Film Institute, 1994).
22 R. Sklar, *City Boys: Cagney, Bogart, Garfield* (Princeton University Press, 1992).
23 R. Hornby, *The End of Acting: a Radical View* (Applause Books, 1992).
24 J. Grotowski, 'Tu es le fils de quelqu'un', *The Drama Review*, 31(3), 1987, pp. 30–41.
25 Lewis-Smith, V. 'Hail the King of Giro Valley', p. 43.
26 M. Berkmann, 'Scot with a taste of Porridge', p. 34.
27 G. Bowditch, 'StringalongaRab', *The Times*, 13 November 1995, p. 6.
28 Cairns Craig, (ed.) *The History of Scottish Literature, vol 4: the Twentieth Century* (Aberdeen University Press, 1987), p. 3.

29   C. McArthur 'Wake for a Glasgow Culture Hero', *Scottish Film and Visual Arts*, no. 6, 1993; R. McColl (ed.) *Lobey's the Wee Boy* (Mainstream, 1992).
30   K. Simpson, (ed.) *Burns Now* (Canongate, 1994).
31   Edwin Morgan (ed.) *Scottish Satirical Verse* (1980), p. xviii.
32   Morgan *Scottish Satirical Verse* (Carcanet, 1980), p. xi.
33   Cited in Morgan *Scottish Satirical Verse* (1980), p. 164.
34   A. Calder, *Revolving Culture: Notes from the Scottish Republic* (I. B. Tauris, 1995).
35   Cited in P. Kane, *Guardian*, 20 November 1993, pp. 26–8.
36   A. McArthur and H. Kingsley Long, *No Mean City: a Story of the Glasgow Slums* (1935).
37   C. MacArthur, 'The Cultural Necessity of a Poor Celtic Cinema', in Hill *et al.* (eds) *Border Crossing*; and 'Culloden: a pre-emptive Strike', *Scottish Affairs*, no. 9, Autumn 1994b pp. 97–126.
38   Alasdair Gray, *Lanark* (Jonathan Cape, 1981), p.243.
39   To speak of any kind of (perhaps especially national) identity as 'authentic' needs some qualification. Much recent writing on the question (D. McCrone, *Understanding Scotland: the Sociology of a Stateless Nation* (Routledge, 1992) and P. Cook, *Fashioning the Nation: Costume and Identity in British Cinema* (British Film Institute, 1996) insists upon the hybridic, impure, provisional nature of all identities. As an ultimate position this can be assented to, but such arguments seem to me to take inadequate account of the dialectical nature of concrete identities which are rarely in a state of rapid slippage whereby they are 'open to all-comers'. More characteristically, identities are formed in the crucible of struggle, usually between a powerful core identity which fashions the identities of the materially weaker groups on its periphery. One such core/periphery relationship is that of England (or perhaps better, the United Kingdom) and Scotland, bearing in mind that in other relationships (the UK *vis-à-vis* the USA, or Scotland *vis-à-vis* the Third World), the core can become a periphery and vice versa. A 'victory' for the periphery over the core, such as I have argued to be the case with regard to *Rab C. Nesbitt*, however fluid and provisional, is ground enough for the application of the term 'authentic'. However, to suggest that the language and 'style' of *Rab C. Nesbitt* is authentic is not to preclude its hybridity. Indeed, the whole discussion of the melding of High and Low Culture is just one example of its 'impurity'. A similar argument could be developed with regard to the presence of American elements in the series, a striking feature of Glasgow working-class life as of so many other milieux. The particular 'enemy' underlying this discussion is the position that would seek to promote the idea of a fixed, essential, unchanging national identity which is exclusive of outsiders. There are too many groups making this kind of argument in Scotland. The case of former Yugoslavia should be an object lesson as to where this argument leads.
40   *Naked Video*, replayed from time to time on cable television, is a useful source of evidence as to how the characters in *Rab C. Nesbitt* have developed. The most remarkable transformation is in the character of Cotter whom Tony Roper played in *Naked Video* without the distinctive whine and the tendency to overreach himself intellectually which are the hallmarks of his performance in *Rab C. Nesbitt*.
41   L. Althusser and E. Balibar, *Reading Capital* (New Left Books, 1970).
42   Roland Barthes, *S/Z* (Jonathan Cape, 1975).
43   P. Macherey, *A Theory of Literary Production* (Routledge and Kegan Paul, 1978).
44   *Cahiers du cinéma*, 'John Ford's *Young Mr Lincoln*', *Screen Reader 1: Cinema/Ideology/Politics* (Society for Education in Film and Television, 1977), pp. 113–52.
45   Robert B. Ray, *The Avant-Garde Finds Andy Hardy* (Harvard University Press, 1995).

Many thanks to Ian Mowat of Glasgow Caledonian University for sharing with me his encyclopaedic knowledge of Scottish radio and television comedy and for supplying materials relevant to *Rab C. Nesbitt*.

8

Peter Keighron

The Politics of Ridicule: Satire and Television

If the 1960s were a 'golden age' of television satire in Britain, the early 1990s must be a second golden age. The analogies that can be drawn between the two periods are obvious and convincing. In the early 1960s a Tory government exuded a moribund political culture. Pomp, ceremony and deference in political life presented clear targets inviting and deserving satirical attack. *That Was The Week That Was* (hereafter referred to as *TW3*) caught the mood of a nation.

By the mid-1990s, John Major presided over another aged, cynical, sleazy Tory government that had long since run out of ideas and credibility. On television *Rory Bremner, Who Else?, Mark Thomas, Have I Got News For You, Saturday Night Armistice, The Day Today, Brass Eye et al.* reflected a cynical disrespect for politicians in general and the Conservative government in particular. But while there are obvious similarities between the two periods, there are as many differences. And those differences say as much about the changing face of television as they do about the political situation. For instance, at its height *TW3* drew audiences of nearly 13 million. *Rory Bremner, Who Else?* rarely touches 2 million.

This chapter is not primarily about the theory of comedy. And while its starting point is *TW3*, it doesn't spend much time directly discussing that show and the history of satire on TV.[1] Rather, it will look at the state of political satire on TV in the 1990s – how and why it survives, and sometimes flourishes, and how television, politics and comedy connect. The arguments that follow have been developed almost entirely from a series of interviews conducted in 1996–97 with comedians, writers and television commissioning editors.

What is it and How Does it Work?

satire 'a literary work in which vices, follies, stupidities, abuses, etc. are held up to ridicule and contempt' and 'the use of ridicule, sarcasm, irony, etc. to expose, attack or deride vices, follies, etc.'

Webster's Twentieth Century Dictionary

satire *n. (Rom. ant.)* poetic medley, esp. poem aimed at prevalent vices or follies; a composition in verse or prose lampooning individual(s), this branch of literature, use of ridicule, irony, sarcasm, etc., in speech or writing for the ostensible purpose of exposing & discouraging vice or folly.

Oxford Concise Dictionary

Two things are worth noting, for our purposes, from these definitions. First, satire is not *necessarily* funny. And, secondly, satire has its roots firmly embedded in *literature*. The satire we're looking at here is not a literary but a *televisual* form and what we're looking at is how political satire can survive on television.

There is quite a lot of political satire on television these days but there are not a lot of political satirists. Or rather, comedians and writers don't seem particularly keen to be labelled as a 'satirist'. It doesn't sound very modern, does it? It sounds a bit, well, literary. It's certainly not the sort of badge that a young edgy, 'dangerous', 'alternative' comedian with a desperate desire for a career in television should be seen wearing, and few of them are. Outside of Bremner, Fortune and Bird, it's difficult to think of anyone who one could call a political satirist. Ian Hislop, perhaps Britain's most clearly labelled political satirist, has established and maintained his reputation mainly through print (*Private Eye*), and it is perhaps significant that on television he courts a well-read 'old fogeyish' image.

Being labelled a 'political satirist' is not exactly a good career move. As Seamus Cassidy, Commissioning Editor for comedy at Channel 4, says, 'There isn't a box into which all the political satire proposals go waiting to be judged against each other because it doesn't come up that often in a particularly good form. In television, satire has to fit into a rather large and untidy box called "comedy".'

But comedians don't just avoid the satire label for career reasons. Some just don't like the literary connotations and, as John Fortune explains, satire has always carried somewhat pretentious and unnecessary added values.

I remember when the Establishment [a club] opened [in the early 1960s] and Jonathan Miller wrote an article in the *Observer* in which he said, this is going to be satire, this is going to be Berlin in the 30s, and Swift and all that. We hated that, because at that stage and only until recently, I think, I've avoided the word satire because satire, or satirist, sound to me like it's got value built into it. Because it seems to kind of elevate the title, whereas we were doing political jokes and were content to do that.

I'm happier than I was [in being labelled a satirist] in that if you define satire as holding up figures of authority to ridicule I'm happy with that. What I'm not happy about is the fact that the great satirists, like Swift and Pope and Hogarth, also had a kind of very strong moral position where they not only ridiculed things ... and mostly all the great satirists have been conservatives, what they talked about was the fact that the world is going to hell and it was so much better in the old days. Whereas I don't aspire to any kind of moral authority, I just want to make accurate descriptions of the world that I see that people recognise as being funny and ridiculous. Ridiculous is the word, really.

Another reason that ambitious young comedians should shy away from the label 'political satirist', besides the danger of portentousness, is that some of the people who matter (both in television in particular and the comedy circuit in general) would interpret that as meaning a comedian who might not *necessarily* be funny. Rory Bremner, while not keen to be defined as *just* a political satirist, is one of the few comedians on television who sees no reason to apologise for the fact that some of his work is intended to be educational and informative – and not necessarily funny. But he also recognises the dangers that entails.

There's a true line on everything and there's a funny line on everything. And what I try to do with satire is to get the two as close together as possible [says Bremner] and it doesn't do to get the balance between the two lines wrong: there's a tendency if you get too angry and you get too sincere and too earnest that it ceases to be funny and in television terms, a television audience, that's a danger.

Jon Plowman, Head of Comedy Entertainment at the BBC, spells out that danger. While Plowman acknowledges that satire *per se* doesn't have to be funny, 'in my area it *does*,' he says, 'because I head the bit of the BBC that's called "Comedy Entertainment", and if it's not funny, I'm fucked, to be honest'. For Plowman, it seems the risk involved in balancing politics and comedy, in the way that Bremner attempts, is not worth the risk:

You know, if you've got something to say of a serious nature that adds to the political debate, the place to say it is *Newsnight*, or in a documentary form. If you've got something to say that's funny, the place to say it is a comedy programme. And the problem is the marriage of the two. In other words, it's not an accident that Rory's show is laden with awards, very skilfully done, hugely right that it's there, hugely right that

Channel 4 does it, but watched by nobody. Well, not nobody but on a Friday night he beats *Newsnight* by half a million.

The implication is that political satire can't really survive on television (or at least on terrestrial prime-time television) because it can't reach the minimum ratings demanded. The most popular satire programme on TV in recent years is, by some margin, *Have I Got News For You* which, significantly, is a comedy programme first and foremost and a political satire programme very much second. The main reason political satire isn't hugely popular, claims Jon Plowman, is simply because it isn't very funny, and, as a genre, people just don't expect it to be very funny.

There's a whole thing about political satire, which is: how much is it that the notion of political satire is actually a way of saying 'I'm going to do you a joke now about Heseltine. It won't be funny but, my God, it'll be satirical.' In the same way that comedy drama is actually something that started life being a sitcom but actually everybody said, 'Hurm, that's not very funny but maybe we could call it a comedy drama.' I mean, with the words 'political satire' I immediately reach for a bit of my brain which says, 'OK, it's probably not going to be hilarious.'

But does absolutely everything that comes under the label 'comedy' *have to* be hilarious? Comedian and writer Jeremy Hardy thinks not.

Ben Elton did do things which weren't funny on television, he made points, and you're torn two ways thinking, it's great that he said that but it's not very funny. And then you're thinking, well, does it need to be funny, does everything have to be wrapped in a joke, does everything need a punchline? We haven't moved away from the idea of jokes, that you have to have a gag every few seconds. And people are so used to television, so used to a high turnover of acts, so used to people not speaking for very long, that it's very hard for people to sit and watch somebody for a very long period of time. If humour could take its place in the arts as simply being part of the oral tradition, that comedy and poetry and political speaking all exist alongside each other and are connected, then there wouldn't be this desperation for everything to be structured in the form of jokes.

Perhaps the closest that political satire on television has come to being 'part of the oral tradition' rather than a string of gags is in the 'Two Johns' sketches in the *Rory Bremner, Who Else?* series (even more so in the extended edits of those sketches shown separately as *The Long Johns.*) Here, the humour and political force of these sketches comes largely from playing around with a discourse that develops through a string of punchlines, attitudes, responses and mannerisms which adds up over the whole series, and from one series to another, to much more than the sum of its parts. The sketches also gain power and humour through familiarity with shifting roles – i.e. the 'George Parr' character (which is switched between Bird and Fortune) can be a civil servant one week and a head of a privatised industry the next – and the whole thing develops into a more or less coherent critique of Thatcherism.

If it appears that television won't let humour 'take its place', find its natural space, that's surely because there is nothing 'natural' about the medium. It changes too quickly in content while at the same time is deeply conservative in form (desperate to hold on to a successful format, always pushing a programme one or two series beyond its sell-by date). Television is the least confident of mediums, the most terrified of rejection, scared that if you stop being funny for a single moment its audience will have reached for the remote. And maybe they will, or at least maybe enough of them will so that 'nobody's' watching anymore.

But what of the argument that while 'hard core' political satire, the political satire that dares to speak its name, like Bremner or Thomas, is a rare beast, that doesn't mean political satire is rare, it just emerges elsewhere, in different forms. As an example of the way political satire doesn't have to be in a programme actually labelled 'political satire', and indeed it might be more powerful if it *doesn't* carry that label, Plowman cites *Blackadder*. 'Was *Blackadder* political satire? Well, it sort of was, really, but actually it was bloody funny.'

Ironically (given Plowman's criticism of Bremner's programme), Bremner seems to back up Plowman's argument.

I think the two most successful sitcoms on television in the last six or seven years have been *One Foot In The Grave* and *Absolutely Fabulous* and I think the reason for that is that both of them were very satirical in their ways and both of them tapped absolutely into the *Zeitgeist*. Because when we look at the world as it was in the late 1980s to early 1990s, there were two responses to it. One was this impotent rage, saying, 'I can't fucking well believe it! John Major! What the hell is this guy doing ....' That was perfectly expressed in Victor Meldrew, this anger. And the second response was *Absolutely Fabulous*, which is to say, 'Oh, Fuck politics, let's just drink Bolly, let's have a glamorous life and behave badly.' And I think they're both sort of satirical in their way, they both tapped into something.

There are plenty of other examples: *Steptoe and Son* (a satire on class mores and values), *Till Death Us Do Part* (a satire on working-class Tory values in the 1960s and 1970s), *Men Behaving Badly* (a satire on new laddism), *The Simpsons* (a satire on the American nuclear family), *The Brittas Empire* (a satire on the management and enterprise culture), *Rab C. Nesbitt* (a satire on surviving Thatcherism), *Chalk* (a satire on the 'education crisis'), etc. All these programmes are clearly of their time, they're all drawing from and commenting upon the political and social situation. The power of their comedy comes not just from the fact that they've got a high GPM (gags per minute) ratio but from the equally important fact that they're about something very real and political. They have a strong truth line.

But, however successful political satire might have been in spreading out from 'political satire' programmes *per se* to all sorts of comedy (and journalism too – one could make a good case for the claim that Jeremy Paxman's interviewing techniques are directly descended from *TW3*), that surely doesn't mean there's no longer a place for that sort of programming, as the success, albeit with minority audiences, of shows like *Rory Bremner, Who Else?* and *The Mark Thomas Show* confirms.

There are other reasons why television, as a medium, is particularly unwelcoming to political satire. Not least of these is the fact that political satire is a dish best served hot and fresh, and it's obviously difficult, risky and relatively expensive to write, produce and broadcast a current news based programme within a few days. While satire exists in many programmes, the traditional (as in *TW3*) weekly review format of shows like *Spitting Image*, Bremner, Mark Thomas, Iannucci, *Have I Got News For You?*, which respond to the week's news, clearly has much to offer. Rory Bremner says:

> There should be, in British life, some place that people can come at the end of the week and thinking, as in that phrase '*TWTWTW*', 'I wonder what they made this week?' It's almost like a review of the week and you touch on the main points – there was a State Opening of Parliament this week, Major was doing that this week, Blair was doing that. And again, it's back to the crossword puzzle job. It's my job to look at that and tease it out and say 'what's the irony here?'

The weekly review format also enables, in fact demands that the truth and comedy lines of satire be clearly exposed and exploited. Which, again, Bremner makes no apologies for.

> I often used to say when I'm being Keith Floyd talking about BSE and all this sort of stuff, he looks to the camera and says: 'There you are, you see. You didn't know that, Dennis, did you? There you are, you learn things on this show.' And I bloody meant it because it was satisfying to think that you're making people laugh but at the same time you pictured a couple on their sofa and one turning to the other and saying: 'Is that true?' And the other person saying, 'Well, yeah.' And us being able to say, yeah, we researched it. Or, yes, if you bought every person in Britain one energy-saving light bulb, the energy saved in one year would mean that you wouldn't have to build Sizewell B nuclear power station. People say, 'Is that true, where did you find that out?' Oh, it

was on Rory's show ... That's a satisfaction. So, it's two things; it's the basic pleasure of making people laugh, it's the more didactic satisfaction that within a comedy show you're still telling people things that maybe they didn't know already. And there is the third thing which is the comic resolution of a sort of gut instinct or anger where you're saying: This cannot be tolerated anymore.

A Question of Balance

When I appeared on *Friday Night Live* the producers came into the room and said, 'I'm afraid there's a density of language, Mark.' And you go, 'Oh, right, OK. Mime, is it, is that what we're doing?' And they go, 'No, I'm afraid it's *bad* language, Mark. You've got a "fuck", a "tosser", a "toffee-bollock" and a "wanker".' And I said, 'Right.' And they said, 'We want the "fuck".' I said, 'Well I want the "toffee-bollock".' They said, 'Well, you can have the "toffee-bollock" if we can have the "fuck".' I said, What about "wanker"?' They said, 'It's yours for the "bastard".' So I said, OK, you've got "toffee-bollock" and "bastard" and I've got "fuck" and "wanker". Thanks.'

As Mark Thomas's experience clearly shows, comedians must tread a delicately negotiable path if they want to get on television. And it's not just a question of naughty words, of course; there's also the *political* question of balance. The BBC, for instance, is bound, by its Charter to maintain 'due impartiality' on political matters throughout its programming. This is a particularly interesting issue when it comes to political satire because there are few if any right-wing satirists on television. There are, of course, more than enough right-wing comedians on television but it's difficult to think of right-wing satire on television (one could cite *Stab in the Dark* as a rare and unsuccessful attempt to rebut the claim that satire is necessarily coming from the left on television) in the way that one could point to right-wing satire in print (the *Spectator* or P.J. O'Rourke). One could make the case that the 'new laddism' includes elements of right-wing satire (for example, on political correctness, feminism) but again this has been much more prevalent in print, in magazines like *Loaded* and *FHM*, than in television where its influence, in programmes like *Men Behaving Badly* and *They Think It's All Over*, has been relatively muted.

So, how does television achieve the necessary 'balance' or 'due impartiality' that is legally demanded of it? And if it isn't really 'balanced' how does it get away with it?

More often than not politics is narrowly defined in broadcasting as meaning *parliamentary* politics and thus the required balance is achieved through a more or less equal distribution of airtime between the main political parties. A sort of balance is thus achieved by the fact that comedians like Bremner and Thomas rarely hold back from attacking the Labour Party, which, even though they're invariably doing so from the left of the Labour Party, does provide a rejoinder to claims that political comedy is anti-Tory. Broadcasters can justly claim that there's as much anti-Labour as anti-Tory material. There is no shortage of complaints on political bias and it is traditional for broadcasters, particularly at the BBC, to claim that as long as complaints are roughly balanced between accusations of left-wing and right-wing bias, they must be getting it just about right.

The *BBC Producer's Guide* (1996) instructs programme-makers that 'Comedy... must be well judged, not gratuitous, unnecessarily cruel or designed to harm or humiliate a person or group.' But, of course, harming or humiliating politicians is *the whole point* of political satire and much of the political satire we see on our screens has been designed to do just that. However, such is the low public esteem of politicians that there's really very little public complaint on that score. Unlike, for instance, the Queen Mum, politicians are almost universally seen as 'fair game'.

Broadcasters do get complaints about comedy programmes but, as Jon Plowman says, 'Most people who ring the BBC duty log and write in and complain are dangerously close to insane anyway, so we're only talking really about how you deal with the lonely.' Anyone who has perused a channel's log book would have to agree with Plowman's analysis. Direct pressure from the public has very little impact on broadcasters. While it's a necessary fallacy for broadcasters, particularly public service broadcasters, to pretend that they do expand much energy wrestling with each and every public complaint, in practice the vast majority of such missives can be safely ignored or placated by a mildly patronising viewers' 'feedback' slot.

But television, particularly at the BBC, and more particularly in times of licence renewal discussions, does have to be seen to be responding to the public or, more often than not, responding to the self-appointed guardians of public morals.

> The BBC in particular, and perhaps broadcasting generally, has got itself on the back foot about reacting to the wishes of the public. We react a bit too much to people's complaints about, 'Oh, this was too filthy to go out before nine o'clock, this was too difficult.' I think we don't treat them as adults enough. There's a growing air of accountability, and when you say to people in the higher apparatchik bits of the BBC, 'But, excuse me, have you done any surveys to see if people do want to be more accountable, or is this a reaction to politicians and the *Daily Mail*?', you find that they haven't.

The public 'accountability' that Plowman talks about here is not accountability to the viewers in general but to pressure groups like Mary Whitehouse's National Viewers' and Listeners' Association and small groups of politically motivated men and women in various editorial offices. The real pressure, on political satire and on all programming, comes from elsewhere.

At the BBC the Board of Governors, made up of the appointed 'great and the good' has long provided a conduit through which the friends and colleagues of the great and the good can have their say, without having to write to Anne Robinson like the rest of us. It would be wrong to overstate the importance of this in relation to comedy programming – *Spitting Image* is not *Death On The Rock*. However, the inherently undemocratic structure of the BBC, coupled with the fact that for almost two decades the BBC was under intense and unremitting pressure from Conservative governments keen to break asunder its public service role, is bound to inculcate a degree of self-censorship.

Stuart Hood, controller of BBC at the time of *TW3*, recalls how the drip, drip, drip of pressure from above eventually proved too much for that programme.

What happened was that Hugh Greene was constantly being pressurised by the Board of Governors about it. The Board of Governors were clearly nervous and worried about it and a lot of pressure was put onto Hugh Carlton to do something about it. And then eventually, I think it was over Christmas or New Year, he had flu and was very depressed and when he came back he said we're going to have to take it off. Now, I was at a meeting where we discussed taking it off and somebody said to Hugh, 'What are you going to say?' And he said, 'I'm going to say we're going to take it off because there's a general election coming up.' It was clearly a relief to him to get rid of it at that point. He'd had enough trying to defend this thing.

The creation of Channel 4, in the early 1980s, did, among many other things, provide a broadcaster that, although legally bound by the same rules and regulations as all the others, could be more challenging and less sensitive to political censorship. The production and broadcasting of *Brass Eye* (1997) provides a telling example of some of the perceived differences and similarities between the BBC and Channel 4 in theory and practice. Chris Morris, the programme's creator, had previously always worked for the BBC, either on radio (*On the Hour*) or television (*The Day Today*), and it was the BBC who originally commissioned a pilot (in 1996) of what was to become *Brass Eye*. However, due to the predicted threat of legal complaints against the programme, it was, says Plowman 'too difficult for the BBC to do'.

Difficult in the sense that there's a perception in the outside world of what the BBC does and what Channel 4 does. And that's a perception that I would suggest goes as far as a legal perception, in the sense of if somebody is thinking of suing the BBC for defamation or slander or libel or whatever, they think, 'Yeah, I'm going to sue the bloody BBC.' Whereas they think, 'Oh yeah, Channel 4, that's what Channel 4 does.' When it came down to it there was talk of, well, if I can't do it here I'll do it at Channel 4. And actually we thought, well, fine, because in a way you'll find it easier to make there.

As it turned out, parts of *Brass Eye* were also too difficult for Channel 4 to do. Seamus Cassidy: 'They can't really bully us that much because Michael [Grade] would just jump up and down and say, "They're bullying us, they're bullying us and we're the champions of independent voice in British broadcasting".'

Cassidy's faith in Grade's ability (or desire) to 'jump up and down' to protect his channel proved over-optimistic in relation to *Brass Eye*. Sections of the programme were pulled (apparently on Grade's personal insistence and in opposition to many people within the channel) at the last moment. Grade's position, and his ability to withstand political pressure, was clearly undermined by a more or less coordinated barrage of right-wing assault on Channel 4 in his last few years as Chief Executive, led by the unremitting editorials from the *Daily Mail*, who famously dubbed Grade the country's 'Pornographer in Chief'. While Channel 4 is immune to the regular licence fee renewal pressure of the BBC, it has for some years now experienced its own political pressures (and responded with its own self-censorship) in the form of threatened privatisation.

For programme-makers, or would-be programme-makers, the rules on what is acceptable (*re* politics, language and the law) is a shifting line. For most satirists, and comedians generally, working in television is simply a case of seeing what you can get away with. For Guy Jenkin, who has worked (as a writer) for ITV, BBC and Channel 4,

It's a balance of some people who really fight to let you get on with what you really want to write and there's other people who are frightened of their own shadow. It's a battle between those two groups and you only get the echoes of conflict coming down to you so it's very hard to work out what's actually happened. It's hard to work out [the BBC line]. I think the BBC is very political now. It's got its own spin doctors and publicists who are very nervous about how the BBC appears so I think it's more running scared of political reaction than anything as complex as a theoretical position on what is right and wrong. I think it's purely practical. But it's a practicality filtered through so many voices that it's quite hard to work out.

Given the hoops that must be jumped through and compromises that must be accepted, not to mention the problems of immediate response that satire depends upon to stay fresh and which TV finds an expensive problem to solve, is it worth it? I mean ...

... it's Not Going to Bring Down the Government, is it?

The *Daily Mail* said it was funny but that it was part of a conspiracy to undermine parliamentary democracy.
Guy Jenkin, on reviews of Crossing The Floor

Jenkin, like most writers and comedians involved in political satire, admits to somewhat more modest political ambitions than the undermining of parliamentary democracy: 'I don't write it to make anyone change their views. I don't think satire often works as political propaganda. If you want to change the world, don't write satire. Become a politician, become a terrorist, or whatever ....'

That sounds like good advice, given the empirical evidence of the last 35 years of political satire on television where one struggles to find any real examples of comedy directly undermining politics or politicians. When asked what practical effect *TW3* ever had on the real world of politics, Ned Sherrin, the programme's producer, said the defeat of *TW3* target Henry Brooke, MP, in an election was 'the only example to which I can point with some certainty'. Guy Jenkin believes that the only thing in *Spitting Image* (for whom Jenkin was a writer) that ever really undermined any political careers was the 'two Davids' sketches (which portrayed David Steel as being quite literally in David Owen's pocket at the height of the SDLP). And when asked for a cause-and-effect example from *Rory Bremner, Who Else?*, John Fortune can only point to the fact that he was told that the government ditched a half-cocked idea to privatise the air traffic control system after a 'Two Johns' sketch.

Not a lot to show for over three decades of biting political satire on television. Indeed there is a theory that after years of being bitten by satire politicians have actually become immune to its debilitating powers and may even be drawing sustenance from it. More worryingly, perhaps, it seems that not only can satire be safely ignored it can even be positively invited.

'It's interesting', says Jeremy Hardy, 'I talk to Labour MPs now and they're obsessed with the idea that comedy is the future of politics. They all want to be funny and they think that TV programmes like *Have I Got News For You* are subversive, which I would question.' Jon Plowman cites disturbing evidence to support the case.

They're gagging to do it. When they started *New Statesman*, Marks and Gran [the writers] rang Michael Portillo's office and said, could Rik (Mayall) come and meet Michael, because we're writing this thing, it's about a Conservative MP, etc. And the reaction of Portillo's office was not, 'Oh God, we'd better be a bit careful here.' The reaction was, 'Oh good, Rik Mayall's coming in – photo-opportunity.' Rik arrived at the House of Commons for what he thought, as an actor, was a kind of research chat with a bloke who was at least in that area and in that thing, and Michael wanted photographs of him and Rik – you know, local MP with funny guy ... Rik high-tailed it out of there as quick as you like. The problem with comedy, as a weapon of political something, is that the politicians are media-savvy and want to join it. They know that being seen as a good sport is worth far more votes than a kind of seriously-thought-through disposition on *Newsnight*.

The logic is simple, says Hardy:

Politicians are not all stupid and they know that publicity is good. They know that people want politicians to be acceptable, they know that it's good to be seen to be a good sport, to be able to take the rough with the smooth and have a sense of humour, to think that things are a laugh, not take things too seriously. There's a sense now that if you can survive Ian Hislop being rude to you or Clive Anderson making a joke at your expense on telly then you're doing pretty well as a politician. It's clearly not subverting anything because they want to take part.

More often than not it's MPs whose ministerial prospects are either behind them or beyond salvation (Roy Hattersley, Neil Hamilton, Cecil Parkinson, Neil Kinnock, Jeffrey Archer, Edwina Curry, etc.) who have been queuing up for shows like *Have I Got News For You* or *Clive Anderson Talks Back*. But even Tony Blair, a man who's political career was hardly in decline, made a carefully calculated appearance on the *Frank Skinner Show* just a few months before the 1997 election (admittedly Skinner did little more than tickle his tummy but, clearly, being seen on a comedy show was thought to be good for Blair's image).

Another factor which blunts the satirical blade is that the public regard of most politicians is generally so low that it's become increasingly difficult to degrade them. As John Fortune says, 'Now I suppose the problem is that you've got to imbue politicians with some kind of dignity before you can kind of take the piss out of them.' For Bremner, Fortune and Bird, and Mark Thomas, one response to this is to find new, more relevant, targets. 'The sacred cows now are quangos,' says Bremner, 'and people like Cedric Brown, the British Gas guy, people who are making monstrous individual profits.' Another, related, response is to look beyond individual targets to attack their ideologies. Fortune: 'In the first series we did with Rory, John and I deliberately concentrated on a theme, which was "the market", whether it was just the market or the market economy, and the fact that any kind of decision to sack 5,000 people or, as in the mining thing, to destroy whole communities was absolutely justified by ... you only had to say "the market", and that was fine.'

It is in the 'Two Johns' sketches (or *The Long Johns*, the extended versions of the Bremner show sketches) that Bremner feels his show comes closest to political satire in its most affective and most politically powerful form.

> Have we influenced anything? I think maybe we contributed to a growing unease amongst the television audience, or amongst the people, that this link between government office and business had become rather too cosy. And so maybe our strongest claim to have made a difference, I think, was the unearthing and the repeated demonstration of the quangos and the quango culture, the Where Are They Nows? and the John Bird and John Fortune dismantling of the market argument. I mean, they spent most of the series, in '93 and '94, lampooning the phrase 'the discipline of the market' which was trotted out time and time again as the justification for what these chief executives, or whatever, were doing. They would take something like libraries where somebody comes up and says, "I've got this idea. I'm going to build this building and I'm going to fill it full of books and people will be able to come in and they'll be able to take these books out and bring them back." And the other person saying: "But that's the economics of the madhouse".'

Comedy and television is part of a multimedia, multifaceted political debate. It is in fact absurd to look for cause-and-effect proof of a programme's political worth. The fact that very occasionally one can point to a programme having had a direct and measurable impact on the political and social world (for example, *Cathy Come Home*) does not mean that all the other programmes have made no difference whatsoever.

Clearly, making a political difference, let alone undermining political democracy, isn't the reason why most comedians tell political jokes. But many of them are politically motivated people. They do want to make a difference, although they know the inherent dangers for a comedian of ever suggesting that that's actually what you're trying to do. Which brings us to the most familiar brick-bat thrown (both from left and right) at lefty comedians: Aren't you just *preaching to the converted?*

Three comedians in defence of 'preaching to the converted'.

Jeremy Hardy

The thing about that expression that annoys me, is the assumption that (a) there is such a thing as an apolitical comedian or it's possible to be entirely non-political, and (b) the idea that some comedians don't preach to the converted. I mean if you do a joke about how it's boring to queue in the post office and everyone laughs, they're laughing because you've told them what they already know. They're laughing because you're preaching to the converted. If you do a joke against Major and everyone laughs, people say, 'What's the point in making that joke? Yes, they laughed but they all agree with you, so what's the point in it?'

And I now actually see political jokes far more in terms of preaching to the converted, far more in terms of being a rallying cry or giving support and cheer to those who agree than trying to change the minds of those who don't agree. Simply for people to know that there's a comedian on their side is uplifting for them. So it's more for that reason that I would do those jokes than thinking I'm going to change the political climate.

Mark Steel

Through comedy I don't think you're going to change anybody's mind about anything. You're not going to make a Tory into a socialist by doing comedy, but what you can do is make people who already agree with certain ideas, you can make them feel more confident about their ideas, which is not to be sneezed at. In a sense you are changing their ideas because you're making somebody who says, 'Well I don't agree with all the injustices in society but nobody else seems to give a shit but me.' ... If you can make them think, 'No, I'm not on my own. There are other people who think it's appalling that people get banged up when everybody knows they didn't do it ... I thought it was just me who thought that.' You can make people feel that. You can make people feel enthused about ideas.

Mark Thomas

I suppose the best way that probably describes it is Robert Wyatt, the singer. He said his music was never going to change anything but he was going to be a cheerleader for change. You know, while the change was going on he'd be cheering. And I suppose that's how I look at it. That you're a cheerleader and you're either a cheerleader for good or a cheerleader for bad. It's a bit biblical, isn't it?

Occasionally it can open up your eyes. Just occasionally it can sort of open up and just say 'Ah', and put words and your feelings, and sort of in a way represent those feelings. But the one very firm thing it does say is 'We're not alone' ... It says 'You are not alone, there's a group of us like this. You are not isolated and you don't have to sit there thinking "Maybe I am wrong, maybe the *Daily Mail* is right".'

New Labour, New Satire?

The purpose of satire is to destroy whatever is overblown, faded and dull, and clear the soil for a new sowing.

Robert Graves

I think one of the achievements of Tony Blair is to make the targets exactly the same. And if the Labour Party wins [the 1997 election] there will be even more necessity for the kind of stuff that John and I did than now.

John Fortune

The Labour Party, frankly, are, to paraphrase Alexi Sayle, the same old shit in a different package.

Mark Thomas

The end of 18 years of Tory government did not leave comedians sitting around scratching their heads wondering where on earth they can get some new ideas for political satire. And that isn't because they've all shifted to the right to attack the Labour Party. As we've already noted, there's plenty of room to attack the Labour Party from the left. Satire should, almost by definition, be in a state of permanent opposition, says Channel 4 Commissioning editor Seamus Cassidy: 'The best satire comes from opposition. Satire is only necessary if you're in opposition. If you're not in opposition, it's propaganda.' But can a position of permanent opposition be detrimental to the body politic? Is it ultimately a negative and corrosive influence? Does it gnaw away at the very fabric of our democratic parliamentary system? Shortly after Labour had lost the 1992 election, Andrew Marr, writing in the *Independent*, spoke of satire as

a tide of acid that can scar as well as entertain ... [W]e should not talk about satire 'pricking their [politicians'] pomposity' without remembering that it can turn them a bit dotty, too. We should not laugh at the lampooning of Mr Major as a gormless wimp without pausing to reflect that these attacks may be damaging a real person and, by distorting the way he responds, may be damaging the country.[2]

Marr's article drew a response from Liberal Democrat Ian Manders who took the argument further by claiming that political satire in general 'hurts the left more than the right' because (even if most of it is aimed at the right) its overall effect is to encourage 'widespread cynicism about politicians',[3] and in such a moral climate it's the right (those who stand for the *status quo*) who benefit most from the belief that all politicians are tossers who can't or won't change anything and that it's not worth voting. It's certainly true that the apathy of some working-class would-be voters who, if they had thought it worth voting would have voted for Labour, ensured a spell of 18 years of Tory government. But it's less certain that any of that apathy was induced by too much satire.

There is some truth, however, in the implication that satire can create distorted characterisations. There is no evidence that John Major ever gave any indication that he was a great green pea enthusiast (as he was depicted on *Spitting Image*). But that image feeds back into the real image of John Major. When we heard his voice we had his grey puppet or Steve Bell's underpants-clad image in mind. When we saw him we could hear Rory Bremner's impersonated voice rather than the real one. And it isn't just comedians who employ satire to distort images. Rory Bremner adds a further twist to the negative power of satire, again citing the 1992 election as an example.

The most effective satire in the early 1990s is what the tabloid papers did to Neil Kinnock. For five years they peddled this image that he was Welsh (true), that he was a windbag, that he was henpecked by Glenys. And by 1992 Neil Kinnock was un-electable ... He was demolished by this public image. It was satirical and he was ridiculed.

But such arguments can only return to the fact that the comedy aspect of satire is only as powerful as the truth aspect. Satire is, almost by definition, a distorted representation of reality but – to work as satire, to work as comedy – it still has to hold to the truth line. It may well not be true that John Major was never happier than when he was pushing his peas around his plate, but the image of a sad, grey man whose most animated conversation centres around the merits of his latest helping of over-cooked vegetables worked because it really was emblematic/symbolic/reflective of a party leader whose leadership and whole public persona was debilitated by a divided and warring Conservative Party; a leader who, when searching for something safe to say, could only think of the peas on his plate. The truth line (an indecisive, middle-of-the road leader) entwined with the comedy line (the pea lover) to create satire.

More importantly, the Marr and Manders argument on the negative impact of political satire is based on a very narrow definition of politics and the political world. They're really talking about the politics of *parliamentary democracy* and the ever narrowing left–right spectrum of Lab–Lib Dem–Tory parties. What has distinguished good (funny) political satire is that it is always coming from outside that spectrum, whether from an ultra-liberal a-pox-on-all-their-houses position or from a left-of-Labour position. As Mark Thomas and Mark Steel explain, there's a lot more to politics than is usually defined by television.

The whole principal of democracy is not enshrined within parliament. The idea that you vote every five years and that somehow counts as democracy, to me that's just anathema because what you're looking at is people's involvement in their life. That is what democracy is. So you're talking about local level of democracy. You're talking about democracy at work. You're talking about accountable leaders and people in parliament. (Mark Thomas)

The problem with talking about political comedy, it's the same as talking about political anything, in a sense, which is that it is assumed that for comedy to be political it must be talking about the government.

Political comedy is about the life that people live, not about the politicians, it is about why is it that when I go to work in the morning I get given a bollocking for turning up ten minutes late by some poncy 25-year-old line manager who's done two years' business studies and knows a tenth about the job as I do. And if political comedy is about real life then I'm afraid that 'smiling boy' [Tony Blair] is not going to change people's real lives, is he? (Mark Steel)

So while a change of government clearly makes little difference, things have changed and will change some more. We've noted earlier how little right-wing satire there is on television but the election of a 'left' government (and disillusionment with what it achieves) could be an encouragement to right-wing comedians. At the time of writing it's unclear how that could affect comedy on television, but perhaps the 'new laddism' which, as we've noted, has up to now been most prevalent in print medium, will find more expression in television.

What it [new laddism] says is that feminism has gone too far. This notion that men are now the victims, people are constantly trying to get this off the ground. In American it's more overt. It's white men who are under threat and the country's men are under threat. It's that whole American thing that the real minority is the white man, that *Falling Down* ethos, that movie with Michael Douglas where he's the angry white male and he's a proud American and he's not anti-black but he doesn't like Korean shopkeepers and Hispanics.

People haven't yet started to push back towards overt racism in the way they have in America. They're more nervous about that. It's okay to be overtly sexist here but not yet to be overtly racist. But it will be soon, it'll be seen to be mischievous and alternative. (Jeremy Hardy)

Yet laddism already looks tired and, irrespective of what happens in other media, it's debatable how much a shift to the right would get past the generally rather liberal-lefty gatekeepers of television comedy. Perhaps, as Hardy suggests, the target of cynicism will shift to the right. On the other hand, Jon Plowman sees comedy moving into a less cynical, politically softer-edged era.

We've certainly lived through a time of media cynicism. We've lived through a time when the trendy thing to be was cynical about whatever it was that one was talking about. We've lived through that as a kind of media trend, but I don't think it is anything more than a media trend. I feel we've gone through that now and we may have come out the other side. It's interesting that the kind of things that people talk about, certainly in the area that I'm in, are the *Father Teds*, the *Shooting Stars*, the *Four Weddings*, the *Vicar of Dibley* bag – that feeling that we've moved through just being cynical to where actually just being nice is quite funny. I mean, *Father Ted* is actually rather *nice*, you know. They are nice people, they are bewildered, they live in a sad and pathetic way but they are ultimately nice. They're not ultimately destructive. *Four Weddings* and all that area of stuff is not destructive comedy, it's quite nice comedy. Ben [Elton] is now writing *Thin Blue Line*, which is 'nice' comedy. I would say that maybe cynicism's been played out ... if you want to call it post-cynicism.

At the time of writing, then, satire on television in the UK has reached an interesting stage. On the one hand we have a lot of 'nice' comedy, 'nice' satire and if not the end then at least the waning of 'new laddism'. We have, too, a new government for comedians to deal with. The smile of Tony Blair may be 'overblown' but its not yet 'faded and dull'. Will we see the development of a right-wing satire?

Perhaps the most promising new direction for satire on television is suggested by the more 'pro-active' formats exploited by the likes of Michael Moore and Mark Thomas and, occasionally, Chris Morris. In *Brass Eye* Chris Morris duped a number of MPs to comment on a fictional new drug, 'Cake' (one even tabled a question in the House of Commons), which brilliantly exposed both the well of ignorance that media coverage on serious issues like drugs creates and the willingness of some politicians to jump into that well. And both Mark Thomas and Michael Moore (the latter more often in an American/Canadian context) have used the camera and the power of television to satirical and political effect – doorstepping authority and setting up 'legitimate' targets (MPs, 'fat cats', etc.). Such formats promise a more confrontational form of political comedy which, while not in conflict with its literary roots, suggests that television, as a medium, has something unique to offer satire.

Notes

1   A. Crisell, 'Filth, Sedition and Blasphemy, The Rise and Fall of Satire' in J. Corner (ed.) *Popular Television in Britain* (BFI, 1991).
2   *Independent*, 8 December 1992, p. 19.
3   *Independent*, 10 December 1992, p. 24.

9

Brian Winston

Not a Lot of Laughs: Documentary and Public Service

Bill Nichols, the totemic ancestor of all recent theoretical work on the documentary, claims that the form constitutes (in a telling phrase) a 'discourse of sobriety'.[1] In this he but echoes John Grierson's dour 'public education' agenda articulated half a century earlier. This spectre of sobriety haunts the documentary, making it unique among the mass-audience film forms created in the cinema's first century in not unreservedly putting the pleasure principle first. In short, documentaries – thanks to sobriety and public education – are not a lot of laughs.

Cinema studies' theoretical approaches in general offer little explanation as to why audiences might then want to watch mainstream Griersonian documentaries. Theory concerned with such issues stresses the sexual 'pleasure in looking', scopophilia (or even the rather more perverted comforts of voyeurism), as the essential psychological reward of cinematic spectatorship. According to this conceptual framework, the transparent mode of mainstream film production is specifically designed to help the viewer not just to identify with the figures on the screen but to 'have the impression of being that subject himself'.[2] But what sort of scopophilia drives one towards endless hours of observing the pain of a children's hospital or a Jamaican emergency room? What voyeuristic thrill, what *jouissance*, arises from contemplating letter-sorting on a mail-train, the fishing techniques of the Netsilik Inuit or the daily round of a peacetime military unit? Do we really want to have the impression of being 'that subject' when he or she experiences nothing but misery in the Borinage or the deprivations of single parenthood in an American slum?

Of course, that psychological theories of the cinema have little to say about the documentary audience could be the result of their 'Gödelian' (as it were) 'incompleteness' in failing to account for all the phenomena

145

they are supposedly addressing. On the other hand, the sort of documentary films alluded to above all come from the canon of the social realist documentary or stand in direct line to it. Scopophilia seems far more relevant when Nick Broomfield explores the dominatrix's dungeon or ITV offers yet another series on the fauna of Hollywood. Moreover, the current fad for 'reality TV' – reconstructions of life's disasters, crimes and sundry other catastrophes – feeds an apparent public appetite for the voyeuristic, the puerile and, if not the pleasures of identification, then at least the dubious empathies of *Schadenfreude*. It could be, then, that the psychological theories are more correct than not, and the canonical documentary's failure to satiate the scopophiliac drive is why it remains a largely marginalised film form.

And a marginalised form is what indeed it is in most parts of the globe, especially outside the anglophone world, even after account is taken of non- or anti-canonical down-market voyeuristic documentary variants. Repeated studies of world television output have shown that documentary does not occupy the scheduler's central ground; it is not, by this crude measure at least, popular.

In 1996, on behalf of the Italian public broadcaster RAI, a new world-wide survey of scheduling practices was undertaken.[3] The RAI study revealed that the documentary output of public service broadcasters fell into two bands. One lay between 5 and 10 per cent; for example, Austria's ORF, the Canadian CBC, Croatian HTV, the Czech Republic's CTV, Denmark's DR, Italy's RAI, the Netherlands' NOS, Slovenian TVSLO and Switzerland's SSR. The second, higher, band included France 2, reporting nearly 20 per cent of time devoted to documentaries, and a second French channel, TF1, 14 per cent; the BBC, reporting 23 per cent; and the American public service system, CPB/PBS, 55 per cent.

Only 6 of the 35 organisations responding were private. Their replies supported the perception that, however badly documentary does on public television, it fares even worse under commerce. Italy's Mediaset, for example, managed 0.1 per cent of output. Finland's MTV3 did double its output between 1994 and 1995 but from only 0.5 per cent to 1.1 per cent.

These figures were the result of a fairly random collection of broadcasters self-reporting via a questionnaire which failed to define documentary closely; yet the RAI study did make the category 'documentary output' distinct from 'classical music', 'education', '"minority" programmes', and a large category called 'Information' which included 'news', 'reportage', 'current affairs', 'magazine' and 'parliamentary reports'. Furthermore, although 'documentary' is almost certainly defined differently in these various countries, nevertheless the RAI study is not seriously at odds with previous analysis. Richard Kilborn cited two other surveys from 1991 and 1994 which also found that European TV stations, commercial and public, between them produced around 4 per cent or 20,000 hours of documentary programming a year.[4] It therefore seems reasonable to suggest that an antipathy to the documentary is almost universal among broadcasters, especially for the new commercial channels and, as we shall see, outside of the anglophone world.

The RAI study further confirmed Kilborn's observation that 'documentaries still fare best in those countries with a long-standing public service tradition'.[5] For instance, the public broadcaster TVE, being in a country, Spain, without such a tradition, claimed no documentaries at all;[6] whereas in Britain even commercial broadcasters did better than the European average.[7] This means that despite the attack on pubic service principles which British television has endured for the last couple of decades an essential mark of such service, the documentary, has more or less weathered the storm.

Kilborn, in suggesting the public service concept as a primary determinant of documentary activity, rather than a documentary film-making tradition *per se*, points up an essential link. As the global neo-liberal attack on the principles of public service broadcasting developed, it became clear that documentaries and the retransmission of high culture in performance were what crucially characterised such a service. The market-place provided, in a generic sense at least, everything else including news. What was threatened or even lost when public service television was commercialised or the public service ethos diluted was, exactly, documentaries and arts features.

This can be seen quite clearly in the United States. Heir, as are British broadcasters, to a tradition of state-funded public education documentary production, the two leading American networks, NCB and CBS, developed significant in-house documentary units. In a commercial sense, the networks' documentary strands were a species of 'cultural loss leader'[8] more designed to maintain public confidence in a system some held to be 'a vast wasteland' than to maximise audiences, which they singularly failed to do. The history of Ed Murrow's journalistic *See It Now* and the more filmic *CBS Reports* or *NBC White Papers* which followed can be read as a chronicle of a species of long-term network public relations exercise, shored up by a sense of civic duty and little else.

This is not to denigrate those films, particularly in the 1960s and early 1970s, which have been written into the record of American television as controversial and influential masterworks. For example, the *CBS Reports* 'Harvest of Shame' on the plight of migrant workers (1960), or 'Hunger in America' (1968) which is credited with facilitating the introduction of the federal food-stamps programme. 'The Selling of the Pentagon' (1971), from the same series, on the military's domestic public relations activities caused such a storm that congressional hearings were held on the matter. Such occasional triumphs of the public enlightenment principle justified the whole commercialised television system and were therefore worth the odd hour of less than optimal audience figures.[9]

Nevertheless, even prior to the Reaganite attack on American broadcasting, the rise of cable and the stunting of the public system, the networks were slowly but steadily giving up on documentary, despite a lingering sense of public duty. Documentary output was increasingly marginalised in the schedule as no sustained audience had been achieved. As Charles Hammond Jr. pointed out: 'Television news documentary regressed only after it was clearly demonstrated that its various subjects had become too heady to be taken steadily. Viewers didn't like to see too much reality.'[10] The result was that documentary was utterly unprotected in the neo-liberal era. In 1984 the Federal Communications Commission's guidelines on programming, which had been outlined in 1960, were formally abandoned. The public service element in American commercial broadcasting was significantly diluted. Gone was any requirement for public affairs programming and, within a few years, the networks' documentary departments were consigned to history. A formal public service mandate and nothing else had been responsible for the documentary's presence in the commercial TV schedules for three decades.

And nothing else – despite the broadcasters' oft-made claim that this demise was the inevitable result of the rise of cable and the exponential growth of competition. The network share of audiences, we are told, has been decimated, falling from over 90 per cent in the early 1970s to some 60 per cent in the mid-1990s. Wilfully sacrificing audience numbers on the altar of public service, especially in the absence of a requirement by the regulator, was no longer possible, it was claimed.[11] This however, is open to dispute. Given the rise in population over this same period and the establishment of 20 million new homes, the fall in the actual numbers of people watching the networks is far less than the fall in share. In 1975 there were 71 million homes with television sets in the US. In prime time the networks reached 37 million of them. In 1995, there were 95½ million and the networks reached about 34 million of them. The networks' advertising take is still in the order of $32,000 million a year.[12] Therefore, the commercial pressure of competition was less significant in the decline of mainstream TV's documentary output than the neo-liberal change in regulatory environment.[13]

This history is in marked contrast to the British experience during the same period. Over the past four decades the BBC has regularly reported remarkably consistent percentages of programming described as 'documentary'. For example, in 1955/6 the Corporation pigeon-holed the 'real' with 'Sport','News', 'Newsreel and documentation films [sic]/outside broadcasts' and 'Talks, demonstrations [sic] and documentary programmes'. These last, at 634 hours, amounted to 25 per cent of output.[14] In 1958/9, the year when Denis Mitchell won the prestigious Prix Italia for *Morning in the Streets*, arguably British television's first critically acclaimed addition to the Griersonian canon,[15] the figures were much the same – 24.3 per cent.[16] The arrival of BBC2 in 1964/5 caused something of a blip as 'Talks etc.', with hours increased to 748 across both channels, nevertheless accounted for only 13 per cent of the output;[17] but a decade later the original range of 20–25 per cent had been re-established with 988 hours on BBC1 (now described as 'Current Affairs, Features and Documentaries'), yielding just under 20 per cent of output, and 712 hours on BBC, just over.[18] A decade after that, in 1984/5, BBC1 had no less than 26 per cent and BBC2 19 per cent in this category;[19] and the RAI survey confirms this sort of level into the mid-1990s.

A similar consistency, albeit at a lesser level, can be noted in ITV's commitment where the 'Documentary and arts' category remains steady at around 10 per cent of output across these decades. Channel 4, the obverse of TVE, devoted a positively non-commercial 22 per cent of its time to such programming.[20]

It is, therefore, perfectly possible to argue that this survival is a measure of the failure of the Thatcherite attack on British public service broadcasting culture. Indeed, it is possible to go further and suggest that such consistencies mask something of a shift in the 1980s to an even greater level of public acceptance for the documentary in Britain.

Before the 1980s, documentaries never figured among the highest-rated shows. The precursors of a change in this were to be found in the occasional 1970s long-form programmes such as Paul Watson's *The Family*, a twelve-parter watched by 5.5 million in 1974, and the military documentary series *Sailor* in 1976. This measure of ratings success was confirmed by the 1977/8 season's sensationalist *Hong Kong Beat*, about the colony's police, and Roger Graef's 1982 *Police*, on their counterparts in the Thames Valley. *Police* marked the culmination of the process as it was the first such series to break through into the Top 10 prime-time list. The same breakthrough was achieved on Channel 4 by a *Cutting Edge* edition, 'Shops and Robbers', transmitted in February 1984.

But it is easy to get carried away. Although the basic point about documentary's survival stands, it is important to remember that these occasional appearances in the Top 10 were, and remain, the exception rather than the rule. For example, despite the high percentage of documentaries in Channel 4's output, in its first decade that single *Cutting Edge* was the only one, at 7.8 million, to figure among its 30 top-rated shows.[21] No documentary of any kind (unless you count Granada's amateur video-bloopers *You've Been Framed!*) made it into the top 100 programmes of 1993.[22]

Thus, the move into prime time does not indicate a significant change in the overall levels of documentary programming as such on British terrestrial television. However, it is this comparatively recent and occasional presence in the top-rated programmes lists which gives rise to an impression, not actually borne out by the historical development of the schedule, that: 'Once there was only *40 Minutes*, now it's forty hours.'[23] Also, there has been no 'rebirth' of the television documentary for the simple reason that it never died.

Increased documentary salience fuels another parallel perception that both BBC1 and ITV were in the early 1990s moving documentary 'down market'. If true, this would rebut the idea that documentary has survived Thatcherism more or less unscathed. On the contrary, market forces, as might be expected, would have debased it; and many, including some of British television's most distinguished 'sober' documentarists, believe this to be the case. David Munro, whose work with John Pilger represents the most uncompromising expression of the journalistic investigative tradition, wrote in 1994:

> I personally don't think the ambulance-chasing, crime reconstruction programmes have any place at all on television; they are voyeuristic and don't achieve anything. ... I believe that every documentary film-maker in this country, every film-maker, every current affairs person, should stand up and say the public deserves better than this.[24]

Such observers find it is easy, say, to contrast ITV's 1980 *Hollywood*, a thirteen-part series made by Kevin Brownlow and David Gill, narrated by James Mason with music by Carl Davis, with Helen Fitzwilliam and Paul Buller's 1996 seven-parter *Hollywood Pets* and conclude that, as far as ITV is concerned, documentary is over, having become instead 'docu-glitz'.

But allowance must be made for the coming of BBC2 and Channel 4. The latter has had an impact on ITV's provision of 'up-market' programming, including documentaries, just as BBC2 had previously done so on BBC1's. Certainly, an increasing tendency to brand slots threatened the one-off documentary, just as it had killed the one-off play. Yet on the other hand, across all four terrestrial channels it is harder to make the case that 'sober' work in general is more marginalised than it has been historically. The supposedly 'new' populist strand is itself at least as old as *Man Alive*, which first imported a tabloid agenda to television and ran on BBC2 from 1965 to 1982. It could be argued, therefore, that such a tradition has not affected serious work as much as the rhetoric sometimes suggests.

Again, it is possible to go further and claim that, outside of prime time, outside of the main channels, the old tradition has survived and even flourished. Practitioners of the dominant observational style have continued their long march through the institutions. Space was found, which it certainly never had been before the coming of Channel 4, for non-anglophone documentaries. Structured attempts were made to revive lost styles; Peter Symes' *Picture This* on BBC2 was more often than not an *homage à* Humphrey Jennings and the more poetic strand of pre-television documentary films. The Community Access Unit's mature attempt to give voice (and camcorders) to 'ordinary people' via *Video Nation* also spoke to an increased range of audience.

Moreover, in the populist heartlands not all has been totally lost. The change in commercial contractors, occasioned by the operation of the 1990 Television Act, which took effect on 1 January 1993, caused the demise of two ITV series, *First Tuesday* and *Viewpoint*, but they were replaced (albeit with one series – *Network First*). Meridian, one of the newcomers, in its first ten months posted *Coltrane in a Cadillac* as its biggest hit; admittedly not as demanding as the Munro/Pilger exposé of Indonesian atrocities in East Timor, *Death of A Nation*, but equally not quite the fly-blown disgracefulness of 'reality TV' either. Even Carlton, which remains a pariah to many British media observers, managed in these early months to insert three current affairs programmes into its top-rated 13 shows.[25]

The strongest support for Munro's position comes from the fact that the sort of expensive investigative programmes he makes are somewhat out of favour. It is certainly true that current managements, Channel 4 aside, do not instil confidence as defenders of basic media freedoms, such as the right to investigate; yet, again, not much of this is new. Managements have never liked controversy; nor have they ever needed ideological hostility to bolster their antipathy towards increased production costs such as those incurred by investigative work.

All this aside, at the end of the day what must be addressed is the reality of documentary's limited audience appeal to what is, after all, a mass medium. When Munro claims that, 'Serious, committed documentaries are popular with viewers here and abroad',[26] one must ask in what sense this is true. In fact, for all that millions of British homes might watch them, documentaries are a lot less popular than most other programming and always have been. Even as Paul Watson was drawing 5.5 million for *The Family*, *Some Mothers Do Have 'Em* had 23.5 million. In the year of *Hong Kong Beat*, a rerun of Richard Cawston's film 'humanising' the Royal Family was watched by 4.5 million but the *Morecombe and Wise Christmas Day Special* was seen by 29 million. *Police*'s 10.5 million did astonishingly well against *To The Manor Born*'s 16.5 million. Any documentary audience above 5 million was, and remains, exceptional.

Documentarists respond to this by making perhaps quite reasonable arguments as to the influence and civil importance of their work, echoing Grierson's (unsubstantiated) concept of the documentary's 'hang-over' effect.[27] Audiences might be smaller but documentaries are more important to them than other forms of programming. Even so, the question remains: Why were they ever introduced into the television schedule in the first place and why do they remain there at all?

In the absence of popularity, at least at the levels achieved by drama and light entertainment, four possible factors can be suggested as documentary's sustaining elements: public duty (as the documentarists claim), ideology, economics and, since none of the previous ones are clear cut, inertia.

First, public duty: the nexus between the public service ethos and documentary, so clearly illustrated by American developments, is more complex in Britain. Obviously, Reith's concept of broadcasting and Grierson's public education rhetoric meshed easily. Despite some small hiccups, such as the Griersonian Paul Rotha's unhappy stint as head of BBC Documentary Department between 1953 and 1955,[28] the British documentary tradition was transferred to the small screen in the 1950s, most ably by Denis Mitchell.

On the other hand, the spectre of audience antipathy to Grierson's public education documentaries was something of a hindrance; for it is not just on television that documentaries fail to attract the public *en masse*. Grierson had demonstrated that they were just as ineffectual at the cinema box-office. 'Why do we spend our pocket money and our leisure hours at the cinema?' demanded a letter to a film fans' magazine in 1933. 'To see our ordinary everyday lives portrayed on the screen over and over again? Emphatically not.'[29] I have argued elsewhere that, as a basic rule of thumb, all audience figures claimed by Grierson and his followers should be treated with caution.[30] Dividing them by anything from 4 to 10 would not seem to be inappropriate. And, as with television, the attractions of competing material need to be remembered, too. For example, the claim of a war-time documentary audience of 18.5 million a year must be compared with the numbers of people visiting the commercial cinema; they were buying some 25 million tickets *a week*.

Twenty years later, the spectre of such audience neglect was still haunting the BBC Documentary Department, counter-balancing the appeal of the Griersonian documentary movement's impeccable public service credentials. *Special Inquiry* which ran from 1952 to 1957 was the department's first major series, disliked by Rotha because of its mixture of studio and film inserts. Norman Swallow, its executive producer, recalled that:

> We were inspired by *Picture Post* and, in television terms, by the Ed Murrow and Fred Friendly series *See It Now*, from CBS New York. They were our two main influences, I think, together with the old British documentary tradition of course. ... actually my favourite pre-war documentary was *Housing Problems*. .... It was probably no coincidence that that was the first *Special* we had.[31]

It was journalism, and the least 'aesthetic', most journalistic Griersonian documentary, that lay behind the programme. In announcing the show, the *Radio Times* said, 'The aim is to forge a new style of television *journalism*' (emphasis added).[32] Public service might be comfortable with public education, but documentarists wishing to reach the new mass television audience needed to disguise documentary as journalism. That inheritance still affects the 'sober' mainstream of work, much of which, as is the case with David Munro for instance, remains essentially journalistic.

This is why the nexus between public service broadcasting and television documentary production levels is complicated. The relationship is muddied by journalism. The journalistic, of course, can embrace sensationalism as well as high-minded investigation – hence the survival of the news in a commercialised, privatised television environment. To the extent that the documentary dons a journalistic mask, then to that extent pure Reithian or Griersonian public service can be compromised; the mask can be tabloid as easily as it can be broadsheet. From the beginning, television documentary, even in the UK heartland of the public education tradition, often adopted just such a journalistic mask.

The impact of specific ideological considerations is no clearer. These constitute a second possible legitimating element, an obverse of the general public service concept just discussed. For Reith public service broadcasting was a 'particularly potent way of creating .... [T]he symbolic community of the nation ...'.[33] For Grierson, public education was also a means of doing this, particularly by depicting on the screen a society moving 'from the negative to the positive'.[34] For this to have effect, though, the image must influence the viewer, essentially by presenting itself as evidence of what the society is actually like. That it might be oppressive to invest some images with a privileged relationship to the real is an idea which emanates from critics of this integrative and paternalistic vision of the social role of media in general and documentary in particular.

Noël Carroll, in a knockabout polemic on documentary, most of which displays a positively comic concatenation of misreading and bombast, usefully reminds us of the validity of this critique.[35] He insists, for example, that quotidian films about killer whales or the value of German glider research during the Second World War to contemporary aviation are, in a comparatively unproblematic way, evidence of the situations with which they deal. They display 'standards of scientific accuracy and attendant protocols of objectivity'.[36] Such depoliticised rhetoric disguises the ideological implications of such texts. Claiming life-enhancing outcomes for Nazi research, for example, is scarcely, on its face, neutral whatever the truth-value Carroll assigns to the argument deployed by the makers of *Wings of the Luftwaffe*. That Carroll has nothing to say about this exactly speaks to the ineffable quality of documentary's traditional claim on the real which he is attempting to embrace. It could therefore be argued that, for the broadcasting authorities, maintaining this sort of ideological power was worth losing the odd hour of maximum audience numbers.

Given the unquestioning nature of the dominant direct cinema style and, in Britain, the veritable uncritical obsession with uniforms and institutions, it is not too far-fetched to suggest that this is exactly what the makers of mainstream television documentaries are about. By this reading, the occasional seriously disruptive programme, *Death on the Rock* for example, is nothing more than a cynical ploy which serves to legitimate the steady drip-drip of integrative hegemonic intentions in the rest of the documentary output. As in America in the 1960s, controversy works to establish the (false) liberal bona fides of the entire television system. It is no wonder that uncommercial documentaries survived in the Thatcherite period.

Attractive as a reading along these lines might be, it seems to me unlikely that such sophistication would be displayed by contemporary neo-liberal political overseers and broadcasting managers who have otherwise shown themselves to be, for example, so fixated on the 'market' that they are prepared, even as the nation creaks and strains at the Celtic edges, to abandon Reith's centralising system. It is not easy, then, to be convinced that documentaries are in the schedule as a result of explicit or implicit ideological conspiracies on the part of such blinkered ideologists who cannot even be relied upon to maintain media structures in their own essential interests.

More persuasive is an argument grounded in the economics of television, the third potential legitimating factor; but, again, the issue is not particularly clear cut. An old-fashioned (pre-neo-liberal) economic argument for documentary might run as follows: since audiences cannot be maintained at maximum levels across all broadcasting hours, it makes sense to transmit cheaper programming in fringe viewing periods, which is when much documentary programming is transmitted. There is no question that even mainstream documentary is cheaper. The most lavish series, the BBC's *A People's Century* for example, costs around, say, £250,000 an episode as compared with the equally lavish costume drama *Nostromo* which cost nearly £2 million per hour. UK-based network documentary budgets are currently running at £150,000 an hour as against £600,000 an hour for drama.[37] A quarter or so of the audience for a quarter or so of the cost does not seem untoward.

However, by the mid-1990s, at the high tide of Birtism in the BBC and the accountants' *Kulturkampf* everywhere else, such rationales no longer worked, so economics is no better an explanation for the British documentary phenomenon than public duty or ideological conspiracy. As David Munro's indignation indicates, cheapness was, of itself, insufficient to offer complete protection for 'sober' work on the more popular channels. There the 'culture' was to push for ever cheaper programming even in maximum viewing periods. Public expectations and competition ensured that this sort of greedy short-termism was kept in check to a certain extent and traditional expensive production values were maintained at least for drama and other entertainment forms. But documentary was caught.

Happy to put cheaper non-fiction programming into prime time for economic reasons, the princes and powers now demanded that it delivered audiences at popular entertainment levels. Cheaper shows for smaller audiences would no longer do. Documentary's occasional incursions into the 'Top 10' ratings acted as a lure and only 'docu-glitz' could feed such managerial expectations. Between the Scylla of mass audience neglect and the Charybdis of voyeurism, the traditional public service ethos foundered. It was in danger of drowning in the whirlpool of Charybdis, but, as yet, it has not quite done so. Despite the current management culture being quite as much for maximising all audiences as they are in favour of maximising share dividends or business 'efficiency', 'sober' documentaries, less attractive to audiences than other equally cheap programming genres, are still commissioned. The mystery of why British television bothers with them remains.

Can it really be, then, that inertia is as good a reason as any? From the 1920s on, the BBC slowly translated a tri-partite vision of British society into three radio services – eventually 'Light', 'Home' and 'Third' – the contents of which were decanted, as it were, into one television channel after the war. Commercial television, although it introduced a world of soap opera and games shows, nevertheless also bought into the main lines of this settlement as programmes such as *This Week*, *World In Action* and *Armchair Theatre*, and ITN, eloquently attest. Included in this was a tradition of documentary production as dedicated to public service as was the BBC's. Doubling these channels allowed both the BBC and ITV to move certain 'Home Service' and 'Third Programme' elements onto the newcomers, but again the programming settlement remained. The same process, with a different mix of programming, can be seen at work in the USA. The American schedule established by their commercial radio networks prewar was also transferred to television more or less intact.

It is as if in these foundational television moments a contract, as it were, was made between broadcaster and audience as to what the new medium actually *would be* – and that, more or less, is where it remains. Decades pass and with a slowness appoaching the glacial, the Western and the variety show, for example, fade from the schedules, the chat show and the crime series rise; but the broad lines of the original settlement persist.

The power of the settlement can best be seen in those new satellite and cable channels avowedly determined to break the contract. Yet a Sky 1 or a USA network looks, repeats apart, more or less like a mainstream terrestrial channel. Within those new schedules, programming forms also survive pretty much intact. Even the most extreme developments, the provision of a 24-hour rolling news service for example, produces no significant new news agenda nor any change in presentational norms.

Furthermore, every time a call goes forth for a new broadcasting dispensation, because of cable or satellite or digital opportunities, back come the same old programming solutions. The only variant is that, in a multi-channel environment, a genre metamorphoses into a whole service. The 1997 UK applications for terrestrial digital licences produced, among the usual sports, movie and golden oldie offerings, the following: 'The Money Channel – a new way of looking at money for a general audience';[38] 'Nature Live';[39] 'Travel – where to go, what to see and how much to spend around the world'.[40] Three more 100 per cent 'documentary output' channels? We go on making documentaries (and everything else) because nobody has a better idea as to what to do with the channels or the slots within them.

This should not surprise us. All communication systems are inherently conservative because senders and receivers need to understand each other; unilateral deviations from the code by the sender run the danger of producing incomprehension in the receiver. The 'news bunny' might be a breathtakingly brilliant deviation from 'sober' news programming but there is no evidence that the audience understands it as such. It is in this comparatively inert environment that the secret of the documentary's survival can be found.

British documentary was, despite an attack on radical radio shows in the 1930s, an element of 'Home Service' content, corseted by sober public education objectives, ideological usefulness and cheapness. It easily survived the move to television (and prospered because of Grierson's legacy) and the subsequent expansion of channels. Now, with everything else, it is part of a more or less fixed television universe; and, it would seem, will remain so because nothing much in Britain ever really changes, whatever the huffing and puffing of politicians.

Inertia might help us understand what drives the broadcasters but it says little as to why the audience, even in reduced numbers, still turns to 'sober' documentaries. Scholarship, as indicated at the outset, is not much help in answering the question of documentary survival.[41] Bill Nichols, for example, manages to ignore *jouissance* even when raising for the first time the question of documentary's cousinage to the porno movie, the one's representation of 'the real world' echoed by the other's representation of the real sexual act: Ejaculation as Truth. But Nichols ignores the potential pleasures of the pornographic text to concentrate instead on the politics of domination in porn films and the validity of the pornographic 'real'. Soberly he sits, the perfect documentary audience member, before the pornographic image, to suggest that 'we watch and listen, we experience and learn from this discursive reality'.[42] As we have seen, not a lot of laughs.

But, as long as there are enough puritans in the land whose epistephilia does not require all programming to provide laughs (or the cathartic equivalent therefore), 'sober' documentaries will be safe – or rather, will be as safe as they have ever been. Not even Thatcherism (and its stepchild, Birtism) has changed that.

Notes

1   Bill Nichols, *Representing Reality* (Indiana University Press, 1991), p. 3.
2   Christian Metz, 'History/Discourse: Note on Two Voyeurisms', *Edinburgh 76 Magazine*, p. 24.
3   Auguston Preta, Mara De Angelis and Marcella Mazzotti, *The Quest for Quality: Survey on Television Scheduling Worldwide* (RAI, General Secretariat of Prix Italia, June 1996).
4   Richard Kilborn, 'New Contexts for Documentary Production in Britain', *Media, Culture and Society* , vol. 18, no. 1 (January 1996), p. 142.
5   Kilborn, 'New Contexts' (1996), p. 143.
6   Preta *et al.*, *Quest for Quality* (1996), p. 9.
7   Kilborn, 'New Contexts' (1996), p. 143.
8   Charles Hammond Jr., *The Image Decade: Television Documentary 1965–1975* (Hastings House, 1981), p. 250.
9   Brian Winston, *Claiming the Real* (BFI, 1995), pp. 134–5, 153, 213, 237; William Bluem, *Documentary in American Television* (Hastings House, 1968), pp. 100–20. Such programming is also significant for the overall development of documentary. The third network (ABC) in 1960 replied to these series by contracting Time-Life for documentary programming. That production team, led by Robert Drew and cameraman Richard Leacock, introduced mainstream audiences to the new hand-held, available style of Direct Cinema which was to dominate the anglophone documentary into the present (Winston, *Claiming the Real* (1995), pp. 148–54; Brian Winston, *Technologies of Seeing* (BFI, 1996), pp. 80–6; Bluem, *Documentary in American Television* (1968), pp. 121–39.
10 Hammond Jr., *The Image Decade* (1981), p. 251.
11 It is also sometimes argued that the new multi-channel world has more than compensated for the disappearance of the documentary from the broadcast networks with whole channels now devoted to such output. However, the truth is that these outlets command very small audiences. The Discovery Channel, for example, has a cumulative rating of 1.1, that is, around 1 million homes (Christopher Russell, Scott Peters, David Wilkofsky, Arthur Gruen and Joe Chung, *The Veronis, Suhler and Associates Communication Industry Forecast* (VSA, 1996) p. 138). The politically battered public television system remains marginalised, also producing about the same average audience penetration; but, from time to time, as with Ken Burns's series on the American Civil War, it can achieve ratings seven to eight times better than that. Nevertheless, the political climate, where other documentary series on the history of Africa and the Vietnam war have occasioned right-wing threats to the funding of the whole system, has slowly undermined CPB/PBS's will to produce effective work. It reported to RAI that around 55 per cent of its output was documentary, but that apparently included all its news and information programming as well (Preta *et al.*,*The Quest for Quality* (1996), p. 52). Despite these high percentages, between PBS, Discovery and other cable output the total American average television audience for documentary cannot be more than a couple of million homes.
12 Russell *et al.*, *The Veronis, Suhler ... Forecast* (1996), pp. 92, 104–5.
13 It should also be noted that there is a further small specialised audience using the art-house cinema circuit to view the occasional theatrically released feature-length documentary. *Hoop Dreams* (1994) took $5 million at the American box-office (Murray Sperber, 'Hollywood Dreams: *Hoop Dreams* (Steve James, 1994)', *Jump Cut* (1996), no. 40, p. 6). Even more rarely, the most notable example being Michael Moore's *Roger and Me* (1989) which was distributed by Warner, a documentary feature will even make it on to the screens in the local mall (John Corner, *The Art of Record* (Manchester University Press, 1996), pp. 165–70).
14 Colin Seymour-Ure, *The British Press and Broadcasting* (Blackwell, 1992), p. 338.

15   John Corner, 'Documentary Voices', in John Corner (ed.), *Popular Television in Britain* (BFI, 1991), pp. 52–4.

16   Anon., *BBC Handbook 1960* (BBC, 1960), p. 226.

17   Anon., *BBC Handbook 1966* (BBC, 1966), p. 42.

18   Anon., *BBC Handbook 1976* (BBC, 1976), p. 118.

19   Anon., *BBC Handbook 1986* (BBC, 1986), p. 148.

20   Seymour-Ure, *The British Press* (1992), p. 138.

21   William Phillips, 'The Fourfront [sic] of Programming?', *Television*, vol. 31, no. 7, November/December 1994, p. 27.

22   William Phillips, 'Top of the Box', *Television*, vol. 31, no. 1, February/March 1994, pp. 28–30.

23   Ros Coward, 'Too many flies on the wall, all wanting a story', *Guardian*, 11 November 1996.

24   David Munro, 'Death of the documentary', *Stage Screen & Radio*, July/August 1994, pp. 18–19.

25   William Phillips, 'Hit or Miss?', *Television*, vol. 30, no. 7, December/January 1994, p. 29.

26   Munro, 'Death of the documentary' (1994), p, 18.

27   John Grierson, *Grierson on Documentary* (Faber, 1979), p. 48; Winston, *Claiming the Real* (1995), pp. 65–7.

28   Norman Swallow, 'Rotha and Television', in Paul Marris (ed.), *BFI Dossier 16: Paul Rotha* (BFI, 1982), pp. 86–9.

29   Stephen Jones, *The British Labour Movement and Film 1918–1939* (Routledge & Kegan Paul, 1987), p. 23.

30   Winston, *Claiming the Real* (1995), pp. 65–8.

31   Corner, 'Documentary Voices' (1991), p. 44.

32   Corner, 'Documentary Voices' (1991), p. 43.

33   Graham Murdock, 'Citizens, consumers, and public culture', in Michael Skovmand and Kim Christian Schrøder (eds), *Media Cultures: Reappraising Transnational Media* (Routledge, 1992), p. 29.

34   Grierson, *Grierson on Documentary* (1979), p. 85.

35   Noël Carroll, 'Nonfiction film and Postmodernist Skepticism', in David Bordwell and Noël Carroll (eds), *Post-Theory: Reconstructing Film Studies* (University of Wisconsin Press, 1996), pp. 283–306.

36   Carroll, 'Nonfiction film ...' (1996), p. 287.

37   It seems quite clear that the rise of reality TV in America was in no little part a response to the impact of the early 1990 recession on American networking operations. The reconstructions in such programming moves them towards the drama but their cost is still closer to documentary.

38   Anon., *Bid For Multiplex B: Summary*, DTN Digital Television Network (DTN), 21 January 1997, p. 4.

39   Anon., *Application for Multiplex License 'A': Summary*, SDN S4C Digital Networks Limited (S4C), ND, p. 4.

40   Anon., *Bid For Multiplex B: Summary* (1997), p. 4.

41   I too am guilty of this, despite a concern with the popularity of the documentary in the 1930s. Only Michael Renov in a recent and as yet unpublished work has addressed this question with any degree of sophistication ('Charged Vision: The Place of Desire in Documentary Film Theory', paper delivered at *The Documentary Turn* Conference, University of Trondheim, Norway, November 1996).

42   Nichols, *Representing Reality* (1991), p. 210.

10

Tanya Krzywinska

Dissidence and Authenticity in Dyke Porn and Actuality TV

This essay explores the idea that so-called dyke pornography on video is a dissident form of audio-visual distribution, representation and consumption. We cannot understand the meaning of its dissidence unless we situate this form of video pornography in relation to the institutional and cultural orders of contemporary broadcast television. It is also useful to identify the technological and aesthetic signifiers of dyke pornographic video. At the level of content dyke porn is clearly transgressive of the aesthetic, ethical and institutional values of broadcast television and its regulation of the representation of divergent sexualities. However, at the level of formal audio-visual language, the dissident voice of dyke porn has a more complex and intricate relation to cultural shifts at work within contemporary broadcast television. The increased use of video within broadcast television and the use of video to produce and consume Explicit Sex videos demonstrates a broader cultural investment in the encoding of 'authenticity' and verisimilitude.[1] At the level of form Explicit Sex videos intersect with realistic representations in the contemporary media-scape, particularly television's current preoccupation with actuality TV, such as Access TV, and the use of home video and surveillance footage in shows such as *Real TV* (Sky), *You've Been Framed!* (ITV), *XCars* (ITV), *Stop, Police!* (ITV), *Cops* and *Coppers* (Sky). This chapter shows how the present media romance with video technology and its rendering of authenticity (intrinsic to the meanings of Explicit Sex videos and to actuality TV) is an attempt to assimilate the dissident status of dyke pornography and other transgressive low-budget independent video productions, such as Richard Kern's sex, death and drugs videos, which is only partially successful.

The dissident value of dyke pornographic videos becomes apparent if we imagine that one should appear on early evening broadcast television. Dyke porn depicts explicit sexual activity between women which does not conform to broadcast television's heterocentrist family viewing agenda. Explicit Sex videos sell themselves through a generic difference to softcore sex films and broadcast television. This difference lies in their promise to deliver real sex.[2] It is the presence of explicit sexual activity that lends hardcore its dissident meaning. Analysts of cinematic pornography have often argued that it is the depiction of the erect penis and the come-shot that convinces the viewer that the sex is indeed genuine. Pasi Falk,[3] for instance, argues that the erect penis and the male come-shot lend the hardcore film authenticity because they indicate real sexual desire. This cannot be the case with dyke video pornography. Furthermore, it is the specific look and sound of the video on which hardcore is now shot that plays a crucial and performative role in framing the sex as real, and not simulated sex. Broadcast television has also, recently, begun to make frequent use of the specific low-grade look and sound of camcorder footage to signify and corroborate the authenticity of footage. This encoding depends on a marked difference to other types of footage used by broadcast TV. For example, actuality TV programmes such as *Cops I & II, Speed!, Coppers, Real TV, The Real Holiday Show, You've Been Framed!, Real Weddings* and *Police, Camera, Action!*, all make use of either domestically produced camcorder footage or surveillance video footage shot by the emergency services or the police.[4] Unlike the BBC's *999: Lifesavers*, these programmes use what we might be termed 'raw' footage and the events shown are not reinterpretations carried out by actors. The reconstruction of rescues in *999: Lifesavers* and Channel 5's *Survivors* are shot and edited in the same way as a Hollywood disaster movie might be shot, using continuity editing, stage-managed *mise-en-scène* and actors to recreate the event. The difference between *999: Lifesavers* and the other programmes mentioned above lies in the different audio-visual formats and languages that are used, rather than in the intent to create 'real' experience on the broadcast screen. Against the high production values of *999: Lifesavers, Survivors* or fictional-based drama, the grainy low quality of video surveillance or home-produced footage has become a fairly ubiquitous signifier in contemporary television culture of an unmediated real event. This, arguably, has originated through the use of the camcorder in the world of low-budget independent film-making, such as that used by the Explicit Sex film industry in the last ten years.

Alongside the particular look and sound of video-produced footage the context of production also supports the creation of the idea that the footage is unmediated and therefore closer to reality than other types of televisual footage. What underpins this meaning is the idea that new imaging technologies give the individual the opportunity to partake in the production of media images. An example would be the BBC's *Video Nation* series. As a latter-day mass observation exercise, this show allows individuals from diverse class, gender and ethnic backgrounds to say their piece about anything that takes their fancy for about two minutes of air-time. The marketing of new media technologies through science programmes, magazines and advertising often makes the case that domestic technologies will be able to give users greater access to the 'happening' world of communication and will give the opportunity for individuals to have a (perhaps dissident) voice in that world, thereby creating a pluralistic and more democratic media-scape. Advertising for domestic media technology thrives on images of a utopian world of free-access communication. The promise offered is that the camcorder will enable families to capture events that hitherto have not made it to the television screen. Video surveillance imagery too offers the promise of being able to show what is normally hidden from the public gaze, such as driving offences and other urban crime. This has important implications for the policing and reiteration of dominant norms, as well as offering the means to create images that might provide critiques or alternatives to them.

The use of the camcorder as a tool for airing dissident voices has been employed by, for example, eco-activists who have often used it to 'police the police'. These images often appear on broadcast news and potentially offer an alternative view to that of the authorities, although while footage may appear to have the potential to show dissident views this does not add up to a pluralist multi-narrative media-scape. This is because these dissident representations are governed by the ideological framework of the broadcast institutions in which they appear. News and other current affairs programmes might use activist footage to demonstrate 'balance', but, nevertheless, the footage itself cannot be outside broadcast television's own regulations. In terms of dissident sexual voices, the use of the camcorder to show alternative sexualities in any detail will always remain off the broadcast television screen. It is this that lends the hardcore film its generic difference and transgressive status. However, broadcast TV recognises the powerful 'aura' of the illicit video-image and is currently assimilating its form, but not its content, into broadcast space through actuality TV. The 'aura' of the transgressive, dissident image has been used to disguise the discursive function of broadcast TV. The nature of the disguise is precisely in the appearance of unmediated reality which gives the impression that new social truths can be screened which have been captured by individuals outside the broadcast institutions. This raises some very serious problems for the consideration of the camcorder as a vehicle for the dissemination of dissident ideas. Can the camcorder become a tool for social change or is it the case that once footage becomes part of broadcast television the political potential diminishes when it is likely to be preceded or followed by cosy adverts for washing-up liquid? The answer to this question hinges on the way in which authenticity is constructed and used in the media.

Within broadcast television the immediacy of the video camera is instrumental to our belief that what we are seeing is real. The construction of this belief is related to the form as well as the content of what we see –

it is based on a temporally specific technological performance. What we might have believed was genuine and unmediated footage 15 years ago, we might now see as a politically expedient construction. This is because in the media culture of the West new technology is taken to be a measure of and intrinsic to our progress towards truth. Technology becomes therefore a kind of magical fetish that is marketed to us by exploiting our desire to see more and know more than we saw or knew in the past. Technology defines our relationship to the present – it marks our present time and our temporally specific identity in that time. This investment in the present is worked through our relationship with the past. Technology sells because it is marketed as showing that which we could not see or know before and in so doing taps into the psychical dynamics of curiosity and power. New audio-visual technologies are often launched into public consciousness through the idea that they can give us access to the forbidden or the hidden. The camcorder, for example, can show criminal activities in urban spaces and also reveal private and intimate sexual behaviour. The pleasure of watching these events is related to voyeurism and power, both of which are symptomatic of our attempt to get the measure of the world we live in and to act upon it, rather than passively letting it act upon us. It is because of the voyeur/power nexus at work within our investment in technology that psychoanalysis can be of use in helping to explain how the pleasures of Explicit Sex films and actuality TV lean upon the psychical dynamics of identity.

Jean Laplanche, the French psychoanalyst, has in recent years sought to reconfigure Freud's idea that the adult psyche is formed through certain problems that face the small child.[5] Laplanche argues that the child negotiates a series of puzzles that relate to its position in the family and the social order. As children and as adults we are constantly driven to question the nature of our relationships with other people and to ask what it is they desire of us. The desire of the other is then a mystery that is constantly present for all subjects and requires investigation (hence our pleasure in the classical narrative format which sets up a series of puzzles or secrets which are solved for us through the closure of the narrative). The seductive lure of the video camera (and both actuality TV and Explicit Sex films) is that it claims that it can reveal what is usually hidden from view. Explicit Sex films, and dyke films in particular, offer the pleasure of allowing the viewer to see the truth of other people's sexual lives. This puzzle is given greater mystery because of the regulation of broadcast television. For example, the British Broadcasting Corporation prescribes that 'actual sexual intercourse between humans should at no time be transmitted'. The Broadcasting Standards Council and the Independent Television Commission's prescriptions on programme context, scheduling, taste and decency and the implementation of a hard line drawn between the public and the private in sexual matters are intrinsic to the transgressive status of dyke pornography because they help to deepen the mystery, and thereby exacerbate the voyeuristic pleasure (for any viewer), of seeing 'actual' explicit sex represented on the television screen.

The growth of the domestic ownership of video-playback in the last ten years has provided the means by which the Explicit Sex video industry can work around the regulation of gatekeeping institutions such as the British Board of Film Censors and the Obscene Publications Act in the UK. Domestic video-playback meant that the sex film could make the lucrative transition from sleazy, public domain, 'club' sex cinemas to the less easily regulated domain of the home. The exhibition and distribution of Explicit Sex videos, such as *Punky Girls*, are illegal under the terms of the Obscene Publications Act in the UK (which outlaws the distribution of hardcore pornography), but through newspapers such as the *Sport*, softcore magazines, the Internet and programmes such as *Eurotrash* (C4), the hardcore video has become a more common and perhaps more acceptable feature of mainstream culture. The use of video format allows a black-market economy to thrive which lies outside the broadcasting regulators' jurisdiction, thereby adding to the transgressive cultural status of these films. Their dissident status lies in their content, and whether we find these videos morally reprehensible or exploitative or not, their dissidence lies in their representation of a diverse range of sexual activities (S/M, multiple, straight, or same-sex sex). The depiction of these is institutionally cordoned off from the mainstream broadcast television which uses the family as its model audience. Ironically this has meant that the use of video-playback for the exhibition and consumption of illicit sex videos can escape the policing bodies that regulate public domain broadcasting. This represents a counter-cultural use of the television set whereby the forbidden can re-enter the domestic arena. What this shows is that juridical censorship and public service broadcasting values are not able to contain the production and consumption of these films and that regulation itself is instrumental to the dissident and transgressive status of these films the form of which has become synonymous, through a metonymic link with their content, with the representation of reality. An examination of *Punky Girls* reveals how the dyke hardcore film presents itself as depicting genuine sex and how this relates to its dissident status.[6]

Punky Girls features two women who are both dress-coded as latter-day street punks.[7] The film centres on a series of linked sexual games played out by the two women and which also implicate the user in their games of sex and domination.[8] The film was shot using a single location which appears to be a low-rent hotel room masquerading, through the use of black sheeting, as a makeshift studio. The entire video is presented as a single event but the chronology is altered through the editing in order to distribute the climactic highlights evenly throughout the film's 70-minute duration.[9] Many hardcore films are composed of different sexual 'numbers' involving different groups of people mostly lasting for 10 to 15 minutes each. *Punky Girls*, however, concentrates simply on the two women.

There is no use of cross-cutting to other scenes and the entire film is located in the makeshift studio.[10] The temporal and spatial organisation of the film is designed to communicate to the user that they are watching a single 'one-off' sexual encounter, rather than a carefully choreographed ensemble of locations and scenes that one might expect from a high-budget Hollywoodised softcore film. *Punky Girls* parallels the temporal and spatial codes utilised by live-broadcast TV – as you might expect a live football event to be covered or the simulation of live action in the geographical and temporal correspondence with real space and time in a British soap[11] or a video number in *You've Been Framed!* The film includes no voice-over or other anchored point of narration which enhances the sense that what you are seeing is live and unmediated. The single-event shot by one mobile camera adds to the transgressive voyeuristic *frisson* experienced by the user – and in conjunction with other features of the film mentioned above creates the sense that you are seeing a live snapshot event which has not been staged specifically for the camera. The form of the film, alongside its content, thus reinforces the communication that you are watching an event 'in the raw'.

What this demonstrates is that Pasi Falk's and Linda Williams's arguments that it is the erect penis that guarantees the authenticity of the sex in these films is misguided. In *Punky Girls* the endorsement that the sex is indeed genuine is not entirely focused on the bodily feats performed by the two women, such as fist-fucking. The coding of these bodily feats as real is achieved by their being framed by two intertextual technological strategies. First, *Punky Girls* parallels cinematic and televisual strategies that are associated with documentary and factual film-making. Secondly, when the film is read against the hyperreal visual and aural codes of special effects Hollywood, the use of low-tech signifiers differentially codes the film as amateur. Because of the exclusion of the penis as a primary signifier of real sex and desire, this means that *Punky Girls* inherently problematises the reading of Explicit Sex film as a phallocen-trically determined ordering of reality, which, in my view as a queer-feminist, adds to the dissident status of the film.

The association with documentary and amateurism is written into *Punky Girls* through the audio-visual techniques used to stage the scene between the two women. Primarily it is the differences from Hollywood narrative cinema that links the film with documentary, actuality TV and domestically produced video. For example, the lighting used in the film is a simple three-point lighting scheme, which functions to reduce shadows and create visual access to the women's bodies. Unlike Hollywood, which uses lighting to sculpt the faces and bodies of Hollywood stars, the lighting here is not designed to mask what in the ego-ideal world of Hollywood and television advertising would be seen as bodily defects (spots, blemishes, bruises, stretch marks, etc.). Through this difference the idiosyncratic bodies generic to low-budget porn become the marks that ratify the authenticity of the sex we see.[12] The lighting in most Explicit Sex films, and *Punky Girls* is no exception, is designed to give the user added voyeuristic access to the parts of the body which are often shadowed out or covered up in broadcast television, softcore or art-house films – female genitals displayed openly to the camera becomes a sign of authenticity through the presence of what is normally hidden. The increased visibility is part of the Explicit Sex video's generic promise to show everything and hide nothing. Because of the absence of close-ups of women's genitals in mainstream media, the close-ups in the hardcore video work differentially and intertextually to signal authenticity. Thereby the guarantee of genuine sex and desire and the construction of an aura of presence is not construed simply, as Falk maintains, through the representation of the erect penis, but instead, in the dyke video, through presence of the, usually hidden, vagina shot in close-up and framed by textual strategies that have become associated with the documentary.

The punk style of the women's clothing also lends another kind of authentic status to the sex depicted in the film, as punk is often associated with transgressive behaviour. Within cultural discourse of the late 1970s and 1980s punk was a style that was often seen as an authentic working-class youth culture (read against hippie culture which was taken as a middle-class sub-culture). The two women's S/M dress and their iconographic coding – one has a mohican and the other a clean-shaven head – lends the video a further authentic *frisson* since the user may construe that their participation in a porn film is typical of the taboo-busting behaviour of punk sub-culture. The S/M dyke, with her inherent rejection of the heterosexist order and her recognition that power is an intrinsic component of sex and desire, constitutes an image of sexual and gender dissidence and it is her clothing that strikingly signals this. The sparkling luciferean light that fetishistically bounces off the metal rings of the two women's body harnesses and their PVC clothing creates a glittering pathway that directs the user's attention to the detail of the women's breasts and genitals. The metal, plastic and leather are also important in the sound-field of the film as they creak and clank, enhancing the visual sway and movement of their bodies. The S/M dress may also add visual and auditory spectacle to the sex depicted in the film, but through its association with punk and its function in the sound-field it also works to communicate authenticity. The sound of the clothing, accentuated through the technique used for recording sound, is instrumental to the representation of real sex and therefore warrants a closer analysis.

In *Hardcore* Linda Williams asks why a genre dedicated to realism uses non-synchronous sound (sound which was not recorded with the image) which tends to produce discontinuities between the sound and the image.[13] The technique of dubbed sound, used by a number of older European and US Explicit Sex films, is a good example of this and is typified by the image of a woman whose mouth is full of an erect penis yet (impossibly) nevertheless still utters loud cries of pleasure.[14] As this example instances, the effect of dubbing often provides an unintentionally comic dimension to the films and, as Williams says, detracts from their realism. Williams suggests that the use of dubbed sound is economically driven because it is easier and cheaper to film silently (she is referring to films that were shot on celluloid) and to dub studio-recorded sound on to the image in post-production.[15] Many recently produced Explicit Sex videos, such as *Punky Girls*, which are targeted at a (so-called) global market, do not use dubbed sound, but instead use subtitles. The main reason for the demise of dubbed studio sound is that camcorders have built-in microphones (which means that the comic effects produced by clumsy dubbing can be avoided); consequently, the industry recognises that for realism to be maintained the sounds must be seamlessly and directly related to the image. The use of synchronic sound provides both a legal and an economic advantage to the industry as the videotape, unlike celluloid, does not have to be specially processed. In the video-wired West, it is now cheaper and less problematic to produce a film using the soundtrack recorded by the in-camera microphone than to add the soundtrack (non-diegetic music or studio-dubbed sound) in post-production. This has implications for the links between low-tech, amateurism and the illusion of presence lent by the presence of the sexual body *in extremis*.

In high production value, celluloid sex films made in the 1960s and 1970s, the inclusion of music and non-synchronous sound accentuates the constructedness of the film, which means that these older films are more likely to be read as orchestrated performances. The lack of music or dubbed non-synchronous sound in *Punky Girls* is due to the sole use of synchronous sound recording (meaning that the recording of the sound occurs during the filming of the scene, rather than being added later). This contrasts with the use of non-synchronous sound and the presence of a musical soundtrack to accompany sexual 'numbers' in older Explicit Sex films.[16] The technological crudeness of the sound in the more recently produced Explicit Sex videos, with all their lack of balance and extraneous 'noise', differs from the booming, synthesised and montaged hyperreal sound of Hollywood and television advertising.[17] The sound-field of *Punky Girls* then resembles that used in 'fly-on-the-wall' television documentaries or real-time news reports at the scene of a crisis or disaster. The particular character of the sound in these examples has come to connote immediacy and direct access to raw reality.

The sound technique used to help produce the aura of presence and authenticity is known as 'close-miking'. This means placing the microphone very close to the sound source during filming. In the case of *Punky Girls*, the camera microphone would fulfil this function as the room in which the action is filmed is very small. The use of close-miking as the sole source of sound creates the impression of a very intimate soundscape. In

Punky Girls, the microphone picks up on the minutiae of creaking of leather and PVC, the sounds of skin brushing against skin, the sounds of well-lubricated penetration and the range of vocal sounds from gentle breathing to loud gasps of impending orgasm. The effect of close-miking in a small room is that the sounds made by the women appear to be very close to the hearer's ears; not necessarily because it is loud, but because the absence of room noise creates a sense of an enclosed space which links the video to the acoustics of domestic space. The consequent intimacy heightens the voyeuristic and eavesdropping dynamic of the scene.

The detail produced by close-miking, its association with other 'realist' genres and the immediacy attributed to camcorder technology (which records the sound on location rather than being produced by a foley artist[18]), are instrumental to the way that sound is used to enhance the verisimilitude of *Punky Girls*. Furthermore, the use of the camera microphone in conjunction with the shaky camera work, the flat, rather grainy image produced by the video camera, and the jumpy editing all work to create a sense that what is being watched is a real and unstaged sexual encounter because its production values are associated with amateurism. How, then, does amateurism become associated with authenticity?

Linda Williams argues that 'stag' films[19] in the early part of the twentieth century deliberately made use of low production values to create a difference between the professional striptease (as a public, revenue-based performance) and the explicit depiction of candid sexual intercourse.[20] The current use of video camera technology mirrors this use of low production values to create the sense that what is being watched is genuine and helps to mask the financial motive for this type of film-making. In contemporary culture authentic meaning is produced because the camcorder is linked with domestic, home-made audio-visual production. What began as the incidental characteristic quality of video production, which has become familiar to us through the use of the domestic video camera to film family occasions, has become a meaning system within its own right. This has been facilitated and institutionalised by the Access TV phenomenon in the 1990s. Programmes such as *Video Dairies*, *You've Been Framed!*, *The Real Holiday Show*, alongside home videos, have institutionalised the look and sound of video camcorder footage within contemporary media culture as amateur – capturing the everyday, private domain much in the same way that Super 8 connoted a difference from 35mm before the advent of video. It is through the association between the camcorder image and its domestic use, in conjunction with the exploitation of the difference from high production values, that camcorder footage is read as candid. Thus an analogue or association has been created between amateurism and authenticity. In terms of dissidence this has interesting implications. Birthday party footage is then linked at a formal level to hardcore footage. Programmes like *You've Been Framed!*,

Blind Date or *The Real Holiday Show* exploit the authentic meaning of the camcorder image in much the same way that a contemporary dyke pornographic video does, and both lean upon voyeuristic and eavesdropping pleasures but with different political status.

The question that is raised by the recent plethora of actuality programmes on contemporary broadcast TV is why there is so much investment in authenticating rather banal types of representation. Despite the frequent postmodern cliche that the real has been replaced in contemporary culture by simulation (which has no original), I would, following Baudrillard,[21] maintain that authenticity has an increased currency in contemporary media. Baudrillard uses the term 'authentic' to denote the way in which the contemporary media disguises its inherent mediating function and to show how postmodern culture masks its lack of raw experience by attempting to persuade us to take representation as if it were reality. Contemporary media promises to deliver first-hand experience to the viewer as a means of countering the inherent second-hand nature of mediation. As a result actuality TV is based on an anxious pursuit of the real. This is nothing new; previous 'new' technologies, such as the stills camera, were sold as having the capacity to capture and freeze time and to validate the reality of our experience (such as the holiday or birthday party snap). While we might know that the camcorder image is always a rendering of an event, and not the event itself, we are encouraged to deny this scepticism and take the audio-visual analogue of an event as if it were the event itself. This operation is intrinsic to the meaning of the camcorder image and the meanings associated with the sexual body in Explicit Sex videos. New technologies help to disguise their own mediating presence because we are seduced by their apparent ability to circumvent mediation. Once a 'new' technology becomes superseded by yet another new technology, this magic dissipates. In other words, the newness of a technology functions as a means for covering over representation's inability to capture the real event. The newness of a technology and its perceived ability to see more than previous technologies helps to stave off the crisis around the status of the real in a media-saturated postmodern culture. Unlike the photograph, once the camcorder became available to a domestic market, broadcast television's growing hunger for cheaply produced programmes began to find ways of exhibiting domestically produced material (*You've Been Framed!*, for instance). While the camcorder has the capacity to enable dissident images, the main use of domestically produced footage is as a form of family-oriented light entertainment (with all its race, class, sexual and gender assumptions). The 'real' footage used by shows like *You've Been Framed!* is not, then, put to dissident ends. The encoding of the camcorder image to signify reality is used to reinforce an image of family life according to a heterocentrist model. In shows based on footage shot by the emergency services or the police, such as *Stop, Police!* or *Coppers*, the aim is to police behaviour by creating bad driving or urban crime as a spectacle of 'otherness' – deviance that can, it is implied, be seen at any time by the policing agents through the ever-increasing surveillance power of new technology. Thus, actuality TV does not use realism to promote social change but rather to produce conformity to the rules and mores of the incumbent system. In contrast, *Punky Girls* speaks a dissident voice against those very rules and whose realism proves the existence of alternative modes of gender and sexual behaviours and relationships

The camcorder's power to signify verisimilitude is built around a question that is posed to the viewer: is what I am seeing here authentic? The question has two distinctive features. First, it is grounded in technology's promise to reveal what has previously not been shown. Second, it relies on a sceptical doubt, borne of representation, about the truth of what is being shown. Truth, as a discourse, depends on doubt and reality-testing which operates as a primary means of actively engaging the user with a given text (for example, wondering if any of the video numbers in *You've Been Framed!* were staged). In *Punky Girls* scepticism is aroused through the appearance of a series of contradictions that interrupts verisimilitude and therefore might burst the closeted voyeuristic bubble. A particular instance of this is the sound of a stills camera motor and flash being used off-screen. This sound jars the smooth rhythm of the sounds of sex and jerks the user into an uncomfortable and/or exciting recognition of their own voyeuristic/eavesdropping position (rather as if you were somehow caught watching what was not meant for you to see and perhaps being photographed doing it). The camera's audible presence also puts into question the motives of the two protagonists by creating an ambiguous tension between their genuine 'innocent' pleasure in the sex and the deliberate manipulation of the user. The sound of the stills camera's motor functions as an extra-diegetic comment on the scene (as well as startling the user) which highlights the sexual performance *as* performance and foregrounds the user as addressee of the scene. The flaw in the verisimilitude is extremely prominent and, rather than distancing the user from the text, it places the viewer in the scenario of being caught watching which leans on what Freud has called the fantasy of 'parental coitus'.[22]

Freud frequently asserted the importance of unconscious fantasy in the formation of the adult psyche. There are, argues Freud, three 'primary' foundational fantasies – parental coitus, seduction and castration – which are produced in response to questions the child has about who they are in the family and in the social order. All of these fantasies purport to explain the origins of certain factors that are important to the life of the child and which relate to identity. Jean Laplanche uses Freud's notion of primary fantasy to make the point that the small child is aware of messages that are carried in the speech and actions of the child's carers. Thus the child is subject to the 'secret discourse' of the family.[23] Primary fantasies are 'like myths' and:

claim to provide a representation of, and a solution to, the major enigmas which confront the child. Whatever appears to the subject as something in need of explanation or theory, is dramatised as a moment of emergence, the beginning of a history ... the primal scene (parental coitus) pictures the origin of the individual.[24]

A key component of the fantasy of parental coitus is overhearing – such as the fantasy of overhearing noises in the night that are not meant for the child's attention but seem to require a response. For the adult particular sounds might then become loaded with extra meaning that is derived from the unconscious fantasy of parental coitus. The sound of the stills camera in *Punky Girls* is one such sound. It further projects the user into the place of the child who, witnessing parental coitus, fantasises about being caught listening or watching. The inaudible whisperings between the two women in the film also evoke the *frisson* of figuring out what these messages might mean and thereby taps into the complex knot of enigmas around sexuality faced by the child which are mapped onto the enigma of same-sex sexual practice. Here dissidence and transgression become entwined because of the ubiquitous but repressed presence of the primal fantasy. Because *Punky Girls* taps into the unconscious economy of the primal fantasy, the experience of seeing its forbidden images of explicit same-sex sex becomes loaded with transgressive, and therefore dissident, meaning.

The fantasy of parental coitus is a response to the child's questions about their place in the family. The adults in that family present the child with half-heard messages about their sexual desire which act as a puzzle to be solved by the child through imagined scenarios. The child further explains his or her own feelings of sexual desire through a further fantasy – that of seduction. Laplanche uses the term 'primal seduction' to 'describe a fundamental situation in which an adult proffers to a child verbal, non-verbal and even behavioural signifiers which are pregnant with unconscious sexual signification'.[25] The child disavows its own desire by projecting its origin onto another person. *Punky Girls* restages for the user the enigmatic quality of sexuality experienced by the user as a child. The sex in *Punky Girls* is presented as an enigma through the dissident status of lesbian S/M sex, through the presence of secret sexual discourse and through the foregrounding of voyeurism created by the sound of the stills camera. The investigative aspect of voyeurism is a means by which the subject is given a pleasurable sense of control purporting to solve the sexual secrets of lesbian sex. However, the glamour (in the sense of seduction) of the Explicit Sex film is that, although the secret life of lesbians is made visible to the user, the mystery is never fully resolved. (This is the case even if the user identifies as an S/M dyke.) The whispered exchanges between the two women are never fully heard, which means that something is always withheld from the user. This is important if the film is to retain its aura of dissidence. So, on the one hand, *Punky Girls* promises the user that it will tell the truth about lesbian S/M sex, a truth withheld by broadcast television, but on the other hand it also maintains the aura of a forbidden discourse through the intimate, exclusive whispering which the user is not invited to hear. The narratives that are proffered as solutions to the enigma of sexuality are never fully successful, if they were then we might 'close the book' on sexuality, as its mystery would be solved and the desire to know would cease.[26] Actuality TV, too, operates with the same type of promise. It purports to show aspects of private life that have hitherto only been represented in a fictional way and which therefore use the same psychic mechanisms (the pleasure and power of knowledge) at work in the Explicit Sex film. Both forms sell themselves through the promise to evade psychic and institutional repression and thereby lean on the drive, which underpins the fantasy of parental coitus, to knowledge. (This provides a dissident reading of actuality TV – because it demonstrates that our investment in this form of TV leans on the same principles as that used in the reception of Explicit Sex films.)

The links between the enigmatic status of certain aspects of private life and the media's investment in authenticity are important to the understanding of the way that reality is represented in today's media. The disconcerting meshing of fantasy and reality which creates a sense of ambiguity is dealt with by strategies that cover over mediation. One such strategy is what Derrida calls the 'metaphysics of presence';[27] wherein the human voice is privileged over the written word. Actuality and Access TV are lauded as giving a voice to the common people and the accessee's voice, according to Derrida's model, becomes the means by which the viewer can measure the integrity and desire of the speaker. In *Punky Girls*, for instance, the whispering voices and the sounds of sexual pleasure are decoded by the user as if they were phenomenal and not representational.

The idea that speech (and the sound of the voice) is immediate and therefore escapes the representational system is revealed by Derrida as a production of a certain hierarchical organisation of knowledge. In this organisation the voice, particularly if addressed directly to the viewer, functions as if it were more authentic than the written word with its connotations of careful thought. This has no immanent basis (even though it draws upon the child's reception of messages as demanding an answer) and operates as a comforting illusion of truthfulness through which hegemonically driven mappings between artifice and reality can be assured. Derrida calls this privileging of the voice 'phonocentrism'; the spoken word appears to be somehow freer and more genuine than the written word. The operation of phonocentrism is evident in on-the-spot interviews with politicians. As the voice is seen to come directly from the body of the politician, it appears to be unique to the individual speaker, as author of their own words, and therefore gives the sense that their words are an expression of their 'real' views. The intonations of the voice, accompanied by non-verbal cues (such as the direction and quality of their gaze) all aid the sense that their words are from the heart, rather than a spin-doctor's prepared speech. Straight-to-camera shots and interviews, or a-day-in-the-life-of footage, maintain the illusion of de-textualised speech through its apparent immediacy, and aids the viewer's sense that duplicitous speech can be detected. The sound of the voice in Explicit Sex films such as *Punky Girls* also gives cues about the authenticity of the sexual activity to the user. The voice is read to test if true pleasure is really being experienced by its enunciator. Because women's pleasure in sexuality is not readily evidenced, the measure of authenticity lies in a close appraisal of the sounds of their voices.

In her book *The Acoustic Mirror* Kaja Silverman links Derrida's phonocentrism to a psychoanalytic reading of the role of the mother's voice for the child. For Silverman the mother's voice becomes a site of fantasy for the child. She states that the mother's voice functions for the child as a 'sonorous envelope'[28] which signifies to the child the mother's power to lull or terrify. The cultural investment in phonocentrism leans on the child's acute investigative reading of the mother's voice (to read the grain of her desire). The sounds of the voices in *Punky Girls* are then closely read for signs of their desire in much the same way as a politician's voice might be read for signs of duplicity and desire. This is perhaps why Margaret Thatcher's voice was worked upon by voice coaches, to make it less like the voice of a terrifying mother; and also why Tony Blair has had recourse to interview in the government's attempt to contain the Bernie Ecclestone/Formula One affair.

The pleasure of *Punky Girls*, for me at least, is the tension produced between the traditionally mutually exclusive discourses of authenticity and performativity which draws attention to my position as voyeur and implicates me as addressee of the scene. The film also offers forbidden images of sexuality that I rarely see on the television screen. Ironically, it is through the Explicit Sex film that the operation of authenticity in actuality TV can be seen to operate at the level of signification and in terms of psychical investments in these significations. My approach to *Punky Girls* might be taken to be a form of reading against the grain (a queer, dissident reading) as might my linking of actuality TV to the pornographic video. For some, *Punky Girls* may be read as simply dissonant rather than dissident. However, I would maintain that the ambiguity created in *Punky Girls* is instrumental to its dissident status, the origin of which can be traced back through the repressed, but still operational, dynamics of fantasy that govern our relation to the world. Sex caught apparently red-handed by the video camera is dependent for its meaning on the technology's exploitation and manipulation of psychic mechanisms, such as the drive to knowledge. This complex relation underpins the contemporary romance with new media technologies by promoting a libidinally charged investment in their power to see the hidden and the forbidden. Although the use of the television set to view Explicit Sex films in the domestic space circumvents broadcasting regulations and as such can be considered to be a dissident use of the television, the re-use of the form of Explicit Sex films in actuality TV and other documentary-style television means that its dissident status is in the process of being assimilated into mainstream media. This consideration of the way in which the hardcore porn film engages the user in terms of the investigative gaze has enabled the libidinal investment in actuality TV to be made more explicit. Whether or not one considers the Explicit Sex film to be a means for the straight viewer to access the private world of dyke S/M, *Punky Girls* relies on its dissident status for its market difference, and because of its content, it will resist assimilation into the heterocentrist, 'family values' agenda of the mainstream media.

Notes

1   Rather than using the term 'pornography' or 'hardcore' to describe these films, I have chosen to use the term 'Explicit Sex' to indicate that I am referring to a specific film genre which uses certain signifiers to define its difference from other representations of sex.

2   This is typified by the inclusion of the following in the mail-order catalogue for a distribution company called Choices Direct:

> Now you can enjoy *genuine*, erotic, uncensored adult entertainment at a remarkable price you can afford ... Are your titles 'the real thing'? Yes, the action in all our videos is completely uncensored and as described in the brief for each title.' (my italics) (Choices Direct)

3   P. Falk, 'Outlining the Anti-aesthetics of Pornography', in *Theory, Culture and Society*, vol. 10, no. 2, May 1993; P. Falk, *The Consuming Body* (Sage, 1994).

4   *Cops I & II* and *Coppers* are all 'fly-on-the-wall' documentary shows that follow the daily routine of US and British policeman going about their daily business of arresting suspects. These shows constitute a staple programming for Sky 1 on satellite. The format is also becoming popular with British terrestrial TV, such as *Stop, Police!* and *999*.

5   J. Laplanche and J-B. Pontalis, 'Fantasy and the Origins of Sexuality', in V. Burgin, J. Donald, and C. Kaplan, (eds), *Formations of Fantasy* (Routledge, 1986); J. Laplanche, *New Foundations for Psychoanalysis* (Blackwell, 1989); J. Laplanche, *Jean Laplanche: Seduction, Translation, Drives* (ICA, 1992).

6   The close focus on a particular film is doubly important here as many analyses of hardcore pornography fail to make close reference to the texts. Catherine Itzin, for example, in her book *Pornography:Women, Violence and Civil Liberties* only makes comment on the covers of a range of hardcore films and rarely mentions the actual content of the films themselves. (C. Itzen (ed.), *Pornography: Women, Violence and Civil Liberties* (Oxford University Press, 1992), pp. 46–9.)

7   There is no date on the videotape, but I would estimate that it was made within the last five years.

8   The term 'user' is used to indicate the active bodily role of the 'ideal' viewer of these films.

9   Hardcore films differ from most Hollywood films in that they are episodically structured. The aim is to 'move' the body and therefore the separate episodes can be used as a prelude to the user's own sexual activity in which case the whole video may not be watched.

10   Multiple locations and the construction of a complex diegetic world is a common feature of pre-video narrative sex-films, such as *Emmanuelle* (Just Jaeckin, 1974, France) discussed in Linda Williams's book *Hardcore* (Pandora, 1990).

11   'The opening credits of the British soap *Brookside* clearly invites us into a geographical space, Liverpool with its cathedrals and municipal buildings' (C. Geraghty, *Women and Soap Opera* (Blackwell/Polity,1991), p. 14). 'The passage of time [in British soaps] is marked by references to the "real" world of the viewer' (Geraghty, *Women and Soap Opera* (1991), p. 12).

12   The presence of 'ordinary' bodies, as opposed to the air-brushed, soft-focus bodies of Hollywood and softcore, are pleasurable to some readers, including myself, because the ordinary body is so rarely displayed in other cinematic and televisual forms. In this sense spots and stretch marks become signs of a lived-in dissenting body which is counter to the hegemony of flawless beauty purveyed by mainstream audio-visual production. Not all Explicit Sex films conform to this, however; many, particularly films produced in the US, feature women who are surgically enhanced and who are much closer to Hollywood's ideal bodies – for example, Michael Ninn's *Latex* (1995).

13   Williams, *Hardcore* (1990), pp. 123–5.

14   In hardcore it is traditionally women who utter louder and more intense noises than men, who tend to moan in a more subdued way and only cry out during orgasm. This is perhaps because women's sexual pleasure in Explicit Sex film is more easily faked than men's therefore women's louder cries are meant to convey the pleasure that cannot be immediately seen (as is the case with an erect penis).

15   It should be noted that Williams's study of hardcore film focuses on the history of the genre – from 'stag' films through to the narrative-based Hollywood-style films made in the 1970s. She does not assess the impact of video technology on the form of recent Explicit Sex films. Most of her information on the production of Explicit Sex films comes from Stephen Ziplow's *The Film Maker's Guide to Pornography*, written in 1977; well before video playback became a common household commodity, which means that she does not address the shifts from celluloid to video formats in the production of these films.

16   Explicit Sex videos which actively target a MTV audience do include music to accompany sexual numbers, and higher-budget films which attempt to construct a story also use music.

17   This difference has made its way into Hollywood movies, for example, *Henry, Portrait of a Serial Killer, Man Bites Dog* and *Natural Born Killers*, in which grainy video footage, with its concomitant limited, low-tech, sound-field, is intercut and juxtaposed with hyper-real celluloid footage with its treated sound field, making the video elements stand out as more authentic.

18   A 'foley artist' reproduces aspects of a sound-field, particularly background sounds, which are rarely recorded on location as it is difficult to control the levels of location background sound.

19   'Stag' films were one-reel films made in the early part of the twentieth century that depicted Explicit Sex. Linda Williams found examples of these films in the Kinsey Institute with titles such as *Am Bend* (Germany c. 1910), *El Satario* (Argentina, c. 1907–12), *The Casting Couch* (1924) and *The Virgin in Hot Pants* (c. 1923–25) (Williams, *Hardcore* (1990), pp. 58–92).

20   Williams, *Hardcore* (1990), p. 77.

21   J. Baudrillard, 'Simulacra and Simulations', in P. Brooker, *Modernism/Postmodernism* (Longman, 1992).

22   'Among the store of unconscious phantasies of all neurotics, and probably all human beings, there is one which is seldom absent and which can be disclosed by analysis: this is the phantasy of watching sexual intercourse between the parents ...' (S. Freud, 'A Case of Paranoia Running Counter to the Psychoanalytic Theory of the Disease', in *On Psychopathology* (Pelican, 1979), p. 154). Freud's view that adult sexuality is

based on the vicissitudes of fantasy, rather than physiological 'fact', means that this theory of sexuality still retains 'dissident' status.

23   Laplanche and Pontalis, 'Fantasy and the Origins of Sexuality' (1986), p. 19.
24   Ibid.
25   Laplanche, *New Foundations for Psychoanalysis* (1989), p. 126.
26   The (perverse) irony here is that discourses of monogamy and celibacy as part of Christianity work to maintain the enigmatic status of sexuality – the translation of sex into sublimity and love is nevertheless based upon sexual curiosity and primary fantasies of castration, seduction and parental coitus.
27   J. Derrida, *Writing and Difference* (Routledge, 1978). Brigitte Sohm, Christina de Peretti, Stephane Douailler, Patrice Vermeren and Emile Maley, 'The deconstruction of actuality: an interview with Jacques Derrida', in *Radical Philosophy*, 68, Autumn 1994.
28   K. Silverman, *The Acoustic Mirror* (Indiana University Press, 1988), p. 73.

11

David Chapman

Downloading the Documentary

The apparatus and institution of the cinema ushered in the twentieth century, offering both a confirmation of technological progress and a promise of new advances and pleasures to come. Heroic times. But as we contemplate the approaching twenty-first century and a new millennium, it appears that we now have emerging communication and entertainment media which seem to offer similar confirmations and promises.

The new digital media, specifically the Internet, have in a few short years made an enormous impact, threatening to supersede or re-model existing media and cultural forms. With the constant proliferation of new hard and software the pace of development is both exhilarating and daunting. The converted confidently anticipate a revolutionary juncture in human communication, with the new technology engendering a whole new world of possibilities and meaning in the way we produce, distribute and consume information and images. Others, less impressed, see a new technological threat to further erode interpersonal relations, cultural values and social cohesion.

The medium of television seemed until fairly recently to have a secure position as the dominant form of mass entertainment and edification. And yet, from whatever perspective you approach it, television will be significantly altered by the new media. Such will become the dominance of the digital media that it is predicted by MIT's Medialab director Nicholas Negroponte that the television set itself, as a distinct piece of domestic technology and furniture, is doomed to extinction.[1] In its place will stand the personal computer which, apart from its current multifarious functions, will also serve as the reception point in the home for the proliferating number of television channels.

This predicted shift from television screen to computer monitor as the dominant site of media consumption in the developed world raises a whole series of questions and some potentially worrying problems. If the entertainment potential and profitability of these new technologies is more or less assured, what will be the effect of these developments on the documentary and the audiences they hope to address?

Why documentaries matter, especially for the left, is a belief in their 'progressive' potential as an educative and political tool, acting as a spur to a wider social activism via information and debate. It is this conception of documentary that concerns me here. In the postwar period the documentary in the United Kingdom, without denying its cinematic tradition, has for all intent and purposes been a televisual form. This is based historically on television inheriting from radio a 'Reithian' conception of Public Service Broadcasting (PSB). This maintained the necessity, in a pluralist society, for the wide range of issues that affected our social and political life to be examined and discussed via the dominant means of communication. In short, as well as entertain, broadcasting should both inform and educate. It also presupposes that there is a persistent demand, by a large section of viewers, for at least an occasional access to factual programming beyond news reports.

The PSB ethos, if always problematic in terms of its implementation and ideological impetus, did secure, at least in the UK, an extensive production and distribution base for documentary. In recent years the combination of ideologically fired media deregulation and the emerging new delivery systems (offering a largely spurious diversity of choice) has without doubt eroded PSB.

These developments have caused concern with regard to the financing of challenging factual programming in an industry becoming increasingly more competitive and deferential to audience ratings. The shift to an even more individuated means of consumption, as represented by the personal computer, could be seen to further undermine the continuation of the television documentary as a mass form and locus for national debate. The 'mass', in this equation, relies on a large-scale television audience with a relatively restricted choice of channels, yet underpinned by a PSB ethos which maintains high levels of factual programming and a degree of diversity. If the aforementioned proliferation of delivery systems is already causing this large-scale audience to diminish, the increasing access to the new media would seem to hasten its fragmentation still further. If this isn't enough, we are soon to witness the coming on-stream of a possible 200 digital satellite channels targeted for the European market, the majority seemingly already destined to be under the control of Rupert Murdoch – not the most heartening of prospects.

It seems that very soon gracing either our monitors or television screens will be some form of 'top box'. This will offer the viewer a personal choice from a vast array of programmes and features. Even the titles of these new forms of consumption underline some of the problems ahead. Video-on-Demand, suggestive as it is of enhanced consumer choice, or the more up-front Pay-Per-View, both clearly place the individual's spending power as the determining factor as to what reaches the screen. In this situation it will be the large-scale audiences for drama, light entertainment and sport that will inevitably prove the most profitable. The relatively small audiences drawn to documentary programming (excluding, perhaps, wildlife programmes and 'reality TV' and docu-soaps) may prove too insignificant to justify the production of challenging documentary programmes on the scale previously enjoyed in this country. These systems must appear ideal to broadcasters as a way of exploiting certain forms, but it is more than likely to be to the detriment of a more pluralistic televisual culture.

If these technological advances and the existing economic and ideological structures are working to the detriment of PSB, in what ways can the new media be co-opted to a progressive practice and perhaps engender new documentary forms? Any developments will be determined by the rate of technological advancement and the developing market for these products. Whatever the hyperbole surrounding the new media, it is clear that computer ownership and access to the Internet are growing, both nationally and internationally, at a phenomenal rate. According to figures published in *Screen Digest* the Internet has been doubling in size each year since 1988 and growing faster than any communications medium, or electronic consumer product, in history.[2] Internet access is also starting to become a standard facility in many schools, colleges and public libraries and the success of the first 'cybercafés' should also see this type of access point steadily increase.

This growing ownership and access suggest that digital media cannot for much longer be considered the preserve of the moneyed or the metropolitan elites. The relative cheapness of the equipment, compared with other communication technology, could also potentially offer some redress to the vast disparity of information flow between developed and developing countries. However, it is important not to fall prey to a species of technological determinism which regards the new media as either valuable in themselves, or to be resisted as yet another advance for consumer capitalism that further erodes our collectivity. But as indicated by the use of the Internet in a wide range of political actions from the anti-roads protests in Britain to the Zapatista uprising in Mexico, these technologies have enormous potential for enhancing, democratising and de-centralising communication, and for the forging of new political and social alliances.

In trying to speculate on a possible future relationship between documentary practice and the new media there is, along with the effect on the wider broadcasting environment, the possibility of a specific documentary practice formed in relation to the new media.

Multimedia, the 'linked' combination of video, stills, graphics, sound and text, most commonly in evidence at present in the form of CD-Roms and Web sites, has great potential as a medium for documentary production. A documentary in multimedia form offers different options for its consumption. The viewer's desire for further information can be fulfilled through hypertext (layered and linked pages of text) which could include additional research information, or provide fuller explanations of issues under discussion or theoretical perspectives informing the work. Yet this information would remain woven into the visual and narrative fabric of the piece, to be accessed when required, without recourse to another medium – as is the case with written support material. Multimedia allows the viewer to create new conjunctures and pathways through the text as desired. In left cultural practice, the question of producing an intellectual engagement with the text has been a key factor in characterising its political efficacy. From this perspective it is tempting to view the possibilities offered by multimedia in terms of opening up some form of 'neo-Brechtian' practice. The characteristics of hypertext and notions of interactivity integral to multimedia could be seen as moving documentaries produced in this form out of a 'passive' mode of consumption into something much more active and dynamic. The ability to break the narrative flow, and to explore issues and perspectives in greater depth as the viewer chooses, moves viewing into a more fluid and discursive mode than a 'linear' documentary format – whatever the formal strategies employed. Of course, interactivity in itself is not 'progressive' unless assigned to a specific social or political understanding, but the way multimedia can be structured allows for a much freer interaction with a text. It could also allow a single text to be opened up, via the Internet, to a whole range of additional work and information, along with inter-personal or organisational contacts.

The greater ease in the manipulation of digital material means that sound and images that are offered in evidence or as part of an expositional strategy are to a greater extent 'liberated' from the drive to objectivity based on the verisimilitude of the image. This will potentially allow for a more vibrant melange of material culled from actuality, fictional construction, or the graphic imagination, to become the stuff of documentary – with the proviso that the audience, through viewing the material, can achieve to some extent a greater knowledge or understanding of the world they inhabit. The exact shape of these developments are difficult to envisage, but new formal strategies for fulfilling the documentary purpose seem likely to emerge as digital technology advances.

The limits on quality that pertain at present could be seen acting as a brake to these types of developments. It is often said of multimedia that it has a poorer image than video, a worse sound than hi-fi, and is more uncomfortable to read than the printed page. However, the rate of technological progress is such that this may soon become less of a problem. Those working in the field of development seem confident that full-screen, full-motion video images will be viable in a multimedia form and over the Internet in the near future.

But as these technological difficulties diminish, some of the problems the technicians seek to address may be less pressing than imagined. If the technical 'quality' of image and sound reproduction will improve, it is perhaps also possible to perceive a shift in the way 'quality' is understood by the viewer. For audiences increasingly exposed to images produced on domestic video equipment and computer games, coupled with the growing volume of footage on our screens shot on 'non-broadcast' formats, the question of image quality in terms of standards of definition is becoming less significant. People are now beginning to find the look of non-broadcast format video pleasurable, in the same way that people enjoy the look of Super 8 film, not in terms of a shortcoming but for its own particularity. Alongside this, as is often reiterated, the issues and concerns that enthuse an audience in relation to television are not generally questions of hi-definition images or hi-fidelity sound, but content.

The growing acceptability of 'lo-fi' images has also acted to weaken to a certain extent the control of television exerted through the maintenance of a quality standard based on specific and highly expensive technologies. This 'broadcast standard' will be further eroded by the new range of digital video equipment coming on to the market which offers extremely high-resolution images at relatively low costs. These technological restrictions, alongside fairly rigid ideas of professional practice, have acted in the past to exclude those who have found it impossible to access the levels of funding and training necessary to become 'players'. The emerging ranks of low-budget video producers are perfectly placed in terms of attitude to seize on the new media to produce and distribute their work. This could revitalise the oppositional independent sector which is already showing new signs of life with the mushrooming of new venues and festivals and initiatives like the 'video newspaper' *Undercurrents*.[3] This venture has proved particularly useful in providing an outlet for the extensive use of camcorders in direct-action campaigns over the last few years. It also makes a clear stand against the control of access to television and the nature of the material that finds its way on to the nation's screens.

The problems of distribution for a cassette-based magazine such as *Undercurrents* are enormous and the opportunities offered by digital media seem certain to allow for a more widespread dissemination for this type of work. The Internet has obvious potential in this area, but the greater availability of channels on cable and satellite may also provide new means of distribution. For example, in the United States the combination of mass camcorder ownership and cheap leasing of satellite channels has led to the establishment of progressive channels, such as Deep Dish TV, broadcasting the work of camcorder activists. It was this system which facilitated the Gulf War TV Project which broadcast anti-war programme from activists across the US, creating an important focal point for national resistance to the Gulf War in the face of almost total media support for US Government policy.[4] However, it remains to be seen, with the tighter regulation of the airways that pertains in Britain, whether these routes will be opened up on this side of the Atlantic.

The future possibilities for the home computer to receive, re-assemble, and send forth over the Internet images and information from countless sources may change significantly what we currently understand as television. Just as sampling and MIDI technology has revolutionised the creation of music and thrown into turmoil the whole concept of authorship, these advances could have similar unforeseen effects on television production. If the whole myriad interactions of social and personal contexts determine the way a piece is read, at least it could be assumed we all saw the same thing, if not always at the same time. In the future this seems less likely. Programmes will perhaps become more like 'bundles' of images and information that are cast out into the unknown to be consumed complete or taken apart, rearranged and re-distributed in a variety of different forms determined by personal requirements and tastes. Although this is true at present in relation to the use made of off-air recordings, the difference will be that any digital reworking of material by 'guerrilla' producers could one day be distributed by the same medium as the source programme and at the *same* level of technical quality. In this context documentary producers may become more like news agencies, producing material available to sell whole or piecemeal and protected by a variety of encryption methods and charge systems. Ownership, and the resources to gather specific high-value material, as opposed to authorship, may become the most crucial factor in determining a professional engagement with the medium.

As it is today, in practice it will probably only be the dedicated few who will produce work of consistent worth to rise above the rest. Yet potential producers will increasingly have the means at their disposal to become engaged, and a new generation of occasional producers may emerge, motivated by passing personal preoccupations or acting in response to specific events .

For all the possibilities this wider access offers there are also potential problems. As individuals become able to collect, re-assemble and produce information in a more fluid manner, the opportunity occurs to produce material that panders to preconceptions and prejudices in a way that far outstrips the current limited ideological perspectives offered by national newspapers and television channels. In this environment the need for more generalised dissemination of information of a consistently challenging type is more crucial than ever, if a broader political debate is to be maintained. And yet how is this to be achieved? One way is for a protected space to be guaranteed through legislation. The present government seem set to protect the existing terrestrial channels from the deluge of proposed new digital services. However, this approach is perhaps a mere holding exercise, politically expedient while the majority of viewers have access only to the terrestrial channels. Quality, in terms of high production values, may give a market edge to maintain audience interest and loyalty in the face of ever increasing viewing options.

Yet, in the long term, perhaps a different understanding of distribution and consumption are required. The potential of the Internet to both advertise the existence of specific material and then distribute direct to the viewer *world-wide* is an exhilarating prospect. In this model, documentaries are circulated in a less concentrated form but over a longer period – and with the possibility for updating the information as necessary; from the triumphal screening to a decreasing national television audience (with, hopefully, a repeat, and an after-life on sell-through, or off-air recordings) to a more haphazard, long-term dissemination based on a viewer-led demand for documentary programmes. It is perhaps also possible to see the potential in this situation for a more equitable distribution of images and information between North and South. The Internet also has the obvious potential to create an 'open access' debate between viewers and to build a new, more interactive relationship between producers and their audiences. The production company Illuminations have shown a lead in developing this potential. When commissioned to produce *The Net* for BBC2, they created a Web site, e-mailed information to interested viewers, and held post-programme discussions on-line. A growing number of other producers have now followed their example.

It should go without saying that at this stage the shape of future economic and aesthetic practices that will emerge are hard to predict, although we can attempt to outline some possibilities based on the current situation and foreseeable developments. If old certainties about the relationship of the documentary to television must change, it should not be seen as all downhill. Much of the best may be maintained. But with the adoption by all major political parties of the free market, the extent of the protected national PSB spaces may be small and the audiences widely fragmented. The economic and ideological 'gatekeepers' who currently control access may be outflanked by the Internet's potential to provide a freer dissemination of information, and a more de-centred, democratic structure. However, the new media comes into a world shaped and dominated by existing media structures and economic systems. As the present struggles by Internet users to fight censorship, government control and attempts by large conglomerates to exploit the Net commercially indicate, it may be just the latest site to contest the same old struggles.

If predictions of television's death are rather premature, it is certainly possible to see a very different environment emerging, one where new patterns of production and consumption seem destined to supersede the space for factual programming previously secured by the PSB ethos. A rallying cry of Internet activists in the US, a country without our extensive Public Service traditions, is 'Don't let the Net become as bad as television.'

This may suggest that those with an interest in the maintenance of a progressive and creative televisual culture should explore the potential of the digital realm and help shape its future.

Notes

1   Nicholas Negroponte, *Being Digital* (Hodder & Stoughton, 1996), p. 47.
2   'On the Internet: Paving the way for the superhighway?', *Screen Digest*, April 1995, p. 81.
3   Peter Sibley, 'Video Power', *Vertigo*, Winter 1994/95, pp. 13–14.
4   Martin Lucas and Martha Wallner, 'Resistance by Satellite', in T. Dowmunt (ed.) *Channels of Resistance* (BFI, 1993), pp. 176–94.

Index

Adorno, Theodor, 26
Althusser, Louis, 122
american TV, 147–8, 154, 155, 180
Anderson, Benedict, 87

Bare Necessities, The, 5, 67–71
Barker, Martin, 23
Barthes, Roland, 45, 72, 79, 87, 96, 122
Baudrillard, Jean, 86–7, 168
Baywatch, 60
British Broadcasting Corporation, 3, 12–13, 20, 27–9, 60, 73–8, 110, 133, 134–6, 146, 148–9, 150, 154, 155, 160, 162, 182
Benjamin, Walter, 6, 56
Between The Lines, 4, 24, 26–30, 33–9
Beverly Hills 90210, 60
Bill, The, 36
Billig, Michael, 102
Bird, John, 128, 131
Blackadder, 8, 131
Black and Blue, 4, 31–2, 38
Bladerunner, 13, 17, 21
Blair, Tony, 13, 86, 138, 141, 143, 144, 172
Brass Eye, 127, 135–6, 144
Brecht, Bertold, 41–3, 179
Bremner, Rory, 128, 129, 131, 132–3, 134, 138, 139, 142
Broomfield, Nick, 146
Brunt, Rosalind, 73, 81
Bryden, Bill, 110–11

Cahiers du Cinema, 109–10, 122
capitalism, 2, 42, 103

Carroll, Noel, 153
Cassidy, Seamus, 128, 136, 141
Catholic, 98–9, 123–4
Cathy Come Home, 22, 139
Channel Four, 3, 12–13, 20, 73, 86, 135–6, 149, 150, 151
class, 17, 29, 50–7, 67–71, 95–7, 102–4, 108, 113–16, 119–20
Cold Lazarus, 3, 13–22
Corner, John, 94
Country, 45
Coward, Ros, 75
Cracker, 4
Craig, Cairns, 107, 112, 114, 117
Crisell,Andrew, 78, 80, 84, 85,
Curtis, Liz, 92

Days of Hope, 41
Death of A Nation, 151
Death On The Rock, 135,
Derrida, Jacques, 171–2
documentary, 9–11, 95–106, 145–58, 164, 166, 173, 176–83
Drew, Robert, 157
Drifters, 96,

Eagleton, Terry, 53
Eastenders, 42
Eisenstein, Sergei, 96
Ellis, John, 75, 93
Empire, 18, 74, 98–9, 101, 109
Ethnicity, 32, 35–8, 86, 91, 92, 103–4, 111
Eurotrash, 163

Falk, Pasi, 160, 164
Family, The, 149, 151

Fanon, Franz, 7, 109
Fiske, John, 93
form, 17, 32, 41–2, 47, 51, 53,
    92–4, 96, 97, 99–101, 109–10,
    120, 163–7, 179
Fortune, John, 128–29, 138–9
Foucault, Michel, 52
Four Weddings and a Funeral, 112
Freud, Sigmund, 162, 169
Full Monty, The, 5

Garnett, Tony, 23, 26, 27, 28–9
gender, 32–3 (and sexuality) 50–7,
    58–71, 159–75
genre, 23–4, 31–2
Glasgow, 108, 110, 113–14,
    116–18, 123
God's Gift, 63–5
Grade, Michael, 3, 13, 136
Graef, Roger, 149
Gramsci, Antonio, 11, 25–6, 36, 92,
    116
Grand, The, 5, 40–57
Gray, Alasdair, 117
Grierson, John, 96–7, 98, 105, 145,
    148, 151, 152–3, 156
Griffiths, Trevor, 45
Grigsby, Michael, 7, 95–106

Hall, Stuart, 101–2, 105–6
Hardy, Jeremy, 130, 137–8, 139–40,
    143
Hartley, John, 93
Have I Got News For You, 127, 130,
    132, 138
Hill Street Blues, 34, 120
Hislop, Ian, 128
Hobsbawm, Eric, 19
Hoggart, Richard, 17–18
Hollywood, 49, 112–13, 164, 166
Homicide, 34
Hood, Stuart, 135
Hurd, Geoffrey, 31,
Hutton, Will, 57

Ideology, 44, 109
identity (national) 7, 15–17, 35–6,
    45–6, 48, 72–3, 77, 92, 94–5, 97,
    102, 107–10, 116, 121–2, 126,
    153

Independent Television (ITV) 3, 28,
    40, 60, 67, 74, 78, 83, 150, 151,
    155
Independent Television Commission,
    28, 162
Internet, 163, 176, 178–9, 181–3
It's a Royal Knockout 6, 82–3

Jameson, Fredric, 16, 43–4
Jenkin, Guy, 136–7
Jennings, Humphrey, 96, 97, 99,
    150
jouissance, 9, 145, 156

Karaoke, 13, 19
Kelman, James, 108–9
Kern, Richard, 159
Kilborn, Richard, 146–7

Labour Party, 7, 9, 19, 25, 52, 88,
    141
Lacan, Jacques, 44
Laing, Stuart, 29
Laplanche, Jean, 162, 169–70
Leacock, Richard, 157
Lenin, V.I., 46, 95, 102, 104
Lifesavers, 160
Lipstick On Your Collar, 12, 18
Listen To Britain, 96, 99–100
Living On The Edge, 97
London, 33–4
Long Johns, The, 130, 139
Lovell, Alan, 96
Lukacs, Georg, 5, 40–3, 48, 49, 51,
    56

MacCabe, Colin, 41, 44, 109
McArthur, Colin, 41
McGrath, John, 23, 29
McIlvanney, William, 115, 118
McNaughton, Adam, 110
Major, John, 127, 141–2
Man Alive, 150
Man O' Man, 63–6, 71
Marr, Andrew, 141–2
Martin, Troy Kennedy, 23, 29
Marxism, 24–5, 91–2, 94
Midnight Movie, 12
Miller, David, 92

modernism, 41–2, 98, 109, 124
Modern Times, 60
monarchy, 2, 5–7, 18, 72–90
Moore, Michael, 144, 157
Moore, Suzanne, 25–6
Morgan, Edwin, 115–16
Morley, David, 102
Morris, Chris, 135, 144
Murdoch, Rupert, 13–14, 16, 17, 84, 177
Mulvey, Laura, 67
Munro, David, 150, 151, 153, 154

Naked Television, 120
Naked Video, 124, 126
Naremore, James, 111
naturalism, 42, 49, 96, 98, 112
Negroponte, Nicholas, 176
Newman, G.F., 23, 30–1, 32
Nichols, Bill, 145, 156
Nietzsche, 49–50, 52–53
Northern Ireland, 7, 91–5, 98–106, 124
NYPD Blue, 34, 36

Obscene Publications Act, 163
Omnibus, 6, 83
One Foot In The Grave, 8, 131

Panorama, 6, 83, 85
Pattison, Ian, 116, 120
People's Century, A, 154
Pilger, John, 150, 151
Plowman, Jon, 129–30, 131, 134, 135–6, 137–8, 143–4
Police, Camera, Action!, 10, 160
pornography, 9, 156–75
Postman, Neil, 14
postmodernism, 11, 16, 18, 40, 44, 168
Potter, Dennis, 3–4, 12–22, 120
Prime Suspect, 4, 31–2
Prince Charles, 2, 6, 76, 80–90
Princess Diana, 6, 76, 83–90
Public Service television, 3, 14, 16, 19, 27–30, 40, 77–8, 146–53, 155, 177, 178, 182
Punky Girls, 163–75

Queen Elizabeth II, 72, 74, 76–9, 87

Rab C. Nesbitt, 2, 7–8, 107, 126, 131
Real Holiday Show, The, 167–8
realism, 44–6, 51, 54, 126, 168–9
Reid, Jimmy, 111
Reith, John, 152, 153, 154, 177
Root, Anthony, 47–8
Rory Bremner, Who Else?, 127, 130, 132, 137
Rushdie, Salman, 4
Ryall, Tom, 24

Said, Edward, 7, 109
Satanic Verses, The, 4
satire, 8, 13, 127–144, 115
Scannell, Paddy, 74
Scotland, 7–8, 107–13, 122
Shohat, Ella, 105
Silent War, The, 98–101, 102
Silverman, Kaja, 172
Singing Detective, The, 15
Soros, George, 2
Spitting Image, 83, 132, 135, 137, 141
Star Wars, 13
Steel, Mark, 140, 143
Stop, Police! 159, 168
Strasberg, Lee, 112–13
Straw, Jack, 25–6
Sweeney, The, 31, 34

Teletubbies, 2
Televising Terrorism, 93–4
Thatcher, Margaret, 15, 83, 97
Thatcherism, 1–2, 6–7, 9, 13, 27, 45, 49, 53–4, 135, 149, 150, 154, 156
That Was The Week That Was, 127, 132, 135, 137
This Life., 42
Thoi Noi, 102
Thomas, Mark, 133, 134, 140, 142, 144
Time of Our Lives, The, 95–7
Too Long A Sacrifice, 98, 100
Trainspotting, 112

unconscious (the) 10, 117, 169–71
Undercurrents, 10, 180

video, 159–75
Video Diaries, 167

Video Nation, 151, 160–1

Watson, Paul, 149, 151
Williams, Linda, 164, 165–6, 167
Williams, Raymond, 19, 93
Wilsher, John, 23, 29–30, 35
Winston, Brian, 98
Wood, Anthony, 46
World In Action, 155

X-Cars, 159
X-Files, 60

Yentob, Alan, 3, 13
Young Mr Lincoln, 122
You've Been Framed!, 9, 10, 149, 159, 160, 164, 168, 169

Z-Cars, 29